Finding a Place for Every Student

Inclusive Practices, Social Belonging, and Differentiated Instruction in Elementary Classrooms

CHERYLL DUQUETTE

Pembroke Publishers Limited

For John, Karras, and Anders

Funded by the Government of Canada
Financé par le gouvernement du Canada | Canada

Library and Archives Canada Cataloguing in Publication

Title: Finding a place for every student : inclusive practices, social belonging, and differentiated instruction in elementary classrooms / Cheryll Duquette.

Other titles: Students at risk

Names: Duquette, Cheryll, author.

Description: Previously published under title: Students at risk.

Identifiers: Canadiana (print) 20220177295 | Canadiana (ebook) 20220177481 | ISBN 9781551383606 (softcover) | ISBN 9781551389592 (PDF)

Subjects: LCSH: Special education. | LCSH: Individualized education programs. | LCSH: Children with disabilities—Education.

Classification: LCC LC3965 .D865 2022 | DDC 371.9/043—dc23

Editor: Kat Mototsune, David Kilgour, Alison Parker
Cover Design: John Zehethofer
Typesetting: Jay Tee Graphics Ltd.

Printed and bound in Canada
9 8 7 6 5 4 3 2 1

Contents

Introduction

We all want to be remembered by our students as teachers who made a positive difference in their lives. Teachers who got to know the students, accepted them, and made learning and academic achievement easier. Teachers who created a classroom where students felt respected by others, where everyone's ideas were valued, and where all students were included in every activity. These principles are central to creating a sense of belonging in classrooms. This book provides strategies for Kindergarten to Grade 8 teachers to develop that sense of social and academic belonging in their classrooms which every student, regardless of age, desires.

Chapter 1 provides several strategies for creating social and academic belonging in your classroom. It begins with the teacher warmly welcoming the students on the first day of school and involves developing a relationship with each student. It also involves the teacher modeling inclusive, accepting, and pro-social behaviors for the students, who in turn use them in their interactions with peers. This chapter also discusses strategies to develop academic belonging among your students through the use of timely and descriptive feedback and increasing motivation, self-efficacy, and growth mindset. Teachers can also use culturally responsive teaching practices and teach social and emotional skills. These approaches are described and practical ways of implementing them are provided.

In Chapter 2, you will find information on differentiated instruction (DI) and how to use it with a class of students with diverse needs. Although DI is mandated in some districts, many teachers' practices only involve alternate ways to demonstrate learning. The focus of Chapter 2 is on differentiated instructional strategies as another way to create academic belonging, and one teacher's experience using the ideas described in this chapter is presented. Together, chapters 1 and 2 provide useful strategies for ensuring *all* your students feel as though they can be successful and that they belong socially and academically in your classroom.

In Chapters 3, 4, and 5 you will find an explanation of a planning process for getting to know the strengths and needs of all your students so that informal individualized goals may be developed. The case studies of Andrew, Alex, and Erik are described along with how their teachers used the planning process, as well as involved parents in establishing learning and social/emotional goals for them. The outcomes are also discussed.

While we want to ensure that every student feels as though they have a place in our classroom, some students with exceptionalities may require accommodations to help them achieve academic success and other strategies to promote social belonging. Chapters 6 to 12 provide information on learning disabilities, behavior disorders, giftedness, intellectual disabilities, mental illness, sensory impairments, autism spectrum disorder, fetal alcohol spectrum disorder, and other low-incidence disabilities. Symptoms and characteristics are presented, as well as practical strategies for instruction and social inclusion. It should be added that many of the suggested strategies for specific exceptionalities may also benefit the entire class.

Chapter 13 discusses how teachers can work effectively with parents to develop effective partnerships where communication is regular, transparent, and focused on meeting the goals for the students. Mutually respectful relationships with parents contribute to students' inclusion in the classroom. Parents know their children well, and teachers can benefit from their experience and observations over time. In Chapter 14, you will find suggestions on how to plan a smooth transition for students with autism (and other exceptionalities) from one grade or level of schooling to another.

You can be that special kind of teacher remembered fondly by your students as one who made an important difference in their lives — perhaps helping them make great academic progress or more friends or that very first friend. This book will help you identify and achieve academic and social goals for your students.

Acknowledgments

Thank you to Tracy Crowe and Natalie Wainwright for their careful reading of sections of this book and their helpful suggestions. Thanks too to Leah Dabrowski, Stephanie Fullarton, and Elspeth Ross for their generous assistance in writing this book.

CHAPTER 1

Developing Student Belonging

Sammy It was November and Sammy, a Grade 5 student, had given up. He did not want to go to school because everything he did was wrong. He felt that he couldn't do the work and that he was being picked on by his teacher, his peers, and the principal. This fall alone, he had been suspended three times for fighting in the playground and seemed to have a detention just about every second day. It was pointless, thought Sammy, and he wondered why he should bother trying. There didn't seem to be any way to make the situation better.

Every school has at least one Sammy, and it doesn't have to be that way. Sammy had clearly lost faith in his ability to "do" school and his relationships with the teacher and his peers were deteriorating. He felt he didn't have a place in his classroom. In this chapter, we will be examining how teachers can ensure that all students feel they belong. Teachers should develop a relationship with each student and get to know their interests and abilities. Many teachers believe that this relationship is the foundation for success for each student. Teachers should ensure that their students experience academic success, which is highly motivating and can make students feel that they can do the work and academically belong in the class. It is also important for teachers to establish a class climate of acceptance and empathy. Students need to feel that they are in an emotionally safe environment and feel supported by peers. One of the ways to achieve this goal is to demonstrate patience and concern and model acceptance for all students in your class.

The last way to support a sense of belonging is to work towards developing pro-social behaviors among all the students. Even though you may be working towards creating an inclusive environment in your classroom, some students may exhibit behaviors that cause peers to become uncomfortable around them. All students need to develop key social skills to increase positive and respectful interpersonal relationships.

Student belonging at school is not a given. It takes a teacher who is willing to work towards developing positive and trusting relationships with their students, supporting academic success, and encouraging peer acceptance to ensure that every student feels as though they have a place in the classroom.

A Sense of Belonging

Belonging is one of Maslow's (1970) basic human needs. It involves the feelings of being connected to others and of being accepted, respected, included, and supported by others. The student-teacher relationship is the foundation of a student's sense of belonging. As a teacher, you should establish a relationship based on trust and respect and through your words and actions ensure that each student is accepted by peers and every student experiences academic success. Research has shown that a sense of belonging is related to motivation and academic achievement. Many students have trouble working and learning unless they feel the teacher likes them and is genuinely trying to help them succeed. Moreover, students need to be able to expect that their peers will not bully or harass them; rather they will collaborate with them in group work and accept them on the playground.

When you feel someone is in your corner and is supporting you to be successful academically and socially, you feel motivated to try to do the work and to behave so that others will not be wary of you. School belonging is also linked to reduced absenteeism, decreased misbehavior (e.g., fighting, bullying, vandalism, disruption), increased happiness, self-esteem, and better transitions (e.g., from elementary to secondary school).

The teacher's role in nurturing a sense of belonging among students is to develop a relationship with each of them. At the same time, the teacher should create a classroom environment where students experience success in work completion, demonstrate positive behaviors, and are accepted by peers. Essentially, for students like Sammy, the teacher plays a pivotal role in nurturing the sense of belonging, and in this chapter, we will discuss some of the strategies that may be used.

> We remember how teachers made us feel and not the content they taught.

Developing a Relationship with Students

Your relationship with your students begins during the first minute of the first day of school or the first day of the new term or semester. You demonstrate your eagerness to get started with a smile and a simple greeting, such as "Hi" or "Welcome to our class." With such an opening you're saying, "There's a place for you in this classroom, and I'm going to help you feel like you belong." Some students may be more nervous about starting the new year with a new teacher, and they may need a few minutes with you to calm their fears. Learn the students' names as quickly as possible. During the first few days, I use name cards that can be propped up on the students' desks. The students write their name on a piece of paper or recipe card that has been folded in half, and sometimes students decorate them as well. You will know some of the students' names, but others will be new to you. Regardless, memorize them as quickly as possible. When you can use the student's name, it sends a message that you actually know who they are. Some teachers in the intermediate panel wonder if they will ever learn all the students' names, particularly when they are seeing 120 a day. Yes, it takes time, but it is well worth it.

Show an Interest in the Students

Students like to have the teacher show an interest in them as a person; it demonstrates they care about them. You can do this by having short conversations with individual students or small groups before the class begins or during a break. For example, on Monday morning, you might ask if the students had a good weekend, which may be followed by the question: "What was the best part?" or "Did you play (name of video game, sport)?" or "Did you see the (name of team) game?" A few teachers introduce themselves to the class on the first day by telling the students about themselves, for example, how long they have been teaching (a particular grade or course), their family life (e.g., having a partner or a pet), and the things they like to do in their free time. However, this type of information will often likely be revealed during informal conversations. Younger students can provide information about themselves in a sharing circle. Sometimes teachers use a puppet or a talking piece to permit students to open up about their favorite color, food, or activity. Some students will be eager to talk about themselves, while others may be shy and should be given the opportunity to decline to speak. The teacher can later follow up with these students on an individual basis.

Some teachers also schedule individual meetings with their students to discuss their interests and out-of-school activities, among other things. One teacher plays the Paper Toss Game with her older students during the first days of the term. On a piece of paper, the students write their goal for the course, one thing they like or dislike about the subject (e.g., English), and one fun fact about themselves. The activity is anonymous; students do not write their name on the paper. The students crumple their papers, and the teacher collects them. The teacher then tosses the papers into the air, gathers them, and reads them aloud. The students learn a bit about each other, and the teacher learns about general feelings towards the subject area, goals, and student interests. Knowing about student interests is important because it may be a vehicle for creating enthusiasm for learning the content. I have worked with students who will not put forth much effort unless the content is of interest to them. Having a topic to which you can relate and know something about is motivating. To arouse motivation, teachers can develop math problems that are based on student interests or explain scientific or historical concepts in terms of everyday occurrences and interests. For example, discussions of families in ancient societies may be linked to students' own families. Or you may decide to talk about leisure activities and sports in ancient civilizations and compare them to the ones we enjoy today. Writing assignments in which students discuss their interests and experiences may also provide them with an opportunity to describe things they find important. I have developed assignments where the students have a choice of topics, including ones not suggested, as long as they have been approved. While students may still grumble at the work, they will appreciate that you took the time to incorporate their individual and group interests. I know one French as a Second Language teacher who coaxed her students into learning vocabulary and grammar through their general love of hockey. She taught the curriculum through discussions on hockey and developed tasks centred on it. The same could be done for any sport or activity. I might add that this teacher was not a big fan of hockey but learned enough about it through reading, watching games, and talking to the students to create motivating assignments and have engaging discussions.

Conduct Check-ins with Students

Teachers gauge how students are feeling and their emotions by using check-ins. They can be as simple as asking students, "How are you?" or "How are things going?", especially for students who seem to be struggling or appear to be "down." For students in the primary grades the teacher can display three emojis showing happy, sad/angry, or neutral and students can high-five or touch the emoji that matches their feelings as they enter the classroom in the morning or after recess. Teachers can follow up with the students touching a sad emoji as quickly as possible and on a one-to-one basis. It is helpful to have a ten-minute cool-down period after recess where students can read silently or write in their journal, and during this time the teacher can speak quietly and individually to students who self-identified as feeling sad or angry. You can ask, "I noticed that you touched the angry emoji. Would you like to tell me about it?" Many students will take advantage of the chance to discuss the problem or issue with you. If the student declines the opportunity to explain the reason for the negative emotion, then say, "Okay. But if you want to talk about it later, we can." You respect the student's decision and leave the door open for discussion. In Chapter 4, we will see that Alex's teacher did this and incorporated social problem solving into the conversation.

Check-ins may also be done with each student on a monthly basis, or more frequently if time permits. Prior to the monthly meeting, older students could list their recent successes, needs, how they're feeling about things, goals for next month, and anything else you or the students feel is appropriate. Try to find a quiet spot in the classroom and position the student's back to the rest of the class while you are facing the class (so that you can monitor what is happening). Speak in a low voice to keep the conversation as private as possible. The students can lead the meeting and the teacher can make notes for their own use. Previous needs may be mentioned to ensure that they were or are being addressed adequately. Over time, the teacher may see patterns in the students' responses. Some teachers conduct more frequent, informal check-ins during times when standardized testing is scheduled. They may ask the entire class, "How are you feeling? Nervous? ... Let's talk about ways to manage the stress." Check-ins send a strong message to students that you care about them and how they are feeling. You validate their feelings and can help them resolve some of their emotional difficulties. For students like Sammy, a teacher who spends time talking instead of scolding and helping instead of blaming could be a turning point for them.

Observe your students

It is not unusual for a student to communicate emotions or cry for help through behavior. Younger students may engage in aggressive behavior or have an outburst, likely because they do not understand their emotions, don't know how to express them appropriately, or want assistance solving a conflict or problem with social interactions. You may notice that some older students suddenly change the way they dress, or start smoking cigarettes or abusing other substances, and skipping school. One person I know told me of doing all of the above simply so that a teacher would ask if everything was okay. She wanted to talk about the trauma at home but did not want to initiate the conversation with a teacher. Instead, she wanted the teacher to initiate the conversation by reaching out to her and showing they cared. Another student appeared to demonstrate total involvement in school activities. She was on many sports teams, served in student government, and participated in the school musical. Moreover, her marks were relatively high, which put her under the radar for all her teachers. She wished that an adult at school had asked why she was overly committed to extracurricular activities so that she could reveal that she wanted to minimize the time she spent at home. She too did not want to broach the subject with a teacher and hoped that one would notice her behavior. Sadly, in the cases of both these girls, teachers did not ask the question, "I noticed ... Is everything all right?" They did not take the opportunity to start a conversation between themselves and their students. Both girls were later diagnosed with anxiety and underwent therapy. However, teachers who noticed behaviors and addressed them when they developed might have helped these students receive the assistance they needed years earlier.

You can also observe the moods of your students. For younger children, observing their selection of emojis to identify moods can lead to the emergence of patterns which might be discussed with the student or the parents. I know of a situation with a Grade 3 student who came to school dishevelled and hungry. He was irritable and angry and indicated his displeasure with the appropriate emoji. Not surprisingly, peers were cautious around him lest they trigger an outburst. The teacher took him aside one morning, and they spoke privately. She began with the I-statement and followed with an invitation to talk: "I noticed that … Would you like to talk about it?" He revealed that his father had a new girlfriend and they permitted him to stay up very late at night playing video games. They slept late in the morning, and there was no time for breakfast. The boy revealed that getting to school was a scramble and he felt tired, disorganized, hungry, and not in the right mood for school when he arrived. While the teacher could do little about the home situation, she was able to provide a small, nutritious snack for the boy to eat when he arrived at school and scheduled the first ten minutes of the day for mindfulness activities, which helped all the students get into the right frame of mind. The teacher's actions helped to open the lines of communication with the student and strategies were put into place to ease the child's transition from home to school. The teacher's caring actions also helped the student and teacher develop a bond of trust between them.

A resource on bringing mindfulness into the classroom is *Fostering Mindfulness* by Shelley Murphy (2020), published by Pembroke Publishers.

Other Strategies for Developing a Positive Student–Teacher Relationship

As we have seen, being open to talking with students is important in building a relationship. Unlike the two girls we saw earlier, some students are quite willing to talk to the teacher. However, they need an opportunity to do so. One way is to provide time for students to meet with you informally by scheduling regular extra help times (e.g., during lunch, before or after school). Teachers may also be able to see students during their prep periods. While some students may attend the sessions to ask questions about the content you're teaching, others may begin with the questions about the work and progress to asking for help with a particular personal problem. I have experienced this situation more than once. In these cases, the teacher can direct the student to the appropriate resources or find out what is available.

In other cases when students reveal personal information to you, they do not want you to act. They just want you to listen. Being attentive, affirming, and focused on the student (and not other things) sends a message that you care about them. Keep this information private unless the student reveals information about which you must legally take action with a child protection agency.

Solid relationships built on respect, and the teacher must earn it from their students. One way to do this is by watching your language. Avoid referring to the class as "guys." Not all students are "guys." Early in my teaching career, a student complained about my use of this term, and I took notice. Immediately, my go-to phrase for gaining their attention became "Grade 8." This term was certainly more inclusive than "guys." Another way to earn students' respect is to challenge stereotypes. Make it clear that negative comments about students with exceptionalities or students from minority groups are not welcomed. When they do, address them immediately. Calmly state: "In *our* class, we speak kindly about everyone. Negative comments are hurtful, and there is no place for them here." This response sends a clear message to everyone that this classroom is an emotionally safe place, which will increase the respect and trust students have in you and their sense of a connection to you.

Having a predictable classroom also contributes to creating an emotionally safe place for students. Predictability gives a sense of security and control to students who may be concerned about what is going to happen during the day. The weekly schedule should be posted on a wall, and some students may need a copy to be taped to their desk. Any changes to the schedule (e.g., an assembly) should be explained beforehand. Routines for lining up, submitting work, going to the washroom, and so on should be established during the first week of classes and followed consistently. Your own behavior should also be predictable. Students need to know that positive behaviors will be reinforced by you (e.g., an acknowledgment for a student helping another find a misplaced article of clothing) by simply saying thank you or placing a sticky note on the student's desk. They should also know that inappropriate behaviors will result in consequences (e.g., writing on a desk will result in having to wash it), and the consequences should also be administered consistently.

Academic Belonging

By developing a relationship with a student, the teacher supports their feeling of social belonging and acceptance. Teachers also want to ensure that the student feels as though they belong academically in the classroom. They can do this by helping the student experience success in work completion and learning. When a student is successful in a task, they feel as though they belong in the group by virtue of being able to do what is expected. By using the differentiated learning strategies described in Chapter 2, teachers can help students with and without special needs learn concepts and master skills, thereby supporting those feelings of belonging. Teachers can also use feedback, motivation, self-efficacy, growth mindset, and culturally responsive teaching to inform their practices and thereby improve academic outcomes and the sense of belonging for all students. These ideas will be discussed below.

Feedback

Feedback should take the form of a non-judgmental description of observed behavior, intended to improve performance. Specific feedback has been shown to be more effective in improving performance than praise, punishment, rewards, and grades. First, students need to know what the expectations for them are, then they need to try out the task. As they perform the task, the teacher should provide descriptive feedback by stating or writing what parts of the task are meeting expectations, what needs to be improved, and how to make improvements. For example, when instructing how to print a small "b", the teacher may demonstrate the steps in forming the letter and say the steps at the same time. They can also state the criteria for a proper "b" (e.g., the circle has to touch the straight line). Students can practise drawing a "b" in the air and then on paper, again with the teacher demonstrating, stating the steps, and noting the hallmarks of a correctly formed "b". The teacher can observe each student printing the letter "b" and state what parts of the "b" are correctly done, what parts need some improvement, and how to improve their "b". To guide the students in their printing, the teacher can post an anchor chart for students on how to make a "b" on the board with arrows and numbers showing the process. Effective use of feedback is important in skill improvement, and it supports a student's feelings that they are able to do the work.

Timely feedback is also important. It should be given as soon after the behavior as possible, otherwise the student may forget what had happened. As well, students need time to practise the correct way to perform a skill. In the case of the printing lesson, the teacher may be providing informal feedback, but feedback may also be more formal. For example, a teacher could provide summative feedback after a major assignment has been submitted for marking. However, the teacher would do well to also provide feedback as formative assessment about halfway through the project so that students could see how their work aligns with the expectations in the rubric, what areas need improvement, and how to make the corrections.

Teachers often find that some students seem to need more supervision when doing their work than others. It is helpful for teachers to observe these students immediately after giving instruction and provide feedback so that the students learn how to perform the skill correctly the *first time*. It can be very frustrating to learn that your work is incorrect because you didn't follow or perform the steps correctly, something that timely feedback can address quickly and easily. When a student experiences failure, they become de-motivated and self-doubt about ever being able to do the task creeps in. They start to feel they don't belong academically in the class.

Without feedback, there is no improvement.

Motivation, Self-Efficacy, and Growth Mindset

When we are motivated to do something, we seem to be more focused and intent on achieving our goal. When not motivated, it is often the case that we postpone or procrastinate and do not put forth our best effort. There are two types of motivation: intrinsic and extrinsic. Intrinsic motivation occurs when a person does something because of a wish they have inside. Extrinsic motivation means that a person does something to obtain a desired result. For example, when a student is personally interested in a topic (intrinsic motivation), they will likely be more motivated to do the work related to learning about it. This is one of the reasons for providing choice on assignments or choice between working in groups or alone. Some students are only motivated to complete assignments and study to achieve a high mark (extrinsic motivation). As well, sometimes students will work hard to avoid negative consequences, such as a low mark and punishment from parents (again, extrinsic motivation). We will see this situation with Andrew in Chapter 5.

How can a teacher promote intrinsic motivation? When you take the time to find out students' interests, you can include them in the curriculum. For example, your students' interests may be incorporated into the examples you use to explain concepts or tasks that are to be completed by them. You can also connect topics to the "real world" and explain why learning about it is important. As well, if you provide choices of assignments, students can select the ones they are most interested in doing. Some students find working in groups anxiety-producing and distracting and would prefer the option of working alone on an assignment. You may also emphasize that marks are not an indicator of someone's worth or value. Moreover, although in some situations marks may be important, in others learning is the goal. For example, not every piece of work needs to be marked. Teachers can provide specific feedback on task performance that is intended to improve performance rather than assigning a grade. If the goal is to use specific elements in a piece of written expression (e.g., capital letters and periods, dialogue, description), the teacher can give feedback on the writing without attaching a grade to it. In this way the feedback can fuel motivation to complete the task and support a sense of accomplishment.

Self-efficacy is a person's level of confidence in their abilities to perform certain tasks. It influences our motivation to try new tasks and persist with them when difficulties arise. One way to give a student more confidence is to express your belief in them. Say, "You have done … in the past. I am sure you can do it this time." I have found that students who are struggling respond well to these types of statements. A second way to promote a student's self-confidence in their abilities is to include their interests in the program. I had a student with developmental disabilities who had experiences with nature and some knowledge about forests. He revealed that whenever discussions or lessons were related to forests and wildlife, he was motivated to listen, participate, and do the work. He was motivated because he knew something about the topic and felt he would be able to perform; he was feeling self-efficacious. My response was to ensure that references to nature were included at least once a day, thereby supporting his willingness to try to do the work. I also provided opportunities for him to share his knowledge with the other students, which helped to make him feel as though he belonged.

Growth mindset is a person's belief about intelligence, which may be malleable or fixed. If you believe that intelligence is malleable, then you are likely to believe that hard work, persistence, and experience can improve it. On the other hand, if you believe that intelligence is fixed, then no amount of practice and feedback will improve it. With fixed mindsets, students choose not to work outside their comfort zone and do not take risks for fear of failure. Subsequently, they may not study for tests, simply hoping for the best. Unfortunately, hope is not an effective study strategy. Obviously, teachers want to support a student's belief that intelligence is malleable. You can do this by demonstrating that mistakes are an opportunity to learn. For example, you can describe a situation where you made a mistake, then changed it, and were successful. Or, when showing how to solve a math problem, you can intentionally make a mistake and demonstrate how to handle the feelings of failure and process of making corrections. Such demonstrations also teach students that mistakes are acceptable, that they can be corrected, and that students need to persist in task completion. Nowhere is this idea more important than in math. Too often, students are defeated by their mistakes and feel that they can never master the skills and complete the work. Some students also need to be encouraged to persist. Sometimes a frustrated student will state, "I give up!" Showing them how to try another way or using the words, "Keep trying," sends the message that you have faith in the student's abilities and that with continued effort they can succeed. Try to remind students that with hard work and persistence, they can be successful. You can also provide one-on-one assistance to the child or seat the student beside a competent peer who will either explain or demonstrate what to do. Feedback can also be used to help students see where mistakes were made and show students how to fix them. Success can be supported using feedback, motivation, self-efficacy, and growth mindset. It is crucial for a student's sense of academic belonging.

Culturally Responsive Teaching

With increased immigration, many schools boast about the number of languages their students speak at home and the different cultures represented in the school population. A culturally responsive teacher is aware that there is no monolithic view of the world and that students' experiences, culture, race, and social class affect their perspectives. Culturally responsive teaching begins with the teacher honestly reflecting on their own practices and biases, prejudices, and stereotypical views. It occurs in an environment that includes content that is relevant to the students and their cultures, takes a constructivist approach, and encourages students to connect new material to their experiences. One example of how a teacher can build bridges between what students know through experience and new material may occur when teaching a unit on immigration in social studies, history, geography, or English. You can discuss the concepts of the push-pull theory of migration and the stages of immigration and apply them to the situation encountered both by early settlers and by more recent immigrants. You can also invite your students to share their experiences and ideas about these concepts. By drawing students into the conversation, you validate their experiences and send a message to their peers that these students are worthy of respect and belong in the class.

Some teachers may view students from minority and marginalized groups through a deficit lens. They harbor a belief that these students cannot learn and consequently have low expectations for them. Unfortunately, this type of thinking often becomes a self-fulfilling prophecy and is reflected in these teachers' instructional strategies. Canada's Indigenous students have felt the effect of deficit thinking for decades. To project an affirming view, teachers should include accurate representations of students' cultures in their lessons whenever possible. For example, read stories and novels about Indigenous people that are written by Indigenous authors, or talk about subjects that Indigenous students may relate to, such as pow wows or hunting and fishing, particularly if you live in a rural setting. When Indigenous students see themselves in the curriculum, they become motivated to participate and learn. While it may take time to find resources that represent the cultures of your students, it is worth the effort to affirm their belonging in the class. One thing that should be avoided is to put the student on the spot by assuming they know everything about their culture. They may not, and asking questions to which they may not know the answer and assuming they are classroom representatives of a particular culture may result in humiliation for the student.

One strategy that may be used to advance a sense of belonging through culturally responsive teaching is the use of activities that involve higher-order thinking rather than simple recall. For example, in addition to asking questions about a character's actions in a novel or story simply to ensure understanding, also ask what students would have done in a similar situation. A discussion in which the ideas are shared respectfully would reveal the different perspectives rooted in culture that students have on a character's situation. Allowing space for different opinions sends a message that they are valued and that difference is part of everyday life. Teachers can also put posters depicting different cultures in the classroom and have discussions about difficult topics, such as residential schools. It should be noted that any discussions of topics involving cultural groups must include accurate information and the perspectives of the cultural groups themselves. These discussions can be geared to any level to include students from Kindergarten to Grade 8.

When beginning a new topic, teachers can ask the students what they know about it and ensure that the students from minority cultures share what they know. Model acceptance of their perspectives and include them in future lessons.

When teachers know about the interests of their students and how they spend their non-school time, they can use examples from this information in their lessons. Again, doing so affirms these students by validating their experiences, gives them voice and opportunities to demonstrate their abilities. When students feel they can contribute, they are motivated to try the task at hand and persist. These beliefs and actions contribute to academic success and help all students develop the sense that they belong academically in the class.

IEPs and Working with Parents

Your students with identified exceptionalities will likely have individual education plans (IEPs) that outline strengths, needs, and required accommodations. Accommodations may be as easy to implement as extra time to write tests and exams or the use of software to assist with written assignments. They may involve more time and effort, particularly with students who have intellectual differences, such as academic giftedness and intellectual disabilities. In these cases, modifications to the curriculum may be required.

You may not be aware if a student has an IEP, especially if the student has moved from a different school district. However, you can ask your resource teacher or administration which of your students has an IEP. Reading the IEP needs to be done as close to the first day of the term as possible. In jurisdictions such as Ontario, the IEP is a legal document and you are required to implement the accommodations that are listed in it. As well, the student needs these accommodations to be successful, and they should be available as soon as school starts. Speak privately to the students who have IEPs to ensure they know you are aware of the accommodations and will be implementing them.

Get in touch with the parents to assure them that you have read the IEP and will be working with their child on them. Ask how best to contact them: telephone call, text, email, or meetings (virtual or face-to-face). As well, before the first test or marked assignment, start off the year or semester with a "good news" call in which you explain to parents what has been covered in your class and how their child is doing. Always have something positive to say about the child to the parent and consider making additional calls to tell them how well their child did in a particular activity. These kinds of conversations open the door to direct communication with the parents. They are your partners, and they can provide you with valuable information about their child. Some will contact you before you call them. Others will be hesitant about answering calls from the school. However, beginning with positive messages can help instill trust in the teacher to support the development of their son or daughter. Chapter 13 provides more suggestions on working with parents.

Supporting Social Belonging among Peers

Belonging does not happen in a vacuum. It involves the people around the individual respecting and accepting them, with no neglect, rejection, or aggression towards them. Developing a relationship with the student and ensuring academic success are things over which the teacher has direct control. We have less control over how peers view some struggling students, such as Sammy. We can stress norms of behavior in the class that emphasize respect, kindness, and acceptance, and we can monitor student activities closely to ensure that bullying does not occur. Whether physical or verbal, bullying generally only happens when teachers are not present, so it is important to supervise the playground, lunchroom/cafeteria, hallways, locker bays, and other areas where it might occur. Every student wants some form of peer support, which includes a sense of trust and closeness with friends and classmates. Unsupportive peers are a source of stress for students. Supportive peers contribute towards academic achievement and foster a sense of care and acceptance, something we all want. Moreover, having friends at school and feeling positive about those relationships make students feel as though they belong socially.

Every student wants to feel respected, and you can model respect by saying "Please" and "Thank you." For example, instead of "Open up your books and get to work.," try "Please take out your books and ..." I actually had a student who stated matter-of-factly that they refused to do the work because the teacher did not say "Please." I took note and ever since have prefaced all requests with "Please." Doing so eliminates power struggles. Thanking students individually for complying with a request or helping someone else should be done quietly, so as not to draw attention to the student, unless, like Sammy, the child feels they cannot do anything right. Then "Thank you" sends a clear message of support and acceptance to the student and their peers. I found that modeling respect positively impacted the quality of peer relations.

Developing Appropriate Behaviors

An observation I have made is that most students are accepting of their peers. However, if a student has a meltdown or is violent, some peers may become cautious about working with them. There are things you can do to teach appropriate behaviors to the entire class to facilitate amicable relations and a sense of belonging among your students. One of the strategies is to teach social and emotional learning (SEL) either through using formal programs (e.g., PATHS) or informally. SEL competencies emphasize the development of skills that may protect students from peer rejection and support acceptance and belonging. Two skills that might be taught are emotional understanding and regulation. Teachers in the younger grades can explicitly instruct their students about various emotions through the use of emojis, pictures, and discussion. Then students practise identifying their feelings. Many teachers use colors to indicate zones of feelings. For example, blue might indicate feeling bored, unhappy, sick, sad, or tired. Green could signal feeling okay, calm, focused, or happy. Yellow could indicate intensifying emotions, and red could show that the student is angry or upset. Every student might have a set of four cards, one of each color. On the back of each card would be strategies. For example, on the back of the red card, strategies could include "I can talk to a teacher or a friend" or "Ask for a five-minute break to walk down the hall." On the back of the yellow card, the strategy might be to do some deep breathing and think about things that make them feel happy. Students could be asked to display their cards on their desks, and the teacher would scan the room looking for students with yellow or red cards. They would discreetly ask the students to select a strategy, then monitor them as it is implemented. The teacher would check in with each student five minutes later to find out how they are feeling and use praise or acknowledgment to reinforce the behavior. This strategy helps to allow the student to cool down and avoid a meltdown or a situation where the student becomes aggressive, which can provoke fear and distrust among peers.

If you need to talk to a student about managing emotions or solving social problems with others, take them aside and quietly ask what the problem is. Listen attentively and summarize what the student said back to them to ensure that you understand them. Then empathize and ask the student to consider the incident from other students' perspectives. Next, direct the conversation towards strategies the student can use to resolve the problem now and in the future. As much as possible, have the student verbalize possible solutions. For example, "I understand that you feel angry because someone hid your hat. What are ways we can prevent this from happening again?" As strategies are generated, ask the student to consider what the consequence of using each one might be. Later, when the student implements one of the strategies, praise or acknowledge the behavior. Say, "I like the way you …" This strategy helps to teach and reinforce emotional regulation and social problem-solving skills that the student has not yet mastered. Your presence, calm manner, and assistance with generating and selecting appropriate strategies will help to develop trust between you and the student.

As part of teaching about regulating emotions, teachers can also help students with conflict management. Some teachers find that when there has been a conflict during recess, taking ten minutes right after students return to the classroom to discuss the problem with individuals or engage in a class discussion helps to restore calm before engaging in the actual lesson. Students who are upset are not ready to participate in instruction. Other teachers have a "problem" jar where students insert a piece of paper describing a conflict, or they can simply place a sticky note on the teacher's desk with information about the conflict. The teacher may organize a class meeting or sharing circle in which students discuss the problem, try to see it from different perspectives, and generate possible solutions. These solutions could be added to the back of the colored cards representing emotions if you're using them, or they may be listed on a large sheet of paper and posted on a wall in the classroom for easy reference. These strategies may also be used to teach other behavioral skills.

Younger children need to be taught basic skills to support peer acceptance, such as turn taking, sharing toys, inviting peers to play, collaborating on joint play and clarifying the rules of the game, and responding positively to others. These skills, however, may need to be reviewed from time to time with older children. Group work is another opportunity to garner peer acceptance for a student. You select group members who may be easy-going, focused, and on task, and who share similar interests with the student. For example, the task may be to research a topic in which there is a common interest or develop a website related to it. As well, structuring the activity following the cooperative learning approach in which each member of the group has a separate task may be useful if the student works better alone but is willing to be part of a group project.

The basic social skills shown in the text box should be developed so that a student is accepted by peers. Some children will require explicit instruction and practice to develop them. As well, this list may be modified to include specific skills that an individual student needs to develop (e.g., following instructions, introducing themself and greeting others, engaging in a conversation, getting the teacher's attention, giving and receiving compliments, and making a request).

> **Basic Classroom Social Skills**
>
> Working collaboratively with peers
> Disagreeing appropriately and receiving criticism
> Respect for others' points of view
> Conflict resolution and social problem-solving
> Regulating of emotions and behavior
> Treating everyone with respect and kindness

Help peers see struggling students through your eyes.

Teachers can also send a clear message to the class that students with less developed social skills are worthy of their positive attention by talking and laughing with them, discussing their interests, and publicly praising them. If there are clubs or extracurricular activities in the school that align with a socially struggling student's interests, then encourage their efforts to join in. Finding others with similar interests may support the development of a sense of connectedness to peers.

Sammy

Sammy clearly is feeling defeated and lacks a sense of attachment to his teacher and his peers. The teacher should change the script. Instead of escalating situations and punishing Sammy, they should be trying to develop a relationship with him. Given his record of three suspensions between September and November, doing so may not be easy. It takes courage for the teacher to change the way they have been working with Sammy. However, the teacher, the peers, and Sammy are going to be together until the end of June, so they should try to make the best of it. What can the teacher do?

The teacher's first priority should be to develop a positive relationship with Sammy. Keeping the lines of communication open and trying to talk to Sammy every day about things other than his schoolwork is a start. The teacher could also find out about his interests and try to talk to him about them. They might also use the colored card system to check his emotions throughout the day and encourage him to use the strategies on the back of the red and yellow cards. A signal for when Sammy feels he must go for a walk in the hallway to calm down should be established. Daily or weekly check-in meetings could be held to see how he's feeling and discuss what he thinks have been successes and where he requires help.

The teacher also needs to ensure that Sammy is experiencing academic success so that he feels he is capable. The teacher can weave his interests into lessons so that he feels he has some knowledge about the topic and is intrinsically motivated to try to do the work and learn. As well, the teacher can provide timely, descriptive feedback, especially when learning a new skill. It will help Sammy to learn how to perform the skill correctly and avoid feelings of failure and re-teaching the skill. Additionally, if Sammy needs something explained more than once, the teacher should be patient and display no annoyance. Once Sammy begins to experience success in his work, he will start to expect success and feel confident that he will be able to do the work (self-efficacy). He will likely be more motivated to persist when there is a problem if the teacher encourages him to keep trying and provides feedback on how to improve. When mistakes occur, the teacher can remind Sammy that it is okay to make them and that it is part of learning. Sammy should also be encouraged to engage in positive self-talk, such as "I can do this work" or

"Everyone is not out to get me." The teacher can also emphasize hard work, persistence, and practice to help Sammy develop a positive growth mindset. As well, the teacher can include higher-order activities in the lessons, such as open-ended questions where there is no one correct answer. Everyone's contributions should be validated. Moreover, the teacher should have high expectations for Sammy, find his strengths, and avoid seeing him as a student with deficits and little hope for success.

The teacher can ensure that the classroom environment is predictable and supportive, a place where everyone feels emotionally safe. Posting and following the schedule and consistent follow-through with consequences for positive and negative behavior are two strategies that a teacher could also use. As well, a norm of acceptance for everyone and kindness needs to be developed so that every student feels they have a place in the classroom.

Sammy seems to have difficulties with emotional self-regulation, conflict management, and social problem-solving. The teacher could teach the skills associated with these SEL competencies explicitly to the entire class, to avoid singling him out. Successes in SEL competencies could be discussed and appropriate behaviors reinforced during regular check-in meetings. With improved skills in social relations, Sammy may experience increased acceptance by peers. Sammy's actions in the classroom and elsewhere in the school can be monitored so that he is neither the perpetrator nor the recipient of bullying. The teacher should model acceptance of Sammy to his classmates by acknowledging appropriate behavior in class. For example, the teacher could say in a positive tone of voice, "Sammy, thank you so much for helping to set up the website."

These strategies will help Sammy develop a positive relationship with the teacher and peers, which will help him feel more connected to them. Once Sammy experiences success in his schoolwork, he will be more motivated and feel he belongs academically in the class. I have always found that when a student feels comfortable in their relationship with the teacher and is successful academically, misbehavior seems to take care of itself, and the student becomes more socially included by peers in the class. I have also found that despite the appearance of not caring, most students want to be successful and accepted by classmates, and it is up to the teacher to find ways to enable that. Ensuring that each student experiences a sense of belonging is central to success at school.

CHAPTER 2

Differentiated Instruction

In the last chapter we saw how the teacher can promote a sense of belonging by developing a relationship with each student, supporting academic inclusion, ensuring a predictable environment, and encouraging all students to be accepting of others. In this chapter we will focus on academic belonging through the use of differentiated instruction (DI), which supports the various principles outlined in Chapter 1, such as the importance of providing feedback, fueling motivation, using culturally responsive teaching, and promoting self-efficacy and growth mindset among students.

The students in a typical class have various differences. These include strengths and preferences in learning modalities, or the sensory channels through which information is received, processed, and remembered — visual, auditory, and kinesthetic/tactile. They likely also have differences in their interests; ability to collaborate with others, self-regulate, and sustain attention; English language proficiency; intelligences; and cultural background. As well, a typical class will have students identified with exceptionalities, and teachers will follow individual education plans (IEPs) to implement the accommodations and curriculum changes required to ensure that these students may participate academically.

Usually, there is no protocol in place to ensure that a teacher receives a student's individual education plan. That said, in the fall, conscientious special education teachers will inform classroom teachers about new students with an exceptionality, and parents may tell their child's teachers about an IEP as part of their advocacy work.

Making Learning Accessible to All

Universal design for learning (UDL) is an approach to curriculum development that makes learning materials accessible to all students. It was developed to reduce the barriers that limit student access to materials and learning in the general classroom. For example, some students have difficulty acquiring information through printed text, and a teacher using UDL would provide multiple media to help those students learn. UDL incorporates many methods of instruction to help all students acquire information; various approaches to engage students, appealing to their interests, challenging them appropriately, and motivating them to learn; and multiple ways for students to express what they have learned. Technology can be used to format documents and texts so that they may be enlarged or are audible, which make the curriculum more accessible and provides students with different ways to express their learning.

Implementing UDL is often compared to designing buildings with electric doors, stairs, ramps, and elevators: some of these features accommodate people with physical disabilities while being used by people without physical disabilities. Similarly, lessons planned using UDL benefit students with exceptionalities (whether disabilities or giftedness) and may also have unintended but welcome outcomes of benefiting students without exceptionalities. When a teacher uses many visuals — for example, makes a PowerPoint presentation, writes key words on the board, posts instructions or important points on flipchart paper, shows pictures and diagrams, demonstrates how to do an assignment, provides a sample of a finished product, or passes around an object that the students can see and touch — it helps students with a hearing impairment, autism, learning disabilities, and attention deficit hyperactivity disorder. At the same time, using visuals and objects supports the learning of students without exceptionalities, especially those who prefer to learn through a visual and/or tactile learning modality.

DI is an approach to instructing students that grew out of UDL. It recognizes that there are students of varying abilities and interests in the same classroom. It consists of strategies that, when implemented, help teachers meet the learning needs of all students. Lessons developed using DI are flexible. Content is varied and challenging for all students, various processes are used to acquire information, and choices in the products that express learning are provided. As in UDL, teachers intentionally plan lessons with DI methods in mind rather than tacking on activities after the lesson is developed.

DI may be used with backwards design, where the expectations, objectives, learning outcomes, or learning goals are kept in mind during lesson development. It guides the selection of the content, instructional strategies, and assessment methods that you will use in your lessons and units. As well, the needs of particular students with exceptionalities may be accommodated as you plan your lessons, eliminating the preparation of individualized lessons. The suggestions in this chapter focus mostly on the process component of differentiated instruction; they will help you understand how to use a range of high-quality instructional strategies to help students acquire information and skills.

How to Use Differentiated Instruction in Your Classroom

DI is a way of addressing the learning needs of specific students without singling them out, but it also benefits the entire class. Using a response to intervention framework (RTI), DI strategies represent how a teacher would instruct the entire class using high-quality instructional strategies (Tier 1).

Response to Intervention (RTI)

Response to intervention is a tiered approach to instruction that provides support to struggling students and is used primarily in reading and math. RTI is organized into three tiers to provide appropriate support for students: Tier 1 — the whole class, Tier 2 — small groups, and Tier 3 — individual. All students would begin in Tier 1 and data would be collected through homework assignments and tests. Students not making progress with the regular instruction would be candidates for Tier 2 interventions. In Tier 2 a small group would receive targeted instruction three to five times a week. It is useful if the resource teacher can work with the small group and one intervention may be explicit instruction. This group's skill levels would be checked regularly, and if students were working at grade level, they would be moved back to Tier 1. If a student was still not making adequate progress, then they would move to Tier 3, where individual interventions would be used. The students in Tier 3 are the most at-risk and may need to be assessed for disabilities to receive special education support.

A multi-tier system of support (MTSS) includes RTI not only for academic skills but also for social and emotional capabilities.

The terms *expectations, objectives, learning outcomes,* and *learning goals* are essentially synonymous, but different school districts prefer the use of one term over the others.

The use of DI strategies does not lower academic standards — teachers should have high expectations for *all* students.

To use DI effectively, you first have to understand the interests, needs, and strengths of your students. As noted earlier, it is important to be familiar with your students as individuals, and the use of a screening checklist can help you know more about them. You also need to know about your class as a group — their preferred learning modalities, interests, and ability to collaborate with one another, the intelligences they demonstrate, the need of some students for enrichment, any need for reinforcement in specific topics, their level of English language acquisition, and their cultural backgrounds. A checklist you can use for your whole class is found on page 39. A teacher must be able to analyze the needs and strengths of individuals and the entire class and put together lesson plans that engage students and ensure that they learn what they are expected to learn. Teachers find that once they start planning lessons using DI strategies, it becomes easy and not as time-consuming as they may have thought.

An Effective Method of Teaching

V   Visual
A   Auditory
K/T Kinesthetic/Tactile

The second thing to keep in mind are the learning objectives of the lesson: what do you want your students to know or be able to do at the end of the lesson? Consider, too, how you will assess student learning. Given the breadth and depth of the content and the number of skills that are to be learned in each grade, as well as the fact that students will undergo standardized testing to determine whether they have learned the curriculum for their grade, "covering the material" is no longer acceptable. Teachers are expected to instruct in ways that will ensure all students learn.

Third, draw on various DI strategies for instruction and assessment of learning when preparing lessons. The easiest way to include all students' learning modalities is to follow the visual, auditory, kinesthetic/tactile (VAKT) method of teaching, as described on pages 26–27. Essentially, ensure that you teach by using visuals (e.g., writing key points to create an anchor chart, writing notes on the board), auditory modes (e.g., expressing important ideas orally or having students discuss a concept and its application in small groups), and, if possible, by providing a tactile (touching, manipulating) or kinesthetic (movement) component. You can then add cognitive supports, explicit instruction, enrichment and remediation, intelligences, group work, and tiered assignments. Be aware of the students' understanding of English and include accurate references to their varying cultural backgrounds. Beyond that, *when appropriate*, give students a choice in the activities they complete as part of the lesson. For example, in a science unit on habitats, students may be given a choice of writing a report, making an oral presentation, or creating a diorama.

The Differentiated Instruction Strategies

DI Strategies to Work With First

1. VAKT — visual, auditory, kines-
thetic/tactile
2. Cognitive supports — attention,
summarizing, chunking, practice,
scaffolding

After you have completed the checklist for the whole class, determined the goals, objectives, or expectations for the lesson, and have ideas for assessment of those outcomes, then plan how to teach the material. Plan your instructional activities with DI strategies in mind. Begin by addressing VAKT learning modalities and then combine them with cognitive supports. Once you are feeling comfortable with using these two DI strategies, add explicit instruction, enrichment, intelligences, and group work as appropriate. The various DI strategies are described on the following pages.

Appeal to multiple senses: VAKT

VAKT is a DI strategy that I have used for years to instruct children, adolescents, and adults. It is a method of instruction in which you present material using multiple senses: visual, auditory, and kinesthetic or tactile. In my experience, most students learn best when the material is presented visually (words, pictures, videos, diagrams, demonstrations), accompanied by oral instruction (auditory), and followed by kinesthetic/tactile (touching, manipulating, printing/writing/typing, doing the task). I recommend combining a minimum of two modalities in a lesson. Many students in your class will learn well when you combine visual and auditory or visual and kinesthetic/tactile. A few students will learn best auditorily — they need to hear you tell them about the concepts, key ideas, and instructions. Combining auditory and kinesthetic/tactile strategies will also increase the accessibility of your lessons to more students.

Below are some ideas about how to use the VAKT strategy in your lesson plans.

Learning Modality	Ideas
Visual	<u>Words</u> — Use PowerPoints, handouts, or electronic documents with key words underlined or bolded. Write important words on the board or flipchart paper. Distribute a handout or electronic document with a description of the assignment and the steps required to complete it. Show an example of a completed assignment. <u>Pictures</u> — Place pictures on your PowerPoints that relate to the concepts or ideas on each slide. Draw simple pictures on the board or flipchart paper to represent ideas. Show photographs or diagrams of items. Show videos to provide information on ideas or instructions on how to do a task. Demonstrate or draw pictures presenting the steps on how to do a task. <u>Other</u> — Show tables or graphs to represent information. Share diagrams to show relationships between things or ideas. Construct timelines. Present figures to demonstrate the steps in a process.
Auditory	Say the important points when describing a concept or event. State the instructions for an assignment or have a student list them. Use songs, chants, or rhymes to summarize main ideas. Have students in small groups discuss ideas and their application.

Kinesthetic/Tactile	Permit students to touch objects that are used in the lesson. Use manipulatives in math and science. Prompt students to make or draw objects that are representative of the concept or process being discussed. Have students demonstrate a procedure or activity. Direct students to practise the skill or activity. Ask students to take notes or copy them from the board. If possible, arrange for students to go on nature walks or trips to museums with interactive displays. Dramatize concepts in all subjects as well as events in history, stories, or novels.

Always use at least two learning modalities, such as visual and auditory, when instructing students to help them remember the material. For example, you could describe a concept or event orally and write key ideas on the board or flipchart paper; talk about an idea or process and draw simple pictures to represent it; show pictures or diagrams and talk about them, writing key points on the board; or orally describe an assignment, demonstrate how to do it while you say what you are doing, write the steps in completing it, show an example of a completed assignment, then have students work in small groups and discuss their ideas with one another.

Provide cognitive supports

Cognitive supports are instructional techniques drawn mostly from cognitive learning theory that help students encode or remember the material you are teaching them. They range from gaining student attention to providing a lot of practice. Some individual education plans (IEPs) call for the use of these strategies (e.g., scaffolding and chunking); however, they are equally effective with all students. Using them as part of your instructional plan ensures that students with exceptionalities are not singled out and feel as though they belong in the class with the others.

1. **Attention:** Before you can teach your students anything, you must have their *attention*. Some factors that affect attention are the meaning that the task or information has for the student, competing sources of information (e.g., a student talking while you are instructing), the complexity of the task, and individual differences (e.g., in age or attention span). One way to increase the meaning a topic has for students is to draw on their interests in your lessons. Another way to improve how meaningful students find new material is to review previously learned material and point out the similarities and differences between it and the new material. As well, you can explain why learning the concept is helpful in their lives. Furthermore, if you have a multicultural classroom, to increase attention, include accurate references to the students' cultures. How Indigenous peoples are portrayed in history is of particular concern.

   There are simple ways to gain students' attention. At the beginning of the lesson, you might say, "Let's begin" or "I need everyone to look at me so that we may begin." Another approach to indicating a lesson is about to begin is to raise a hand as a signal for students to stop talking. Some teachers also use a "hook," such as showing a clip from a video to introduce the topic or conducting a quick experiment related to the lesson. To focus student attention during certain parts of the lesson, use a different color of marker or chalk, bolded words, gestures, or cue students with words, for example: "This is important." Other ways to help hold students' attention involve novelty, as in having students discuss their responses to an open-ended question in small groups or conducting a short opinion poll; visual aids, such as a slide or photograph of a person, place, or thing related to the topic; or an object that illustrates a point, such as a model airplane to demonstrate Bernoulli's principle. Your enthusiasm for the subject and topic will be infectious.

2. **Summarizing:** Teach by summarizing a concept or series of steps into three or four key words. For example, in a lesson where you want your students to know the three main elements of a story, review what they already know about writing stories, then read a brief story to them as they follow along, using their own copies of the same story. Introduce the term *introduction* and show them that part of the story using your finger. Have each student circle the introduction, using a finger. Talk about what information appears in an introduction. On flipchart paper, write the title and the word *introduction* below and three or four points about the introduction. Continue in the same way with body and conclusion. Then verbally summarize the elements of a short story for your students by pointing to and underlining the words *introduction, body,* and *conclusion* on paper. Post it on a wall so that the students can refer to it later. Then reinforce the three key ideas by dividing the students into groups and giving each group copies of a short story that is familiar to them. If possible, provide each group with a different story. Have the groups analyze their stories according to the description posted on the wall. Encourage them to say the three key words, use their fingers to circle the various sections, and explain to the others in their group how the criteria for each section apply to their story. Then, ask each group to discuss their stories and as an exit activity have students write the three key words on a piece of paper which is given to you. Post the flipchart paper on the wall and use it to review the parts of the story; have students refer to it as they compose their own stories. In this lesson the strategies of using VAKT and summarizing the writing process into three words will help your students remember the components when they write their own stories.

3. **Chunking:** Divide the material you want to teach in a lesson into parts, or "chunks." Teach one chunk at a time and follow it by a summary of the important ideas (use three or four key words), a short question-and-answer session, or a discussion of the concept in small groups or pairs to consolidate this first phase of the learning. In physical education, you might also have the students perform the step you have just demonstrated. Proceed then to the next chunk of material and link it to the first part verbally or by drawing a diagram or even a timeline. Follow this segment of the instruction with a short activity to consolidate this part of the learning. Continue until all the chunks have been presented and review the entire process or concept. Have students apply what they have just learned (e.g., steps in a dance).

Chunking works because some students have short attention spans and need to change activities frequently (e.g., watching and listening to talking or doing) and some students' working memory allows them to hold only small amounts of information at a time. Breaking the explanation into chunks or steps followed by a short consolidation activity helps them to process the information.

4. **Practice:** When students practise printing or cursive writing, for example, they learn how to form the letters. We incorporate a lot of practice for some tasks because we want students to over-memorize: the goal is for the task or concept to become automatic for them. Simple repetition usually works for arithmetic facts, vocabulary words, or a memorized script. It should be noted that each student will require different amounts of practice to learn a concept or how to do a task. Students identified as gifted generally need much less practice learning concepts or procedures than other students.

   We must also acknowledge that *perfect* practice makes perfect. When students are just beginning to learn how to do something, they need your attention to ensure that they are doing it correctly. If they are not, then they need your feedback on how to improve. For example, in physical education, students need to know if they are throwing the ball correctly, and in math, they need to know if they have executed the proper steps in doing a subtraction question with borrowing, dividing a fraction by a mixed number, or solving an equation. Providing feedback on how students are doing things is one of the best ways to help them improve their performance.

5. **Scaffolding:** I use the imagery of a construction site as a way of understanding this fifth cognitive support. Think of two parts of a building that are joined by a board that acts like a bridge to lead from one section to the next. The board is the scaffold, and in lesson planning we use scaffolds to lead students from what they can do independently to being able to do something new, first with assistance and later independently. I see scaffolding as being a broad concept that involves almost anything a teacher can do to help students learn a concept or perform a task. Scaffolds can include demonstrations, think-alouds, explanations, drawings, pictures, videos, hand-over-hand activities (e.g., place your hand on the student's hand when showing a student how to print or write a letter or word), and tracing activities with dots to follow (e.g., for printing and writing letters). Knowledgeable peers working in heterogeneous small groups can also explain a concept or demonstrate a procedure, thereby using scaffolding to advance the learning of the others in their group.

Give explicit instruction

Explicit instruction (also known as "direct instruction") is a way of organizing your lesson plans so that you follow a process of gaining students' attention, introducing the material or skill, providing opportunities for guided practice, and finally, enabling independent practice. This strategy can be used when implementing a response to intervention (RTI) approach to reading and math. It works well if you are able to co-teach with the resource teacher in your school. The students can be divided into two groups with the smaller group instructed by the resource teacher, who will focus on re-teaching skills using explicit instruction (Tier 2). You can teach the larger group that is working at grade level, using explicit instruction or other high quality instructional strategies (Tier 1). If the resource teacher is not available, you can re-teach skills using explicit instruction to a small group of students while the rest of the class works independently. The steps in teaching a lesson using explicit instruction are on the following page.

1. Gain students' attention by announcing that the class or group is ready to begin, introduce some sort of novelty, or "hook," related to lesson content (e.g., a picture, a short video, a short story), or draw on students' interests, culture, or past experiences.

2. Review the previous day's work to ensure understanding and present a basis for the lesson; explain what will be learned by the end of the lesson; provide an advance organizer (e.g., a diagram or short and basic explanation) to show the big picture or main ideas. If possible, explain why knowing the new skill or information is important.

3. Present the lesson whereby you teach the steps or concepts. Use the VAKT methods described above, demonstrate the skill or process, chunk the information into segments, or steps, checking for understanding after teaching each one. Explain a concept and provide many examples of how the concept or ideas are linked to students' lives. Focus on the important information and repeat key ideas or words. Ask questions to ensure understanding or to have students think more deeply about a point. Prompt students to discuss specific points or questions either as a large group or in small groups (e.g., pairs).

4. Provide opportunities for guided practice, where the students practise the task or apply the information individually or in small groups. When working in small groups, the students can discuss what they are to do and solve problems together. Be aware of what the students are doing and how they are following the process. Provide corrective feedback as necessary.

5. Once the students are ready, have them perform the task or apply information independently and without your close attention. Students may work alone or in small groups. You can provide rubrics or a checklist so that students can engage in self-assessment.

6. Assessment is the final step, and you need to check the students' work to see whether the learning objective or expectation was achieved. Consider offering choices to students about how their learning is assessed (e.g., choice of topic for a written expression assignment and how the information will be presented: completely in writing, some writing with a hand-drawn picture, or typed). If the expectation was not met, then analyze students' work to find out what they know and what they do not know; reteach accordingly.

Open up enrichment activities

You can also differentiate instruction when including enrichment activities in your lessons for those students whose individual education plans require them and for others who may be interested in a topic and want to explore it further. Simply showing students where to learn more about a topic by providing links to websites and books may satisfy most students' curiosity. You can also have students identified as gifted work on individual research on various topics of interest. This opportunity may be made available to all the students (including struggling students), thereby giving them an opportunity to investigate a topic of interest. After completing their projects, students may reflect on what was learned by filling out the Personal Enrichment Exploration form on page 31. They can then use the finished form as a prompt to discuss their project with a small group of students, the entire class, or individually with you. Engaging in research activities or "passion" projects allows everyone to demonstrate areas of competence, which can lead to a sense of academic belonging. Applying Bloom's taxonomy and instituting tiered activities are two other ways of providing enrichment, and they are discussed on page 32.

Personal Enrichment Exploration

Focus Topic or Question:

_____

_____

What I Learned:

_____

_____

_____

_____

_____

_____

_____

_____

_____

_____

_____

Other Topics or Questions That Arose:

_____

_____

Resources Consulted (e.g., Books, Internet, People):

_____

_____

_____

_____

_____

_____

Pembroke Publishers © 2022 *Finding a Place for Every Student* by Cheryll Duquette ISBN 978-1-55138-360-6

Endeavor to incorporate Bloom's taxonomy, with its six levels of thinking skills, into your questioning and assignments. Doing so will allow all students (including the ones with cognitive disabilities) to demonstrate understanding of ideas and concepts, not just basic recall. Consider these examples of lower-order questions: "How many Loyalists fled to present-day Canada during the American Revolution? What was the Underground Railroad?" On the same topic, here is a question that requires students to synthesize and evaluate information: "If you were a farmer in the Thirteen Colonies in 1776, would you have supported the Patriots or joined the Loyalists? Outline the reasons for your decision." Chapter 8 provides more ideas on how to do this.

Tiered activities can also be used to provide enrichment. You can give students the choice of completing a basic required assignment, as well as one or two other options that extend their knowledge of the topic. The first tier, or level, consists of an assignment that would be completed by all the students. It would likely be one that most students could do independently, one that involves the use of materials accessible to all students, and one in which students applied information just acquired. Second and third tier activities would involve deeper research and higher-order thinking. Students who need enrichment activities would be required to select at least one additional assignment, and completion of the second and third tier work would be optional for the others. For example, in a history lesson on the First World War, the basic activity would be to read the print materials, view the videos on the life of a soldier fighting in the trenches, and write a journal entry from the soldier's point of view. A second tier activity could involve comparing and contrasting the information already discovered about fighting in the trenches to the points made about military life, as described in the recruitment material used in the First World War. A third tier activity might be to explore specific military technological advances made during the war and to evaluate their contribution to the war's outcome. Hence, the three tiers of activities related to the First World War constitute a range of levels of research and thought about the topic in which students could engage.

In addition to tiered activities, you can include *extension activities* in many of your lessons. For example, if the students are showing patterns in art using only two colors, an extension activity may be to have the students who finish first ("fast finishers") complete another pattern using three or four colors. If you are working on geometric figures in math, an activity for fast finishers is to construct figures using tangrams. Providing extension activities helps to extend and reinforce learning and ensures that all students are engaged in learning activities throughout the class. Some teachers also observe that making popular extension activities available for all students changes the atmosphere in their classroom. Students are focused on their work so that they will have time to do some extension activities.

Recognize intelligences

As seen previously, individuals have learning style preferences that relate to the modality in which they acquire new information and process it (visual, auditory, and kinesthetic/tactile). It is also known that students' areas of strengths or intelligences are diverse. It is posited that when students are taught according to their strengths, academic performance improves.

Robert Sternberg (2008) and Howard Gardner (1983, 1999) have each proposed key ideas about intelligences.

The Intelligences, According to Sternberg

Analytical
Creative
Practical

Multiple Intelligences, According to Gardner

1. Verbal-linguistic
2. Logical-mathematical
3. Musical-rhythmic
4. Visual-spatial
5. Bodily-kinesthetic
6. Naturalistic
7. Interpersonal
8. Intrapersonal

Sternberg developed the theory of successful intelligence. One element is that individuals have different abilities that can be used to learn and ultimately achieve success in life. Sternberg contends that teachers should vary instructional style so that students are required to "analyze, evaluate, compare and contrast, judge, and critique; other times encouraged to create, invent, discover, imagine, or suppose" (2008, p. 153). He says teachers also need to ask students "to apply, put into practice, implement, and use what they have learned" (p. 153). Essentially, these three intelligences — analytical, creative, and practical — should be used to ensure that all students have an opportunity to learn in a way that matches their strengths.

Gardner proposes eight specific intelligences, or domains of strength: verbal-linguistic, logical-mathematical, musical-rhythmic, visual-spatial, bodily-kinesthetic, naturalistic, interpersonal, and intrapersonal. It is proposed that Gardner's multiple intelligences (MI) can be used as ways to vary the teaching of material to a class and how the students demonstrate their learning. While including all eight intelligences in a single lesson is unnecessary, it may be possible to provide students with choices as to how they might express their learning: these choices can be linked to multiple intelligences.

Sternberg and Gardner believe that students have diverse learning strengths or intelligences. They propose that teachers should endeavor to vary their teaching strategies and fit their instructional and assessment methods to the intelligences of their students to improve learning. Given the currency of their ideas, during the course of a unit, try to include as many of their intelligences as possible; in so doing, you can appeal to many student strengths.

Use group work

Group work is another way of incorporating differentiated instruction into your practice. It is recommended that for the purposes of differentiated instruction, short-term, flexible groupings be used to tap into students' interests and strengths to complete assignments and to provide remediation. Consider using *heterogeneous groups* so that students' varying strengths may be used to do an activity. For example, an assignment may require that a group of students read, write, construct a table, and produce some artwork. Arrange the groups so that there are students with these abilities in each group.

Some teachers also use cooperative learning, in which small groups of students each have an assigned task that is integral to the completion of the assignment. One component of cooperative learning groups is that each member either instructs the others about the part of the task they completed, or all the members help one another learn the material. Here are two popular cooperative learning strategies:

- In Think-Pair-Share (also known as "Turn and Talk"), two students in close proximity think about what the teacher just presented and then discuss their thoughts about it.
- In Jigsaw, members of a group are each given a different topic on a subject to research; they then leave the home group and work with members of other groups that are investigating the same topic as they are. After completing the research, the students return to their home groups and teach one another what they learned. A teacher can select the members of each group on the basis of their ability to complete the tasks and collaborate effectively. Group composition may vary according to the task requirements of each assignment.

Homogeneous groups may be used to provide enrichment and remediation. For example, if two students in the class either require enrichment or are keenly interested in pursuing research on a particular topic, they can be paired to delve more deeply into the particular subject matter. Likewise, if a few students need to have a concept retaught or reviewed, they can be brought together into a small group so that you can provide remediation. In both cases, the homogeneous groups would be formed on a short-term basis to address specific needs.

For review or consolidation activities, teachers may also use peer tutoring where students are paired to complete an activity. Reading buddies is an example of this type of activity, where older students are paired with younger ones to read passages or books. The older, more experienced student can read a passage, followed by the beginning reader. As the younger child reads the passage the older one can provide immediate feedback in the form of correction, help the partner sound out words, or explain the meaning of words. Having the children in pairs ensures that the less experienced reader is receiving individual attention and corrective feedback. Peer tutoring may also be used to review concepts in a unit of study, and for reinforcement of sight words, number facts, or vocabulary.

Getting Started with Differentiated Instruction

When implementing differentiated instruction for the first time in your classroom, begin by making observations on the students as a group, introduce the VAKT strategy, and then add the other DI strategies when you feel comfortable. As you try each of them, take a few minutes and think about how well it worked in the lesson, what went well, and what did not work so well. Continue to use the strategies that seemed to help the students learn and make adjustments to how you use the ones that did not result in the students achieving the objective or expectation of the lesson. Through trial, reflection, and revision, you will develop a repertoire of DI strategies that work with your students.

What to observe about your students

When observing your students, you may want to use the checklist on page 39 to focus. Note through which modalities your students generally learn best. Visual learners may be subdivided into two groups: students who learn best through print and students who learn best through pictures and videos. Students who learn best by print are usually good readers and understand what they read. They are likely able to express their ideas in writing reasonably well. Students who prefer to learn via pictures or videos like to see a photo or video of what is being discussed. These students also learn when a skill or task is demonstrated and when concepts and ideas are summarized in figures, diagrams, or tables. Visual learners like to see instructions in some sort of visual form, for example, in an itemized list in words or pictures. Auditory learners prefer to hear the ideas and discuss or talk through what is being learned. These students are able to follow oral directions. Kinesthetic or tactile learners prefer to touch and manipulate objects and get out of their seats to be directly involved in their learning (e.g., role play, making a model). As noted above, try to incorporate at least two learning modalities in each of your lessons.

Make observations about the interests of your students, as well. Listen to their conversations about sports, video games, music, and other topics, as these will give you some clues as to their interests. Incorporating these interests into your lessons will serve as a motivator, or "hook," for the students.

Be sure to note to what extent your students are able to collaborate during in-class activities. Some students seem to work better in small groups than others. In some cases, you may have to select the groups and give each student a particular task to complete in order for group work to function smoothly.

Take note of the intelligences that students display. You may find that you have more students with naturalistic intelligence than you expected, for example, so you would be wise to include their specific areas of interest in your instruction. Observe, too, if students seem to be more analytical, creative, or practical in their learning and expression of learning.

You will also want to identify which students require enrichment or remediation and in what areas. It is possible that most of your students have a weak knowledge of a particular math concept or skill in writing that you will have to review in depth with them. Note the number of students who are learning the English language. If they make up a large proportion of the class you will likely have to structure your lessons to give greater emphasis to visual and kinesthetic/tactile learning modalities as opposed to auditory.

Finally, note the different cultures of the students in your class. Take the time to learn about them and refer to them in your instruction as much as possible. For example, discuss the teachings of the Anishinaabe people's seven grandfathers in your lessons on character development. Students like to see their cultures represented positively and accurately at school.

Build on VAKT strategies by adding cognitive supports

You will likely notice that you have students who seem to learn best through each of the three modalities (visual, auditory, and kinesthetic/tactile). With this information, you can plan lessons with VAKT in mind. Include the elements described above in the presentation and application parts of your lessons. Once you begin implementing VAKT, reflect on how well these strategies are working and continue or make adjustments. The next step is to combine VAKT strategies with some cognitive supports, as described above. Again, keep adding and combining the cognitive supports as you feel comfortable, and make adjustments depending on the needs of the students.

Provide enrichment and remediation

The next component to include in your lessons is *enrichment and remediation*. As noted above, enrichment can be incorporated in your lessons through using Bloom's taxonomy to guide your questioning and activities. Consider trying out tiered assignments, too, to ensure that there are extension activities in the lesson. Students can choose whether they want to do just the required level of activity or that component plus the extension activity. Students with individual education plans stating that they need enrichment should complete all the activities for the lesson. When planning a unit, ensure that there are extension activities available for students to pursue when they are finished their work and that there are specific projects for students identified as requiring enrichment. It is easy to set up a spot in the classroom where students can explore concepts or do some research on a particular topic related to history, science, geography, math, art, health, or language.

If you are planning a lesson using explicit instruction, remediation can occur when students are working on the independent practice part of the lesson. Work with individuals or small groups of students to reteach or repeat concepts. You can also provide feedback and support as some students may still be in the guided practice phase.

Plan lessons that draw on the intelligences

Another DI strategy that can be included in your lesson planning is intelligences. Plan lessons with Sternberg's successful intelligences and/or Gardner's multiple intelligences in mind. Giving students the opportunity to select from activities that are analytical, creative, or practical or that follow one of the eight multiple intelligences is an easy way to address students' strengths when they are completing assignments. Students appreciate having a choice of activities to show what they have learned, and often these activities may be done in pairs or small groups. Offering this type of choice allows students a chance to be successful, which supports academic belonging.

Incorporate culturally responsive teaching

Draw on students' various cultures to motivate students to want to learn and pay attention. While it is often difficult to find accurate resources depicting students' various cultures, teachers report that it is well worth the effort. Common resources are story books, novels, and posters. When teachers include references to students' cultures it promotes a sense of validation and belonging.

Promote discussion in groups

The last step is to use partner work, small-group work, and cooperative learning in your classroom. Most students enjoy the opportunity to talk about the concepts the teacher has just presented or to work with a partner to apply an idea or practise a skill. This focused talk can help them consolidate and extend their learning.

You can use flexible groups to provide opportunities to discuss an idea, apply a concept, or practise a skill for short periods of time at certain points in your lesson. For example, break up the content of your lesson into chunks and have students discuss what they have just learned through a Think-Pair-Share activity, or have students practise a skill, such as using a metre stick or ruler to measure a particular object. Once you can see that students have mastered this part of the lesson, move on to the next segment so that they can build on the initial learning. I tend to use small groups for in-class activities for students to discuss and apply ideas rather than for assignments that are completed outside of class and that will be marked. You can also work with a small group of students who need to have a specific concept or skill retaught before they are ready to do the activity. Often, this type of session involves a quick review of the ideas or skills you presented and some guided practice whereby you give immediate feedback to them. There is no stigma attached to this sort of small-group session because it does not involve the same students all the time. Including peer tutoring is another way to reinforce learning.

The DI template

DI is an approach to teaching in which students' interests, strengths, and needs are considered when planning lessons. Including students' interests and strengths into lessons is motivating and gives them a sense that they can expect to succeed. As well, the needs of students with exceptionalities may be included into your lessons, and they will likely benefit all the students (e.g., using visuals and manipulatives). DI builds on high-quality instructional strategies and allows the teacher to develop a single lesson that will be used with the whole class. Although specific accommodations for some students may be required (e.g., the use of a computer or preferential seating), they are easily implemented within the lesson. I have used DI strategies throughout my teaching career and have found that using them just becomes part of the way you teach. They are effective and have helped my students be successful and feel as though they belong academically in the classroom.

Below is a template for implementing differentiated instruction in your classroom. It summarizes the steps.

1. Make observations of your students as a group (see "Class Observation Checklist for Differentiated Instruction," page 39).
2. Plan lessons using visual, auditory, and kinesthetic/tactile learning modalities —VAKT.
3. Add cognitive supports (e.g., gaining students' attention, demonstrating what has to be done plus three or four key words, summarizing ideas plus three or four key words, chunking, practice and feedback, scaffolding) — VAKT + cognitive supports.
4. Add other DI strategies (explicit instruction, enrichment, intelligences, group work, and cultural references) — VAKT + cognitive supports + other strategies.

As a student teacher, Leah Dabrowski tried out DI strategies during her first practicum, using a template based on the above. She found that focused observation helped her to know more about her students as a group and the steps in implementing differentiated instruction helped her structure her lessons for them. In the text box on the next page, Leah shares some of her experiences using differentiated instruction.

Implementing Differentiated Instruction: One Teacher's Experience

Walking into your first practicum as a student teacher can be a nerve-wracking experience. Differentiated instruction (DI) helped me begin my teaching practice with an open mind and the willingness to let myself try and fail a number of times to find which strategies worked best. I can't stress the importance of knowing the students in your class as a starting point for implementing any teaching strategies. Before my practicum began, I spent a day getting to know the students and the school, thereby gaining some basic information before I had my first official day. I found this extra day let me get to know the students and structure of the class. It was a real treat being able to walk in the first day with the students knowing who I was and that I would be staying with them for a few weeks.

I took a good three days only teaching read-alouds and immersing myself in the students' world in order to figure out which strategies I thought would work best for my class. VAKT was particularly helpful, and in each lesson I conducted, a minimum of two learning modalities were used. My class was predominantly male, and they responded best to incorporating tactile and kinesthetic modalities. Believe it or not, dance was one of their favorite activities. Throughout my practicum, I observed how the lessons went and in a log I reflected on what went well and what did not go as planned. Using trial and error, I tweaked strategies until they worked or until I figured out they were not going to work with this group. For example, when I tried group work the first time, it was not very structured and it ended in chaos. The second time I divided the students into two groups and subdivided them into smaller groups of four. I supervised one larger group, and the teaching assistant worked with the other one. This method of organizing group work was mildly effective. The third time I used a form of cooperative learning whereby I structured the activity so that the students could not find the overall answer without each of them contributing. Then I organized the students into groups of four, assigned them each a task, and rotated the students through all the tasks. This time the group activity worked well, and the students understood a concept related to measurement. So through trial and error I was able to figure out how to structure group work for this group of students.

My advisor, Cheryll Duquette, developed a template on how to implement DI, which I used throughout my whole practicum, especially when planning out units. I found it easy to follow, and it was also a tool for reflection on my own practices in the classroom. This template accounted for any special needs I had and the ways in which I could address them. After a while it became automatic to implement DI as I had used the template so much that most of what I did happened automatically. I became more effective in planning and teaching my lessons and felt that using DI helped my students learn. The increase in confidence, motor skills, collaboration, and basics skills such as writing and arithmetic among them was amazing to see!

Class Observation Checklist for Differentiated Instruction

Predominant Learning Modalities

☐ Visual Print
☐ Visual Pictures/Videos
☐ Auditory
☐ Kinesthetic/Tactile

Interests

_____

_____

Ability to Collaborate with Others

_____

_____

Intelligences

☐ Multiple (verbal-linguistic, logical-mathematical, musical-rhythmic, visual-spatial, bodily-kinesthetic, naturalistic, interpersonal, intrapersonal)
☐ Analytical, creative, practical

Enrichment

_____

_____

Remediation

☐ Generally
☐ Specific areas

English Language Development

_____

_____

_____

Cultural Backgrounds

_____

_____

Pembroke Publishers © 2022 _Finding a Place for Every Student_ by Cheryll Duquette ISBN 978-1-55138-360-6

CHAPTER 3

Observing Students

We have all been in the situation where a student's performance or behavior caused us some concern. Perhaps a student seems to understand things orally but can't express themselves on paper. Maybe a student's behaviors disrupt the learning of the other children. Or you wonder what you might do about a student in your classroom who grasps new concepts quickly, is among the first in the class to complete their work, and usually has the work done correctly. You may suspect that these students have a learning disability, a behavioral disorder, or a gift. But because the referral process usually takes months, even if the child is identified as having an exceptionality, they may no longer be in your class by the time an individual education plan (IEP) is written. Nevertheless, you want to have high expectations for all your students and do your best for them when they are with you.

While you may have some ideas about how to work with these students, what you need is a framework or process to help them. One that works well consists of the following steps: (1) observing, (2) formulating goals, (3) developing strategies, (4) implementing the action plan, and (5) reviewing the action plan. This framework is based on the classic process of problem solving, which is widely used in administration. It is also similar to the process used in action research by teachers who want to improve their practice.

In this chapter we will examine how to observe students, especially those who have not yet been identified as having an exceptionality.

Know Your Students

One of the most important things to do as a teacher is to know your students: their strengths, weaknesses, preferred learning modalities, and interests. You may do this in several ways. Simply observe their classroom work and behaviors and keep formal and informal records. Examine the files in which are kept report cards, records of achievement testing, and so on. Pay particular attention to the comments made by previous teachers on the report cards. These will give you a sense about earlier achievement levels, work habits, and behaviors. The results of any formal assessments, psychological testing, or medical examination will tell you about the child's intelligence, specific learning disabilities, and the presence of attention deficit hyperactivity disorder (ADHD) or other exceptionalities.

You may be surprised by what you discover. Perhaps a particular student tested as gifted, which may explain why they finish work before everyone else and fills in time by talking to others. Or another student proves to have a hearing impairment, which may explain why they rarely seem to participate in group discussions or follow oral instructions. Another student may not be

The Process of Working with Students at Risk

Whether students have identified or not-yet-identified disabilities, behavior problems, or gifts, follow this basic process:

1. **Observe students.**
2. Formulate goals.
3. Develop strategies.
4. Implement the plan.
5. Review the action plan.

A Formal Assessment and Plan

A student who is identified as having an exceptionality has undergone a formal assessment consisting of standardized tests that measure intelligence and achievement, and other tests related to the area of the suspected disability, disorder, impairment, or gift. A committee reviews the results of the tests and decides whether the child has an exceptionality and what special accommodations are required. An individual education plan (IEP) is then prepared. An IEP is a legal document that states the student's strengths and needs, and ways to accommodate the student's special needs. It is based on the results of the assessment and is written by the classroom teacher, the special education teacher, and sometimes the parent and child. The student's progress is noted and reviewed at least once a year; the IEP is updated accordingly.

wearing their glasses, and you may realize why they are constantly talking when copying work from the board.

Speak to the student, the parents, and previous teachers as well. I have found that by about Grade 4, a child will be able to tell you why work is not being completed (e.g., *can't see the board, don't want to do the work and prefer to play with my pencil, don't understand the work, can't write what's in my head, can't copy very quickly, it's too easy*). Parents can also provide information about the child's previous progress, abilities, and home life, effective teaching techniques, and so on. Previous teachers will likely be able to provide information about academic levels, social and emotional skills, classroom behaviors, and teaching techniques that worked for them.

You need to make observations and gather information about a student to determine their academic strengths and weaknesses, as well as learning style preferences, extracurricular interests, and activities. The strengths, interests, and learning style preferences may be used to plan lessons and weaknesses then translate into the goals for improvement.

You may be able to use a student's strengths to achieve the goals. For example, I once taught a Grade 7 student who knew *everything* about 18-wheelers. That year, almost all their creative writing was on the one subject they knew: trucks. Because the student felt confident about the subject matter, they were able to accept my spelling and grammar corrections. Through the corrections and individual conferencing, we were able to improve their skill levels in those two areas.

Academic Performance in Elementary Students

The observations you make at the beginning of the process serve as the baseline of academic performance or behaviors so that you may measure improvement. Below are some ways to observe students.

Observe over time

Record keeping is extremely important in making observations about a child's academic performance. Generally, you can use published checklists and anecdotal reports recorded in a private journal or password protected file. In the primary grades, keep track of whether the work is completed and handed in. This may be done by checking off the child's name on a class list. You may also want to make some informal notes in a private journal or file about whether the child seems to understand the concepts. You will notice this through the written work that you correct every day, during class time as you teach the material, and when you circulate around the classroom as the students work on an assignment. While you circulate, you will observe who seems to be struggling to understand the instructions or concepts. You will also see who grasps the ideas easily and finishes the work well ahead of the others. As you make your observations over time — for example, two to four weeks — notice how often work is incomplete, not understood, or completed accurately and quickly.

Note, as well, in which subject areas these work trends are occurring. For example, you may have a student whose oral reading and comprehension are not at grade level and who has difficulty with spelling and written expression. In this case, you would note the performance of the child in these three subject areas over a few weeks.

Be specific

The more specific your observations, the easier it will be to develop a plan for the student. For example, if the child struggles with oral reading, try to note the specific areas of difficulty, such as phonological awareness, phonics, decoding skills, omission of words, or insertion of words. Be discreet about making the observations. Note them during the oral reading sessions and record them using the published checklist that may accompany your reading series or that is distributed by your district. You may also consider recording observations in a private journal when the children are not in the classroom and keeping the journal in a locked cabinet or as a secure electronic file.

You should also note the student's academic achievement. One way to do it is through teacher-made tests and assignments. Subject-based skill-development checklists that have been developed by your board of education are another option. For oral reading, you may use word lists for a specific grade that are prepared by the publisher of the language texts. The child would read these words, and you would note those that were read correctly and those that were read incorrectly. For the words read incorrectly, note whether they were guesses or whether the child tried to sound them out. In the latter case, write what the child pronounced. For example, if the word was *mate* and the child pronounced /mat/, write what was said beside the word that was pronounced incorrectly. When the child has finished reading the words, examine the words that were pronounced correctly and incorrectly to determine specific patterns. After examining the list, you may notice that the child knows short vowels, but not long vowels, for example. Be sure to make many observations over time to determine whether or not the student really does know the long vowel sounds. A single observation is insufficient because the child may not have been feeling well or may just have been inattentive. Track the child's performance in daily work and on tests and assignments for a few weeks.

Note clusters of strengths and weaknesses

Be aware of *clusters* of difficulties, such as those in the language area: reading, spelling, and written expression. Note the child's speech and language development. Listen to pronunciation, vocabulary used, and sentence structure. You may notice difficulties in math, too, particularly in remembering the facts and procedures about how to do the operations involved in adding (such as carrying), subtracting (such as borrowing), multiplying, and dividing. Consider that a child who has difficulties with problem solving in math may also have problems with reading comprehension. Note, too, the motor skills of the child: fine motor, as shown in printing or writing; and gross motor, as in running, jumping, or climbing. Observe whether the child can organize their work, how long an attention span the child has developed, and how well they collaborate with others in groups. You should also make observations about the child's preferred learning style (visual, auditory, kinesthetic/tactile — VAKT), ability to think critically (analyze text or statements and evaluate them), and creativity (ability to develop new ideas or solutions that may be useful). Social and emotional development should also be observed (e.g., emotional awareness and regulation, persistence, understanding of others' thoughts and feelings, relationships with others, and ability to make responsible decisions). Also note indicators of mental health, such as being connected with others, engaged in the work, and changes in behavior (e.g., suddenly misbehaving in class, not completing or submitting work, hanging with a new group of friends). Beyond that, if the child's first language is not English, make notes about their English language development and cultural background. You may want to use a screening checklist, such as appears on pages 45–46, to record your observations. It provides a general guide for observing a student's development and skill levels. A reproducible version appears immediately after it.

Verify your observations through previous records

Another area to examine is the child's file. Look for the results of an IQ test. Some boards give group IQ tests to all students at certain grades, such as Grade 3 or 4. You would find a statement of the child's intelligence, such as low average, average, high average, or superior. A child may have also had an individual IQ test, such as the Wechsler Intelligence Scale for Children (WISC), which would have been administered by a psychologist or psychometrist. A full report would indicate the child's areas of strengths and weaknesses, such as language, arithmetic, or visual-motor skills; their IQ; and suggestions for classroom accommodations, if required.

You may also find a copy of an IEP that, for whatever reason, is not being followed. This may sound surprising, but if a student has arrived at your school from a different board or even from a school within your own board, the file may not arrive until mid-October. If the child or parent has not informed you of an exceptionality and an IEP, you will not know that one exists unless you read the student's records.

As you go through the file, read the previous report cards and note the marks and teachers' comments. These records may support your own observations. Sometimes, the report cards offer no clue as to the present functioning of a student. In this case, trust your own observations and act upon them.

Next, read any other pertinent documents. These may include the results of an eye examination, hearing test, or standardized achievement tests, such as language and math at Grades 3 and 6. In summary, read the file to find out about the past academic performance of the child and clues as to why the child is performing at his or her current level.

When making observations about academic performance, the important things to remember are to observe over time, to be as specific as possible, to note any clusters of strengths or weaknesses, and to verify them with previous records.

What to Focus On in Intermediate Grades

Making detailed observations on each of your 120 students is difficult because you may not see each student every day. However, you may have noticed some whose academic performance is well above or below the standard or those who frequently exhibit inappropriate behaviors.

The most important things to concentrate on are the student's marks, ability to hand in work on time, and attendance. They may offer indicators of mental health issues. Record keeping is obviously important here.

Patterns of achievement

You likely record the results of all tests, and after three tests you will begin to note the obvious patterns of achievement. In other words, you will notice whether a student has done well on two or three of the three tests. You will also see which

Screening Checklist

Name: _____Tyler_____   Grade: ___4___   Date of Birth: ___June 25, 2004___

Language

☐ Oral Reading — *some hesitancy, doesn't pay attention to punctuation, slow pace, little intonation, reads a rehearsed passage better*

☐ Reading Comprehension — *can answer most fact and detail questions, some difficulty with main idea and inference, seems to understand more when listens to a tape and reads*

☐ Spelling — *weekly spelling tests are well done, everyday spelling is weaker, has trouble sounding out words, sequence of letters in middle and end of words is sometimes a problem*

☐ Written Expression — *can express sequential thought, ideas are usually expressed logically, does not put much effort into creative writing, applies punctuation and capitalization rules most of the time*

☐ Oral Expression — *extensive vocabulary, no articulation problems, expresses ideas logically and sequentially, volunteers answers regularly*

☐ Oral Comprehension — *follows directions, understands passages better when read orally*

Math

☐ Concepts — *good understanding: numbers, operations, measurements, patterns, geometry*

☐ Facts — *knows +, −, ×, and ÷ to 12*

☐ Problem Solving — *better understanding of what is asked when problem is read orally*

Motor Skills

☐ Fine Motor — *handwriting is slower, well formed (cursive and manuscript), stays within lines*

☐ Gross Motor — *able to throw and catch, maneuver a ball with right and left feet*

Work Skills

☐ Ability to Organize Time and Resources — *locates materials when required, organizes own homework, able to anticipate time limits*

☐ Ability to Focus on Task — *can usually focus on work until completion, not easily distracted except when reading*

☐ Ability to Work Collaboratively — *works well with others, plays with a small group of same-sex friends, accepting of authority*

Other

☐ Learning Style Preference (VAKT) — *mostly oral with some kinesthetic/tactile and visual (pictures)*

☐ Critical Thinking — *is beginning to be able to analyze statements and texts and to support an evaluation*

☐ Creativity — *occasionally comes up with novel ideas*

☐ Social Skills — *fairly well developed*

☐ English Language Development/Cultural Background — *English is his first language*

☐ Interests — *was on the school soccer and cross-country running teams; doesn't seem to do much reading for pleasure*

Summary

Math, motor skills, work skills, oral skills (receptive and expressive), and writing are average to above average. He is able to collaborate with others.

Reading and spelling need reinforcement: review phonics and segmenting words and suggest books that may be of interest.

Seems to be primarily an auditory learner, who also needs some kinesthetic/tactile components.

Screening Checklist

Name: _____ Grade: _____ Date of Birth: _____

Language

☐ Oral Reading

☐ Reading Comprehension

☐ Spelling

☐ Written Expression

☐ Oral Expression

☐ Oral Comprehension

Math

☐ Concepts

☐ Facts

☐ Problem Solving (individually and collaboratively)

Motor Skills

☐ Fine Motor

☐ Gross Motor

Work Skills

☐ Ability to Organize Time and Resources

☐ Ability to Focus on Task

☐ Ability to Work Collaboratively

Pembroke Publishers © 2022 *Finding a Place for Every Student* by Cheryll Duquette ISBN 978-1-55138-360-6

Other

- Learning Style Preference (VAKT)

- Critical Thinking

- Creativity

- Social Skills

- English Language Development/Cultural Background

- Interests

Summary

students have done poorly on two or three of the three tests. If possible, note the areas in which a student may be having difficulty, for example, questions that require memorization, understanding of the passage, logical thought, or ability to express ideas in writing.

Homework completion

A second area in which to keep records is whether the students are submitting assignments on time and if daily homework is completed. You might use a class list and check off each student's name when an assignment is submitted. At the beginning of each class, have the students open their notebooks to show you their homework. Make note of those students who have completed or not completed it. You can follow this same record-keeping procedure for bringing equipment to class, such as shorts and T-shirts for physical education, geometry sets for math, and textbooks and notebooks for other classes. If you notice a pattern of homework incompletion, it may indicate a lack of understanding, insufficient time (e.g., responsibilities at home), mental health issues (e.g., anxiety, depression), lack of a place to do the work, or an unstructured or hectic home life.

Attendance matters

The third area in which to keep records is attendance. Note all absences or late arrivals. If there are many, examine your records and note the day of the week and the day in the school's cycle. You may observe that the student is away every Friday or every Day Two in your school's cycle. If no pattern is apparent, then consider what was taught, done, or had to be submitted on the days of the absences. You may see a pattern of behaviors motivated by avoidance of a particular type of work, for example, oral presentations or written assignments. Note the *number* of absences, as well. They may be linked to things happening at home (e.g., babysitting, lack of clothing such as a winter coat), changes in living conditions (e.g., no longer living at home and couch surfing), time spent acting as an interpreter for their family, bullying and/or lack of social connections, or mental health issues. Excessive absences often result in poor academic performance, so it is important to monitor attendance.

The student's file

Another opportunity to make observations about your students is during the teaching of your lesson. Note who answers questions and who appears to understand the concepts. When you circulate after giving the instruction, make the same notations about degree of understanding, speed of work completion, and attention span. Note, too, if a student avoids work by skipping class, talking to others, not bringing materials to class, requesting to sharpen a pencil or visit the washroom, or putting their head on the desk — these types of observations may be written in a protected file. Note the frequency of behaviors over time. A single occasion of incomplete homework or classroom chatter is not a behavior pattern; many observations of specific behaviors over two to four weeks will help you determine patterns.

After noting patterns of academic performance and classroom behaviors that may contribute to that performance, read the student's file. Note the marks in the subject area from past years and the teachers' comments. This information may support your own observations. Be sure to read any psychological and medical

What does it signify when you see a score in the student's records that looks like a decimal? Interpret it in this way: a reading comprehension score of 5.6 means that the student is comprehending at the Grade 5, six-month level.

reports in the student's file. A psychological report will provide information about a child's level of intelligence and areas of strength and weakness.

You may also find an IEP that may or may not be in effect. A child may have an IEP that is supposed to be followed but has not been read by the teachers. As we have seen, when a student changes schools, the files may arrive at the new school months after the classes have begun. Furthermore, parents may have assumed that the school is aware of their child's needs and not informed the teachers. When a student moves on to middle school, an IEP may no longer be followed. The student's progress may be such that accommodations are no longer needed, a student may choose to do things without assistance, or a student may have decided against taking part in a gifted program offered by the district.

Note any reports on hearing or vision. In upper elementary, students may not want to wear their hearing aids or glasses, which can prove to be a hindrance to their academic performance. There may also be a report from a physician on attention span or attention deficit hyperactivity disorder (ADHD). Finally, the file may contain the results of standardized group achievement or ability testing that could give clues to present academic performance. If, for example, a student's reading comprehension and vocabulary are both 18 months below grade level, the student may have difficulty with tasks that require reading (e.g., multiple-choice tests, instructions, and problem solving in math). Another example is a student whose verbal comments suggest high intelligence, but whose assignments and tests are of average quality. By reading the files, you may find that this student used to be in a gifted program; by talking with them, you may discover that they purposely achieve average marks to fit in socially.

Disruptive, Withdrawn, or Unusual Behaviors

You will readily notice those students who behave disruptively within the first two hours of the first day of school. Students who show signs of being withdrawn, however, may go undetected for several months as you concentrate on setting routines and dealing with the disruptive students. Do make note of avoidance behaviors, particularly in play or social situations, such as recess or group activities. Make note, too, of autistic-like behaviors (e.g., rigid adherence to schedules, poor social communication and interpersonal skills) or the appearance of day-dreaming, which may indicate attention deficit disorder.

There are two basic ways of recording behaviors: tally charts and anecdotal reports. When reviewing your observations over two to four weeks, note the frequency and intensity of the behaviors. Note any *patterns* of occurrence, for example, avoidance behaviors right after certain tasks have been assigned. Whichever method of observation you choose, be discreet about collecting the data.

Tally counts

Tally counts are a method of counting the number of times a behavior is observed. They involve making a vertical stroke every time you note a particular behavior. When you have four vertical strokes, the fifth stroke is a horizontal through the other four. A tally count may be used to establish the frequency of such behaviors as wandering, pencil sharpening, calling out, and going to the washroom.

A tally may be done for the entire day or for certain intervals or periods of the day. For example, an elementary teacher who notices that a child is out of their seat often may want to make observations of wandering over a three-day period.

In one tally count, the teacher discovered that a child was out of their seat five times during a 40-minute period.

— 卌 —

The A B C Method of Description

Antecedent
Behavior
Consequence

A teacher of the intermediate grades may want to use a tally sheet to note the number of times a student talks during the class period over a three-day time span. Or a teacher may want to use a tally count to observe off-task behaviors in five-minute intervals. In this instance, it's best if there is another adult in the class who can spend time observing a particular student.

Either method of tally counting will give you an idea as to whether the behaviors are excessive. Then, from your observations, you can decide if the behaviors are interfering with the student's academic performance. You will also have baseline data with which to compare the behaviors after you have implemented your strategy for managing them.

Anecdotal reports

This method of observing children involves making entries in a private journal or secure electronic file. The short reports may be written in full sentences or in point-form notes. They are your personal means of noting details about specific behaviors, such as arguing, temper tantrums, or defiance.

When describing the incidents in which these behaviors occur, you may find it helpful to adopt the A B C method.

First, note what happened before the negative behavior occurred, in other words, the *antecedent* action. For example, just before the disruption occurred, a task that the child did not want to do was assigned, group work was announced, or they spoke to another student. Note what happened just before the student became defiant or angry.

Next, note the *exact behaviors*, such as the words the student used to challenge your authority, the nature of the fight between two students, the gist of the argument between you and the student, or the actions observed during a temper tantrum. Make note, too, of the intensity of the behaviors and their duration.

The final observations to record are the *consequences* of the behaviors or how the incident was resolved. A student who swore at you would have been sent to the office, as would the two students who were fighting. A student in the midst of a temper tantrum may have abruptly begun to cry. A student who was arguing with you about the senselessness of an assignment may have stormed out of the room. The behaviors immediately after the disruption are recorded under Consequences. You may also record how the incident was resolved, for example, with an apology, a suspension from school, or a return to work.

Reviewing your anecdotal records for a student over a two- to four-week period will give you some ideas as to behavior patterns. For example, you may notice that a child avoids unpleasant tasks by putting their head on a desk, wandering, or defying your authority. The third type of behavior may land the child in the principal's office, where the work could be successfully avoided. When making anecdotal reports, be discreet; record your data in a secure electronic file or place the journal in a locked file cabinet when you are not making entries. The more richly described the incident, the easier to note patterns of behavior.

Cautionary Notes on Making Observations of Students

Sometimes, especially where child behavior is involved, a teacher engaged in observing a student may find it difficult to keep the right balance between objectivity and involvement. Here are three ideas to keep in mind as you observe.

Keep developmental stages in mind

When reviewing your observational data, ask yourself if what you are seeing is within the broad range of normal behavior for the child's age group. For younger children, consider whether the lower academic performance or behavior problem is due to a short-term developmental lag. In other words, the child does not have a developmental or a learning disability but is simply not as ready to learn or as mature as others in the class. This may be true of some children born in the fall of the year, assuming that the enrolment cut-off date is December 31.

Some academic problems and behaviors may be explained as a developmental lag up until Grade 5 or 6. For example, some children may struggle with reading until the end of Grade 2 but suddenly catch on in Grade 3. Other children may be able to think abstractly at age 10, while others yet may need a lot of concrete materials to learn concepts at age 14. Therefore, remember to consider the normal stages of development when reviewing your observational data, and note those areas that seem to be outside the normal range. If you need to refresh your memory on developmental stages, consult a credible online source or any textbook in child psychology or educational psychology. You may also ask the special education teacher at your school about specific students.

Consider whose problem this is

For disruptive or unusual behaviors, always ask yourself this question: "Is this beyond the normal range for a child of that age *or* is it that I am intolerant or haven't planned this lesson properly?"

Every teacher has different tolerance levels for certain behaviors. For example, some teachers permit more talking and movement in a classroom than others. It must also be noted that some children require more opportunities to talk and move than others. Sometimes, teachers blame the child when they should be examining their own tolerance levels and ways of conducting lessons. Ask yourself how much talking or wandering you expect to see in a given activity. If you are having the students work in groups or at centres, then there will be more talking and moving than if you are conducting a teacher-centred lesson. Ask yourself, as well, how much talking and moving you can tolerate. You may find that you will reassess the amount of talking and wandering you will permit.

One important act of teaching is to plan your lessons carefully. Aim to have all the materials prepared ahead of time and in place for use by yourself and the students. Strive to plan lessons that involve the children as much as possible, incorporate a multisensory approach (visual, auditory, kinesthetic/tactile) and cognitive supports (e.g., scaffolding such as demonstrations and think-alouds), and include opportunities or activities for children who need reinforcement and enrichment. Know the students' interests and incorporate them into the lesson, which will improve motivation. The lesson should have no "dead" spots to tempt students to exhibit off-task behaviors. Through thorough planning, you will find that you are well organized and deliver the lesson effectively, thereby allowing the students to learn more.

Learn all you can about students who have identified exceptionalities

The previous comments have related to *unidentified* students who are at risk or who may have a gift. If, however, a student has been identified as having a specific exceptionality, you have resources to turn to. Read the child's file and, in particular, the IEP, which will state, among other things, the accommodations that are required by the student, and supporting documents, such as a physician's report or the psychological report. Beyond that, read as much as you can to gain a *general* idea of the exceptionality. Talk to the parents and the child about specific needs. For example, a student with low vision may tell you they require more or less light as the day goes on to accommodate levels of eye strain. Talk to the child's previous teachers to find out what strategies worked with them. Finally, make your *own* observations in the context of other information. For example, a report on a student with Down syndrome may state that during testing the child was able to do only certain things; however, you may see that in a more relaxed situation, the student can perform much more than was reported.

Referring Students for Testing

After making observations, you may find that your hunches about a possible problem in academic performance, disruptive behavior, or potential giftedness were justified. You may want to refer the child for testing.

First, discuss your findings with the principal, vice-principal, head of special education, guidance counselor, or any other designated person. Review your data with this person or team to determine whether the student should be referred for testing. You might decide in favor of an immediate referral for testing or you may introduce some accommodations or behavior management programs *before* the child is referred. Given that it takes so long for testing to occur, the latter course of action is usually taken.

If it is decided that testing is desirable, discuss your observations with the student's parents. The conversation about testing will *not* have been the first held with the parents. You would have already spoken to the parents by telephone or in a meeting after collecting your data about a child's academic performance.

When testing is recommended, most schools want to meet with the parents to review the observational data and any initial achievement testing or screening done by the special education teacher. At the meeting, the parents may state that they have similar concerns and may approve the testing; however, the parents may not want the child to undergo any tests at this time. Each district has different rules about parental approval for testing, and you need to know whether any formalized testing can occur without parental consent.

If you and your colleagues decide that you should implement an *informal plan* to address the student's needs, then describe your observations to the parents and explain how you intend to accommodate the child's needs. Whenever you speak to parents, have all your data with you so that you can state specific marks on specific tests given on specific dates, or the precise dates that the child was absent from your third-period class, or the exact inappropriate behaviors that were shown in which situation on a specific date.

Be prepared for a negative reaction, at least initially. No parents like to hear that there is a problem with their child. *Listen* to what the parents say about the child. Ask if the parents have noticed any difficulties or specific behaviors at home. Let the parents know that you want to work with their child to make improvements and tell them that you will call them again in a week or two to provide an update. Since a parent may want to meet with you to discuss the plan, you should be open to this suggestion and offer to arrange a meeting at the school or on a digital platform.

Bear in mind two key points: if you raise a problem about a child with a parent, then you have to address it — *never* call a parent just to complain — and be sure to inform the parents of the progress of the child as your informal plan is being implemented. In this way, the parents will know that before testing was recommended, the school tried to address their child's problems.

Whether the child is slated for testing or not, you will have to develop a plan for working with the student in the classroom. As soon as the student is suspected of having a disability or a behavior problem, or as requiring enrichment, you have a moral obligation to adapt your teaching strategies and possibly modify the curriculum to meet that child's needs. However, as you will discover, meeting the needs of these students is not necessarily burdensome. More often than not it involves making some minor adjustments to your teaching behaviors and lesson/unit planning. And remember: by making observations, you have already begun the process of working successfully with that student.

CHAPTER 4

Formulating Goals, Developing Strategies

Should you make a plan for every student? No. Just develop informal plans for those who have not been through a formal identification process and who seem to have some strengths or weaknesses that you, as the classroom teacher, can address.

After making observations of a student and deciding that some action is needed, think about targeting specific areas to address the child's strengths or weaknesses. List those strengths and weaknesses. For the weaknesses, include any observational data you may have, for example, the number of times the student is out of their seat, their reading level, the number of absences. Writing down this information may help you prioritize the weaknesses or strengths, beginning with the ones that require immediate attention before those that can wait.

The next step is to select the top two or three areas and develop them into your goals to address the needs of the student. As you address these goals, introduce the next ones on your priority list. You may do these two activities on your own or with the resource/special education teacher at your school. I recommend identifying strengths and weaknesses and developing possible goals before talking with the parents. In this way, you can present them for discussion at the initial meeting and make revisions based on the input of the student and parents. This meeting should enable you to proceed with making agreed-upon adaptations for the student.

The Process of Working with Students at Risk

Whether students have identified or not-yet-identified disabilities, behavior problems, or gifts, follow this basic process:
1. Observe students.
2. **Formulate goals.**
3. Develop strategies.
4. Implement the action plan.
5. Review the plan.

Three examples of observational data translated into goals are outlined below. The students whose cases are presented are composites of children with whom I have worked in Kindergarten to Grade 6 and intermediate schools. I have used or seen used all the strategies suggested for each child. I know they all work. The teachers in each case study are modeled on some of the caring and inspirational educators with whom I have had the privilege to work.

The Real Problem Identified

Andrew

Andrew was a Grade 7 student who was initially viewed as having a behavior problem. At the meeting of the Grade 7 teachers with guidance and resource personnel at the end of September, the vice-principal noted that within the first month of school Andrew had skipped two classes (both in English and on days when written assignments were to be submitted). The English teacher added that on four occasions Andrew had arrived late for her class and when he did, he appeared sullen, making random negative statements about English class. The vice-principal then made a comment about this boy "heading towards a year of office detentions." Andrew was thus "flagged."

The English teacher's thoughts turned to the weaknesses she had observed in Andrew's written work. She wondered aloud if Andrew was practising avoidance behaviors to get out of doing the written work required in English. She was also concerned about his negative attitude towards English and his refusal to do some assignments. Over the next two weeks, she collected data on Andrew's strengths and weaknesses. (The results are shown in the margin on page 54.)

- Arrives late (4) and skips classes (up to 10) (ongoing)
- Easily off-task (ongoing)
- Refuses to complete some assignments or portions of some assignments (ongoing)
- Hands in assignments late (7/9 were late)
- Doesn't always bring his notebook and pen to class (6 times in 6 weeks) (ongoing)
- Written assignments too short (1)
- Handwriting very messy (2)
- Has a negative attitude towards English

Strengths
- Participates in oral discussions
- Is able to express his ideas well orally

Goals
1. **To lengthen written responses**
2. **To improve neatness of written work**

The English teacher discussed her observations with Andrew privately. He stated that he disliked writing because he found it difficult to organize his thoughts and he was embarrassed to hand in his work due to his poor handwriting. With some probing the teacher learned that Andrew hated English because he felt he couldn't do well and didn't want to be embarrassed. She wondered if his behaviors and negative comments were a cry for help.

The teacher decided that the most important goal at this time was to lengthen Andrew's written responses to test questions and the assignments that he submitted. Andrew's marks in English were below average, and she felt that if he learned how to organize his thoughts on paper, his grades would improve. She also believed that if Andrew experienced some success in her class, he would be more motivated to arrive on time and not to skip. He might then feel more academically included in the class.

The teacher's second goal for Andrew was to see the neatness of his written assignments improve. Andrew's handwriting was difficult to read; the letters were crowded and poorly formed. He also wrote slowly. The teacher felt that if Andrew could submit more legible assignments, then he might be more willing to hand them in.

Finally, the teacher wanted to ensure that Andrew experienced more success in her course generally: she wanted to give him opportunities to use his oral strengths. Her hunch that many of the avoidance behaviors he practised were due to a feeling of being unsuccessful in English seemed to be accurate. It was now almost the middle of the semester, and the progress reports would soon be issued. Andrew's achievement mark in English was only in the 50-percent range, and she surmised that a low mark in English would not be warmly received by his parents. So the teacher felt that this would be an opportune time to discuss the goals with Andrew.

The teacher was able to look beyond Andrew's behavior to see the real problem: written work. Her hunch was that Andrew's "behaviors" were a means of avoiding the activities in which he was unsuccessful and served to communicate a need for help. The teacher felt that by addressing Andrew's weaknesses, the symptoms of a behavior problem would decrease.

In our next case study, we will see how an elementary teacher handled another "behavior" problem.

The Reason behind the Behavior

Alex

It was mid-November, and the Grade 3 teacher was at her wit's end with Alex's behaviors. Alex seemed to be even more active in the classroom than earlier in the fall. The girl left her seat many times during the day, constantly jiggled her right leg, and talked continually. Her attention span seemed to be shorter than that of the other children these days, and she blurted out answers constantly. Alex was finding it difficult to work with others, arguing about various things, and had been in two fights during recess. She seemed to be on edge and not as in control of her emotions as a few weeks earlier.

Alex's behaviors were now at a level that the teacher was finding intolerable. Her constant talking and wandering were disrupting the other students in the class. The teacher had nagged, threatened, and raised her voice occasionally, but none of these techniques were working. When asked privately if everything was all right, Alex responded, "Yeah," and in a tone that said, "Don't bother me!" The teacher responded, "Okay, but if you want to talk to me, I'm here to listen." However, matters got worse. Alex began to argue with the teacher, who now felt quite frustrated. The teacher wanted to ensure a reasonable learning environment for all the students, but Alex's actions were disruptive. The teacher was also concerned that Alex's social and emotional skills were declining rapidly.

After one exhausting day with Alex, the teacher sat at her desk and asked herself whether the problem was Alex's — or hers. Was she becoming less tolerant of Alex's behaviors, or were the behaviors increasing to such a level that no one could tolerate them? In short, whose problem was this?

After thinking about Alex's behaviors in September and October, the teacher determined that the impulsivity and restlessness had increased. The other students were now complaining about Alex's excessive talking and about being bothered when she was out of her seat. The teacher also acknowledged that her own tolerance might be lower than in September.

A similar list of characteristics appears in Chapter 7.

As she examined a list of characteristics of children with attention deficit hyperactivity disorder (ADHD), the teacher wondered whether Alex had suddenly developed ADHD. She put aside that idea, however, as she doubted that the symptoms had persisted for at least six months. She then thought that she should try to see Alex's strengths, that maybe she was focusing too closely on the irritating behaviors. The teacher did think of three positive characteristics. Alex was a good athlete and a member of a swim team, and her creative writing showed that she had a vivid imagination. As well, until recently, Alex had demonstrated good social and emotional skills.

The teacher then wondered if something at home was causing Alex anxiety because some children react to stress by behaving in the ways Alex was. She decided to check Alex's file to see whether comments about this type of behavior had appeared on previous report cards and to talk to Alex's parents.

The teacher read Alex's file, its comments suggesting that the girl had previously had problems "focusing." Many youngsters have short attention spans, however. She did notice that in Grade 1, Alex's teacher had commented about aggressive behavior in the final term. The teacher also observed that Alex's marks were well above average on all report cards.

Before she contacted Alex's mother, the teacher decided to do some tally counts and make anecdotal reports about the girl's behavior. Over a three-day period, she noted the following:

- Alex was out of her seat between 15 and 17 times a day.
- She talked constantly while doing her seatwork.
- She blurted out answers during the instructional part of any lesson between four and seven times.
- An argument occurred with peers during the completion of a group task.
- An argument occurred with the teacher during a creative writing assignment.

In the latter instance, it was obvious that Alex didn't want to write an alternative ending to the story they had just read in language arts. She stated that she didn't know what to write and argued. The teacher raised her voice, and Alex continued arguing. The teacher then threatened to send her into the hall to write her story, and Alex still argued. The teacher moved Alex's desk into the hall, and Alex wrote nothing. The teacher was surprised that Alex didn't want to do the creative writing, because her stories were always well written. She was also surprised at how quickly the argument escalated and how readily she used threats to try to control Alex, when in reality she had lost control over Alex.

Weaknesses/Priority
- Out of seat 15–17 times per day (1)
- Talks constantly (2)
- Blurts out answers 4–7 times per day (ongoing)
- Short attention span (ongoing)
- Argues (3)

Strengths
- Athletic; is on a swim team
- Vivid imagination; writes well
- Had demonstrated good social and emotional skills

Goals
1. To decrease the out-of-seat behaviors
2. To decrease the talking

The teacher telephoned Alex's mother and discussed the changes in the girl's behavior. She inquired about whether things at home might have affected Alex's behaviors. Alex's mother responded that her husband had just been diagnosed with a heart problem and was now on a waiting list for treatment. In the last few weeks, there had been much tension in the house over the husband's medical condition. She also said that she, too, had noticed that Alex was behaving more aggressively, particularly towards her younger brother, and that Alex was arguing more with her over the bedtime hour and about making her bed in the morning. She said that at the most recent swimming practice, Alex had sat alone on the deck instead of swimming in the pool. The mother assumed that Alex had misbehaved but did not pursue it. She wondered if anything could be done to help Alex in school. The teacher told her that she would talk to the special education teacher and get back to her.

The next afternoon Alex's teacher and the special education teacher met and reviewed observational data that had been collected. They also discussed Alex's strengths and possible behavioral goals for her.

Alex's teacher prioritized the two behaviors that the other students found disruptive to their own learning, that is, the wandering and the talking. She knew that she couldn't eliminate these behaviors, but they had to decrease in order to be tolerable to others. She also didn't want her peers to marginalize Alex. The teacher also felt that the arguing had to stop, as again constant friction could damage relations with others. Finally, she thought that if she made some adjustments in her teaching style, Alex's shorter attention span and habit of blurting out answers might be manageable in the classroom. She also decided to work with Alex individually on emotional awareness and emotional and behavioral regulation.

The teacher examined not only Alex's weaknesses, but her own. After much thought, the teacher realized that she could improve her curriculum planning, teaching techniques, class management, and discipline. She reflected that if she changed the environment, then Alex's behaviors might be improved.

Indeed, I have found that how I act affects the way a student acts. It seems so obvious, but sometimes we are so "stuck" in our ways that we automatically blame the student when our actions can improve the child's behaviors. Keep in mind that you will not likely be able to eliminate all of a student's inappropriate behaviors, but you can usually improve them so that the child's social inclusion remains intact.

Collecting Data on Strengths

In the two previous cases, we have seen teachers looking beyond negative behaviors and examining the strengths of the student, as well as their own teaching styles. For Andrew and Alex, the teachers took time to collect data to have an accurate "read" on avoidance and disruptive types of behaviors. With these data in hand, they were able to identify patterns and verify that specific behaviors were occurring.

These teachers collected data not only on weaknesses, but also on strengths. Too often, we focus on weaknesses and ignore the positive things that are happening for a child. As will be discussed later, strengths can be used to address weaknesses.

In the last case presented here, we meet Erik, who shows no behavior problems.

Recognition of Gifts

Erik

Erik was a Grade 7 student attending the intermediate program that was housed in a high school. Erik's father was in the military, and the family had moved three times in the last six years. They had just settled in the area this past August and believed this move would be the last.

At a meeting of the Grades 7 and 8 teachers at the end of September, the boy's homeroom teacher expressed delight in teaching such a capable student. He had noticed that Erik had some strong abilities in math and computers. The music teacher then stated that he too had noticed that in the last month Erik had made exceptionally strong progress in music. (At this school every student had to learn how to play an instrument, and Erik had chosen the saxophone.) However, the other teachers commented that Erik was a quiet boy who was performing in the average to above-average range. The special education teacher was perusing the file and noted that there was no record of any ability testing, likely because Erik had missed scheduled group tests during his frequent moves. The group also discussed Erik's social skills and agreed that although he seemed to be easy-going and accepted, he had not yet developed a group of friends. He often ate lunch alone and rarely talked to others during breaks.

The homeroom and music teachers spoke privately to Erik about their observations and recommended that he participate in enrichment activities in the areas of math, computers, and music. They explained that they would develop ideas and have a meeting with him and his parents within the next two weeks. Erik responded favorably. He explained that he was bored in school and was happy that the two teachers had finally noticed his abilities. He agreed to consider the enrichment activities in math, computers, and music as long as he had a say in them and that his work wouldn't be obvious to his peers. He was a reserved and quiet student who was trying hard to fit in and didn't want to be ostracized before he had a chance to make a few friends. The teachers hoped that involvement in these activities would help him find friends who shared the same interests so that he would feel more social belonging at school and in the classroom.

In this case, teachers and Erik agreed to set informal goals related to enabling Erik to take part in enrichment activities. Because nothing as formal as the observational data and numbered goals for Andrew and Alex was prepared, Erik was free to take part in suggested activities or not.

Translating Goals into Strategies

It took willingness and courage for all the teachers described above to make changes in their programs and teaching approaches that would benefit their students. These teachers cared about their students and wanted to make a positive distance in their lives. Whether a student needs remediation or enrichment, the development of strategies to achieve the goals set for students is an important step.

Consult the special education teacher

Let's assume you have undergone the process of observing a student, as described in Chapter 3. Discussing your observations with the special education teacher is always wise: you will gain some ideas on what accommodations would be appropriate. In many schools, the special education teacher or resource teacher works with small groups of students, but also acts as an in-school consultant for teachers, providing them with ideas about classroom accommodations. Once you know possible ways to provide remediation or enrichment, then you can begin to decide which ones will work in your classroom with a particular child.

Hold a meeting about your informal plan

After developing possible strategies to meet each goal, write an informal plan and then arrange a meeting with the family and school personnel. Meet with the child, the parents, the special education teacher, and the principal to discuss your observations, goals, and plan to address the needs. The meeting should occur as soon as your informal plan is written and at a time convenient for everyone. It will allow you to present your observations and proposed plan. It will also provide an opportunity for others to react to your ideas and have input into the informal plan. During your discussion, new information may be presented or other ideas may be added to the plan.

Once you have agreed on strategies to implement, decide on a time frame in which to implement them: one school term is usually long enough for any improvements in academic performance or behavior to be sustained. By the end of the time period, you may safely conclude that work habits or marks have improved, or that enrichment work has been appropriate.

Further to the meeting, you can implement the teaching techniques, accommodations, and curriculum adaptations you have planned. As you do so, be sure to collect more observational data and to determine whether your measures are working. Adjust them if they are not.

You may encounter some resistance during the process. Most parents will support your ideas to address the needs of their child; however, parents may not feel that any plans or accommodations are necessary and likely would have told you this during your telephone calls before the meeting. In this case, respect their opinion, but file the observations and plan in a secure spot. You may also be in a situation where the student refuses to take part in such things as self-monitoring of behavior, a reward system, or enrichment activities. In this instance, it's best to identify what the student is willing to do and to begin with this. If the student refuses to participate in the plan, you can do little else but explain the possible consequences of receiving no assistance and acknowledge that participation is voluntary. Place your plan in a secure place — namely an electronic file requiring

The Process of Working with Students at Risk

Whether students have identified or not-yet-identified disabilities, behavior problems, or gifts, follow this basic process:
1. Observe students.
2. Formulate goals.
3. **Develop strategies.**
4. Implement the plan.

See pages 70–71, 73–74, and 78 for examples of informal plans, as well as the planning sheet on page 83.

Always respect the wishes of parents and students.

a password or a locked file cabinet. However, be open to the possibility of implementing it when the student is ready to work with you.

Let us return to examining how the teachers who worked with students Andrew, Alex, and Erik dealt with the need to provide adaptations for them.

Introduction of Coping Strategies

Andrew

To avoid drawing hasty conclusions that may be incorrect, collect your data systematically, compare them with the information you have on learning disabilities, and talk to the special education teacher.

Andrew's English teacher, who had taken a course in special education, thought that this Grade 7 student might have a mild learning disability in the area of written expression. She believed that his attempt to hide his weakness was turning into a behavior problem.

After the meeting of the Grade 7 teachers, the teacher talked to the head of the special education department about her observations, goals for Andrew, and possible accommodations. In response, the special education teacher showed her a list of learning disability characteristics. Andrew seemed to be showing some of them in the area of written expression, but perhaps he had just never learned how to organize his thoughts before writing. Furthermore, the English teacher couldn't say that this problem had persisted over several months. What she did know was that by the time any formal testing results would be available, the school year would be over, and Andrew would no longer be in her class.

The English teacher decided that a plan was needed *now* to help Andrew during the remaining part of the year. She sought to give him opportunities to use his oral abilities and to teach coping skills to help him improve his written work in English and other subject areas. She wanted to open up more opportunities for Andrew to succeed. She believed that if he were successful, then he would come to class with his notebook and pen and remain on task. The English teacher also wanted to use Andrew's strength in oral communication whenever possible. Finally, she decided on accommodations that were appropriate for the *entire* class so that Andrew would not feel singled out. She also hoped that with success, Andrew would feel more academically included and appear happier in her class.

As a teacher, be very careful about diagnosing a student as having a disability or attention deficit hyperactivity disorder (ADHD) without proper assessment by a psychologist or physician. You may have a hunch about a student, but it is important to examine all possible causes of low academic performance and negative behaviors.

In mid-October the teacher met with Andrew, his parents, the head of the special education department, and the vice-principal. She described what she had done thus far and sought their input. Andrew's parents were surprised that an intermediate teacher had taken the time to work with their son. They admitted that Andrew was a "master" of avoidance behaviors and that since Grade 4 some weakness in written work had been detected, but not seriously addressed. They also confirmed that Andrew would rather talk than write if given the choice, and they gave their consent to have their son tested for a possible learning disability. They expressed their disappointment in Andrew's attendance record but were happy to be informed of it.

Andrew was quiet throughout most of the meeting; however, he did agree to cooperate with the English teacher and try her accommodations. He was feeling desperate as his parents knew about the skipping and the low mark in English. He felt as though he had to make some effort to turn things around. The next meeting was scheduled for February.

What follows is an outline of the accommodations that Andrew's teacher developed to help him.

Written assignments

For pieces in which Andrew had to state and argue a point of view, the teacher adopted the practice presented in the box below.

> ### Writing from a Point of View
>
> 1. Discuss with the entire class the points of view an individual could have on a topic, as well as possible main ideas to explain each perspective. Write key words on the board. Students can also meet in small groups and discuss their points of view and main ideas to support them.
> 2. Give students a copy of Frame for Writing a Five-Paragraph Essay (see page 61), which they can use to organize their ideas into major and supporting points. Each grouping of one idea and its supporting points would become a separate paragraph.
> 3. Ask students to rank their ideas from 1 to 3, with 1 being the strongest and 3 the weakest.
> 4. Direct students to write the introduction, then a paragraph with idea 2, a paragraph with idea 3 (the weakest in the middle), a paragraph with idea 1 (to send a strong message), and the conclusion.

In support of this model, the teacher demonstrated to the whole class how to use the model and provided samples of completed assignments to illustrate how to organize the material or points. She also worked with Andrew and two other students in formulating their points.

The teacher decided upon the following ways to accommodate the student:

☐ Discuss with Andrew privately the answers to questions related to the study of novels, short stories, or plays. Discussing the answers to questions with the student allows him to show that he knows the material, even though his written work may not reflect it. The struggling English student will also feel more confident that he has the correct answers and may volunteer answers during discussions.

☐ Talk to Andrew about the possible need for more time to complete written assignments. Make it clear that if an extension is required, he must request it before the assignment is due and the due date must be mutually agreed upon. This option was made available to the entire class.

☐ Provide all students the choice of completing some assignments as a written or an oral report, video, or podcast.

Handwriting

☐ When Andrew writes by hand, encourage him to use every second line and to space out the letters of the words so that they may be read.

☐ Inform all students that they may type their assignments. Encourage Andrew to choose this option and use the editor function. Typed copies usually look neater and motivate students to write more than they would if handwriting an assignment. Typewritten text takes up less space than hand-written text, and students feel that more ideas are needed to add length.

Frame for Writing a Five-Paragraph Essay

Title of Essay: _____

Introduction (Present your thesis or main purpose or focus):

_____

_____

Body (After noting your ideas, prioritize them from 1 to 3, with 1 being the strongest and 3 being the weakest. Write your essay so that 2 is presented first, followed by 3 and 1 — save the strongest to the last):

Idea 2: _____

Supporting Points: _____

_____

_____

_____

Idea 3: _____

Supporting Points: _____

_____

_____

_____

Idea 1 — Strongest: _____

Supporting Points: _____

_____

_____

_____

Conclusion:

_____

_____

_____

_____

Pembroke Publishers © 2022 *Finding a Place for Every Student* by Cheryll Duquette ISBN 978-1-55138-360-6

General accommodations

☐ For tests and examinations, try to arrange the following: that Andrew have up to one-third more time to write them; that he write as much as he can for each answer and then tell an adult what he wanted to write (the adult will write the sections of the oral answer that did not appear in written form); and that Andrew be permitted to write answers to test and examination questions in point form. Tests and examinations may be written in the resource room. Even though Andrew had not had a formal assessment, the special education teacher arranged for him to write in the resource room if he needed more time. You can set up a similar accommodation for a student who writes very slowly.

☐ Encourage Andrew to take part in large- and small-group discussions. Structure small group work so that Andrew does not serve as the recorder. As much as possible, let students use their strengths. Oral communication was Andrew's.

☐ Set up a chart with Andrew whereby he records how often he arrives on time, brings his notebook and pen, and submits assignments; however, continue to record late arrivals, absences, and late or missed submissions. Praise Andrew discreetly for coming to class and submitting assignments.

☐ Have three-hole paper available for Andrew to use, if required; be prepared to lend him a pen in exchange for collateral for the length of a class period.

☐ Try to develop a rapport with Andrew and other students before the class begins by talking about topics that interest them, for example, sports, music, or events at the school. I have always found that greeting the students with a smile or a simple "hi" as they walk into the classroom is an effective way to open the door to a possible conversation. It also says, "Welcome."

☐ When marking a student's assignments, provide as much specific feedback on strengths and suggestions for improvement as possible through written comments in the margin.

☐ Have check-ins with Andrew every week to see how the strategies are working and to provide encouragement. Urge students to monitor their own behaviors. They then have something to base a change upon.

☐ Discreetly acknowledge work that is well done (e.g., with a sticky note on his work) and call Andrew's parents with the good news.

We saw that Andrew was noticed by his teachers due to the poor quality of his written work and his passive avoidance behaviors. Alex, on the other hand, presents a very different case. Her academic work is at grade level, but her aggressive and non-compliant behaviors are disturbing the entire class and making peers cautious around her.

Ways to Address Disruptive Behavior

Alex's teacher had discussed goals for Alex with the special education teacher, and they later met to develop some ways of addressing the Grade 3 student's disruptive behaviors. The following are the strategies the classroom teacher adopted.

Wandering

☐ Plan some lessons that enable Alex to move around. Allowing her (and the others) to stand while working, using manipulatives, and organizing learning centres should enable this.

☐ Break an assignment into smaller pieces ("chunking"). As Alex completes each section, praise her and permit her to go for a drink of water. Remind her that when she goes for a drink, she has to be back within one minute and is not allowed to touch others or talk to them.

☐ Have Alex monitor her own behavior by keeping a daily tally count of her wandering. The tally count should be divided into four sections to correspond to the time blocks of the day. Keep an independent tally count to compare numbers with Alex. Once students become aware of how often they behave in a certain way, they may be motivated to reduce it.

☐ Establish the number of times per day that Alex may be out of her seat and reward her each day with a sticker in her planner if she stays within that limit.

☐ Reteach the class the rules on moving about the room and not bothering others. Be prepared to remind Alex of these rules whenever required.

Talking

☐ Assign Alex one desk at the front of the room and a second desk at the back. Have Alex come to the front for the instruction part of the lesson and complete her seatwork at the desk at the back. If necessary, turn the desk to the wall so that her voice will not carry. Providing a student with two desks works when the classroom is large enough to place a desk away from other students.

☐ Plan more lessons involving groups. The talking would be less disruptive and might even be focused on the task.

Arguing

☐ Provide more choices in classroom work, such as in creative writing, so that Alex can find something that interests her.

☐ Use the broken-record technique in response to her arguing about not doing work. For example, say, "In our class, we do our work." Repeat this sentence in a calm, firm voice, moving close to the student and looking her in the eye. For most students, the arguing stops after three repetitions.

☐ Enforce the hands-up rule when the children are answering questions and call on Alex as soon as she raises her hand. Use nonverbal cues to remind Alex to raise her hand or return to her seat.

☐ Plan interesting lessons featuring a variety of activities (e.g., teacher-directed activities, small-group work, and individual work). Consider planning a shorter instructional part to the lesson, if necessary.

☐ Use a multisensory method of teaching that incorporates visual, auditory, and kinesthetic/tactile stimulation (VAKT). [See page 91 for an example of how it may be used when teaching spelling.]

☐ Use I-messages in an assertive, quiet, and calm voice when Alex does not follow the rules. (See the third strategy in the margin to the left.) *An example of an I-message:* The teacher could say: "I am concerned when you are out of your seat because you are not completing your work. I want you to stay at your desk and finish this assignment."

For example, say, "In our class, we do our work." Repeat this sentence in a calm, firm voice, moving close to the student and looking her in the eye. For most students, the arguing stops after three repetitions.

If the activity in the lesson changed about every 10 minutes, Alex's attention might be more focused than if she were just listening to the teacher talk.

An example of an I-message: The teacher could say: "I am concerned when you are out of your seat because you are not completing your work. I want you to stay at your desk and finish this assignment."

- ☐ Monitor Alex's behavior in the classroom as much as possible to prevent some problems from developing. Re-direct inappropriate behavior.
- ☐ Provide as much individual assistance and positive feedback as possible.
- ☐ Give Alex opportunities to shine. For example, in physical education ask her to demonstrate certain skills she can perform well. It will boost her self-confidence and allow peers to see her strengths.
- ☐ Develop a rapport with Alex by discussing her swimming and other interests.
- ☐ Conduct daily check-ins with Alex to ensure that things are okay.
- ☐ Review the types of emotions we feel and how we can regulate them and our behavior with the entire class.
- ☐ Establish a signal or way to communicate that Alex needs a break and allow her to take a walk to the end of the hall and practise deep breathing.

The overall strategy was to bring more structure to the classroom and to monitor Alex's behaviors more closely. At the same time, however, the teacher realized that she had to "give" a little, too. She had to make shorter presentations and provide more activity when teaching, behave more calmly in the classroom, and recognize Alex's strengths whenever possible. She needed to alter the classroom environment so that both she and Alex could thrive.

Alex, her parents, the special education teacher, the classroom teacher, and the principal held a meeting to discuss the observations, goals, and plan of action. As soon as the teacher finished speaking about the goals, Alex burst into tears and said that she didn't want her daddy to die. Her father quickly gathered her into his arms and explained that his medical condition was treatable, that he wasn't going to die. The adults realized that Alex had been very anxious about her father's health, which likely had been responsible for the sudden increase of disruptive behaviors. After Alex calmed down, the teacher explained the plan, and Alex agreed to try it. She said that she knew she had been "bad" but couldn't help the way she was feeling and acting these days. She said that the teacher's ideas might help her get back to "normal." The group decided to meet at the end of March, and over the next three months the plan would be implemented.

The stories of Andrew and Alex show how you can develop an informal plan to address the needs of students with academic and behavioral difficulties that will help them develop and maintain a sense of belonging in the class. The next case focuses on providing enrichment to an intermediate student who possessed some obvious gifts but was having difficulty finding a group of friends in his new school.

Encouragement for Enrichment

Erik

At an end-of-September meeting of Grades 7 and 8 teachers, Erik's homeroom teacher stated that he was very impressed by Erik's abilities in math and computers, while the music teacher wanted to allow Erik to advance his talent in playing the saxophone. Both teachers wanted to recognize Erik's strengths in a way that would make him feel comfortable in developing them. They both expressed concern that if Erik remained unchallenged, he might not develop good work habits and could become disruptive in class. The teachers also said they noticed that Erik seemed friendly but shy and observed that participating in smaller groups

devoted to areas in which he had abilities would make it easier for him to socialize and have a group of friends.

A few special meetings followed. The next week the homeroom and music
teachers met with the special education teacher to brainstorm possible enrichment opportunities. The parents, Erik, the special education teacher, and the
vice-principal were later invited to attend a meeting to discuss the teachers'
observations and ideas for enrichment. After the teachers spoke with the parents
and the administration, the parents decided that Erik would not be tested. No
gifted classes or enrichment programs were available at the school, and Erik's
abilities in other subject areas were only above average. Moreover, Erik made
it clear that he was willing to engage only in informal enrichment activities in
math, computers, and music. Several options, outlined below, were identified.

Many students, like Erik, have gifts, but that alone does not make them candidates for IQ testing, which measures ability in language and logical thinking. In
Erik's case, he had abilities in logical thinking, but his language scores were not
in the superior range. Moreover, he was not interested in attending a special program. Testing was therefore not considered. As well, Erik was new to the school,
and it was not easy finding friends. Participating in activities with peers who had
similar interests would help Erik develop friendships in his new school and help
him feel more socially connected.

Math/Computers

The word *encourage* is key to working with adolescents. You can acknowledge their abilities and talk to them about how they might enjoy participating in a competition, club, or team. You can also provide them with information about the activities. Teenagers, however, need to choose their own activities; your job is to recognize needs and provide opportunities.

- ☐ Encourage Erik to join the Engineering Club, whose members enter math and engineering contests and solve real-life problems.
- ☐ Encourage Erik to enter the school's Science Fair, where winners go on to compete in provincial and national contests.
- ☐ Encourage Erik to do at least one extra project in computers by the end of the term. Make use of a Learning Contract for Independent Study to struc-
ture and record discussions on topics, the process of collecting data, final product, and evaluation. (A reproducible form appears on page 66.) Allow all students to do this kind of independent work and earn extra marks, in part to prevent Erik from feeling singled out.
- ☐ During class time, ask open-ended questions that stimulate higher-order thinking, include a problem of the day in math at the beginning of the period, and provide enrichment questions in both math and computers for Erik and other students who finish their work ahead of the others.

Music

- ☐ Encourage Erik to join the Grade 7 Band.
- ☐ Encourage Erik to go through the Grade 7 music book at his own rate. Offer individual tutoring about the theory and technique as required. Give Erik sheet music of more challenging pieces that could be practised at home.
- ☐ Informally acknowledge him as the first saxophonist for the Grade 7 Band and find pieces for that band where the saxophone is featured.
- ☐ Later in the year, encourage Erik to join the Jazz Band for Grade 8 and promising Grade 7 students.
- ☐ Speak to Erik's parents about the possibility of providing private music lessons.

Learning Contract for Independent Study

Title of Project: _____

Description of Project (Include the purpose and the process for gathering data):

_____

_____

_____

_____

_____

_____

_____

_____

Type of Product (Describe what will be produced):

_____

_____

Criteria for Evaluation:

_____

_____

Breakdown of Marks:

_____

_____

Due Date: _____

_____   _____
Signature of Student and Date   Signature of Teacher and Date

Responding Appropriately to Student Needs

In this chapter you have seen teachers move from formulating goals based on observation of students to working with others to develop adaptations to their teaching style and the curriculum that might provide the accommodations necessary for a student to succeed. In each case, the special education teacher was consulted for ideas on possible modifications. (You will find many adaptations identified in Chapters 5 to 12 of this book.) The teachers also worked with the parents, the student, and other school personnel in developing an informal plan of action.

What teachers do depends on their students' needs.

The student's age is one factor to consider. For example, to address an academic weakness in a child in the primary or junior division, the teacher would normally develop a strategy focused on remediating the area of weakness. For someone in Grade 7, such as Andrew, the strategy would be to teach coping skills to help the student perform better now and in the future. Providing *remediation* helps elementary students to gain skills; teaching coping skills, such as using a calculator or editing functions, helps enable older students to perform well to obtain the highest possible marks. If a student has previously had remediation work, then more of the same is unlikely to be helpful.

Student interests and need to develop friends should be taken into account. Erik had a few specific gifts, so the first strategy was to present as many opportunities for enrichment as possible and to allow him to engage in those of interest. It was thought that involvement in these activities would help him find a group of friends.

Alex was in a different situation. Her needs were not in the academic area at all; they related to emotional stress. In her case, the teacher worked with Alex and her parents to change the disruptive behaviors that signaled her worry about her father.

These stories confirm how caring and committed teachers can help their students improve and extend their performance. In the next chapter, we focus further on implementing the action plan, which, in this case, is the informal plan, and on reviewing its success.

CHAPTER 5

Implementing and Reviewing the Action Plan

The Process of Working with Students at Risk

Whether students have identified or not-yet-identified disabilities, behavior problems, or gifts, follow this basic process:
1. Observe students.
2. Formulate goals.
3. Develop strategies.
4. **Implement the plan.**
5. Review the plan.

Wandering

Before Plan Implementation

~~+++~~

After Plan Implementation

/

The final stage in the process of working with any student who needs remediation or enrichment is to discuss the student's progress in order to make decisions about future directions. First, though, you need to implement the plan you have developed for your particular student. Typically, you would do so during the remaining weeks of the term or school year. As you begin to use your plan, consider how to collect data to determine whether changes and improvements are occurring.

When assessing a child's progress, it is helpful to use the same methods as were used during the observation phase a few weeks or months ago. For example, if you used informal teacher-made tests or tally counts when you began observing the child, use these methods again when you want to assess the child's progress since implementing the plan. In this way, you can make valid comparisons of pre- and post-implementation behaviors and achievement. The tally counts at the left show the number of times a student wandered in a 30-minute period, before and after a plan was implemented.

Jointly Making Decisions Based on Plan Outcomes

After collecting this second set of data within a predetermined time, arrange to meet with the parents, the child, the special education teacher, the principal (or designate), and any other involved people to make decisions about future adaptations. Present the initial data, provide a brief statement of the goals, describe the strategies and adaptations that were implemented, and summarize the final set of observational data. If psychological testing has been conducted, the results may or may not be available at the time of your second meeting. If these results are available, they will tell you about the student's total IQ score and the areas of cognitive strength and weakness. The psychologist who wrote the report will also note any learning problems or academic giftedness.

Once everyone has had a chance to discuss the adaptations and outcomes, the group can make decisions about continuing parts of the informal plan, making modifications to it, or incorporating it into an individual education plan (IEP) that will be written later. The decisions will vary. In some cases, it may be decided that testing would be inappropriate, that a specific goal has been achieved, or that work should continue in specific areas.

As you read more about Andrew, Alex, and Erik, you will see how each of the students progressed with the accommodations and understand the rationale for the decisions that were made for each of them.

Steps towards Success

Between mid-October and the end of January, the English teacher let all her students choose how to best present some assignments: in writing, orally, or with a video. Andrew, whose strength was oral communication, gave oral presentations whenever possible. He also began taking part more often in large-group discussions and small-group work. For five-paragraph papers in which he expressed his views, Andrew followed the writing guide. He found that when his ideas were organized in point form on paper, presenting them was easier. His ideas were better organized, but still not fully expressed.

The teacher initiated other ways of supporting students such as Andrew. She told the class that she would grant extensions, but only if they were requested before the due date. The maximum length was two days. Andrew now felt safe to ask for an extension and needed only one between mid-October and January. When taking tests for English, he wrote his answers in point form, which helped him to complete the questions within the allotted time. However, he knew that he could go to the resource room if he needed extra time for English tests. He chose not to take advantage of this option because he did not want to appear different. Essentially, he sought ways to cope with his weakness in written expression by doing oral presentations, answering questions in point form, and taking extra time with assignments when full sentences were required.

Resolving one problem, in this case, legibility, can lead to the discovery of another. For Andrew, it was spelling.

When Andrew began writing on every second line and spacing his letters so that the teacher could read his work, she discovered that the boy had a spelling problem. He admitted that he was not a good speller and "sort of scribbled" to hide the spelling mistakes. The teacher gave him a list of spelling rules, and Andrew began typing his assignments and found that the spell check helped his spelling because he could see the correct version. He discovered, too, that the neat, typewritten pages looked much better than handwritten pages, and he started putting them into plastic covers instead of just stapling them.

Students like positive feedback that acknowledges good work, so be sure to explicitly say or note what they do well and make suggestions for improvement. For older students, write comments on the last page of an assignment or in the margins. You can also talk to students about improvements in behavior, such as completing homework and arriving to class on time.

The teacher asked Andrew to monitor his attendance, late arrivals, bringing of a notebook and pen, and submission of assignments. She did the same. After the middle of October, he skipped only one class (the day before the winter break) and was late for three (all in October and early November). While self-monitoring, Andrew was amazed at how often he thought about skipping, particularly in October and early November, but he knew his parents would be telephoned immediately and he decided to go to class. On the three occasions when he was late, he seriously thought of skipping, but changed his mind.

In case Andrew and any other students forgot basic classroom tools, the teacher was ready. She kept extra three-hole paper in the classroom and gave Andrew a sheet or two when necessary. If he forgot his pen, she loaned him one. To receive a loaner, however, he had to surrender his bus pass for the period. She extended this policy to all students and found that it had the greatest effect on those who had to give a shoe as collateral. Once was all it took to have those students find a pen to bring to class. At the end of each week, she and Andrew met quickly after class (which was just before lunch) and examined tally charts. They also used this time as a check-in so that Andrew could discuss how things were going.

Andrew's parents had agreed to have him tested as it was suspected that he might have a mild learning disability; however, the testing wouldn't occur until April.

Planning Sheet

NAME: _Andrew_   IMPLEMENTATION DATE: _October_

GRADE: _7_

STRENGTHS

– *participates in oral discussions*
– *is able to express his ideas well orally*

WEAKNESSES

– *arrives late (4) and skips class (up to 10)*
– *easily off-task*
– *refuses to complete some assignments or portions of some assignments*
– *hands in assignments late (7/9 were late)*
– *doesn't always bring his notebook and pen to class (6 times in 6 weeks)*
– *written assignments too short*
– *handwriting very messy*

GOALS

1. *To lengthen written responses*
2. *To improve neatness of written work*

ADAPTATIONS

1. *Length of Written Assignments*
   – *use the Frame for Writing a Five-Paragraph Essay for five-paragraph essays and work individually with Andrew*
   – *demonstrate how to write a five-paragraph essay and provide samples of completed assignments*
   – *discuss the answers to questions about the novel, short story, poem, etc. before he writes the answers*
   – *give extensions if required*
   – *occasionally give a choice as to how to complete assignments (e.g., orally)*

2. *Neatness of Written Assignments*
   – *encourage Andrew to write on every second line and to space out letters of words*
   – *inform all students as to when the school's computer lab is open*
   – *encourage Andrew to type assignments*

3. *Other*
   – *accommodations for tests and exams — point form, extra time, part written and part oral*
   – *encourage Andrew to participate in group discussions*
   – *seat Andrew close to the front to monitor off-task behaviors*
   – *set up a chart for Andrew so that he can keep a tally count of lates, skipping, bringing notebook and pen, submitting assignments*
   – *have three-hole paper available*
   – *loan a pen with collateral*
   – *praise Andrew discreetly for submitting assignments on time, etc.*
   – *develop a rapport with Andrew*

POST-IMPLEMENTATION RESULTS: *February*

1. *Length of Written Assignments*
   - *the writing frame helped him organize ideas*
   - *he needed only one extension between mid-November and January*
   - *chose to do as many assignments orally as possible*
   - *tests answered in point form — effective, extra time available in the resource room*
   - *written answers and assignments were longer, but not substantially*
   - *mark rose from 52% to 64%*

2. *Neatness of Written Assignments and Spelling*
   - *typing the assignments and using the spell check feature helped*

3. *Other*
   - *tally sheets helped him monitor his own behaviors*
   - *having three-hole paper to give and pens to loan helped*
   - *Regular check-ins helped to develop a relationship*

DECISIONS

- *referred for testing for possible learning disability in area of written expression*
- *teacher will continue using these adaptations and the resource teacher will monitor next year*

Meanwhile, the teacher was implementing accommodations designed to teach Andrew how to cope with his writing problems (through organizing his thoughts before writing and using the computer) and to use his relatively strong oral abilities whenever possible. By the end of the semester, his mark in English had risen to 64 percent from 52 percent, in large part due to the marks accumulated through oral presentations. Although his written work was legible, his ideas were still not fully expressed. This area required further work, which would be done after the results of formal testing were made available.

With the help of his teacher and parents, Andrew was finally taking responsibility for his work. However, this change in behavior might not have occurred if Andrew had not been "ready" to make some changes. In the fall he felt that his marks in English were so low that his parents would be upset. He was thus motivated to try the teacher's plan to avoid punishment. He had been successful at submitting typed assignments and doing work orally. As well, his attendance was no longer a problem, he was bringing his notebook and pen to class, and the sullenness and negative comments about English ceased. The teacher's hunch had been correct: Andrew would attend classes and work if he knew he could be successful.

At the beginning of February, the English teacher, the special education teacher, the parents, and Andrew met. The English teacher gave them a copy of the planning sheet she had prepared (see pages 70–71), described the accommodations she had implemented, and outlined the progress Andrew had made. It was decided that they would continue the plan until the end of June. For Grade 8, the special education teacher would monitor Andrew's progress and work with his new teachers. Andrew's parents expressed their gratitude, and Andrew mumbled something about English not being that bad after all.

The Value of Positive Reinforcement

At the initial meeting with her parents, it became known that Alex was greatly distressed about her father's medical condition. It appeared that this anxiety had triggered the girl's increasingly disruptive behaviors, but something else emerged from the meeting. When the teacher spoke to the special education teacher about possible strategies for use with Alex, it became painfully obvious to her that she should alter her teaching approach. The teacher realized that she was overly rigid, talked too much, and was not providing the kind of structure that Alex (and a few other children) needed. She also felt that she was too quick to become angry and punish Alex. In short, the teacher realized that *she* would have to make some changes to her teaching style that might benefit everyone.

Addressing behavior problems

The teacher planned the next social studies unit using centres at which the students took part in activities in groups, writing answers to questions, dramatizing certain events, drawing pictures, making maps, and doing research using books and the internet. Setting up the activities at the centres and tracking the students' work were time-consuming, but it allowed the children to move about the classroom, and the teacher was able to monitor Alex's behavior. She was also able to provide individual assistance to Alex and other students who needed it.

Planning Sheet

NAME: *Alex*   IMPLEMENTATION DATE: *November*

GRADE: *3*

STRENGTHS

– *athletic; is on swim team*
– *vivid imagination; writes well*

WEAKNESSES

– *out of seat 15–17 times a day*
– *talks constantly*
– *blurts out answers 4–7 times a day*
– *short attention span*
– *difficulty regulating emotions*

GOALS

1. *To decrease the out-of-seat behaviors*
2. *To decrease the talking*
3. *To increase the emotional regulation*

ADAPTATIONS

1. *Wandering*
   – *plan lessons that allow some movement in the classroom and touching of objects to maintain attention (e.g., centres)*
   – *chunk an assignment into smaller pieces, praise when each segment is completed, and reward with the opportunity to get a drink*
   – *have Alex monitor her own behavior, using tally counts for the number of times she is out of her seat*
   – *establish a number of times each day that she may be out of her seat without teacher permission*
   – *reteach the classroom rules about moving in the room*

2. *Constant Talking*
   – *assign Alex one desk at the front of the room and a second one at the back of the classroom*
   – *plan more lessons involving group work where talking wouldn't be disruptive and might be focused on the task*

3. *Emotional Regulation*
   – *daily check-ins with time to engage in individual social problem solving after recess, if required*
   – *discussion on emotional awareness and strategies for managing feelings*

4. *Other*
   – *enforce the hands-up rule when calling on students to answer a question*
   – *use nonverbal cues to remind Alex to raise her hand or to return to her seat*
   – *plan interesting lessons in which movement, manipulation of objects, and discussion are included*
   – *provide more choices in classroom work*
   – *use a multisensory method of teaching in which instruction is presented using the visual, auditory, kinesthetic, and tactile learning modalities (VAKT)*
   – *use "I-messages" when Alex does not follow the rules*
   – *Use the "broken record" technique when Alex argues*
   – *monitor Alex's behaviors in the classroom*
   – *provide as much individual attention as possible*
   – *give Alex opportunities to shine*
   – *develop a rapport with Alex*

POST-IMPLEMENTATION RESULTS: *March*

1. *Wandering*
   - *using centres helped to provide Alex with opportunities to move; monitoring of her behavior was possible*
   - *chunking worked — the assignment didn't seem overwhelming, and she was motivated to do the work and get the drink*
   - *self-monitoring of wandering helped her realize how often she was out of her seat — effective because it helped her make a link between wandering and completion of work*
   - *reward program with stickers was successful; most of the time not out of seat without permission more than five times a day*

2. *Constant Talking*
   - *the desk at the back worked — less talking; working at the back of the classroom was not viewed as a punishment*
   - *group discussions were successful, especially with tolerant, on-task peers*

3. *Emotional Regulation*
   - *check-ins were done at the beginning of the day and after recess, Alex identified her mood and feelings*
   - *scaffolding emotional problem solving was usually successful, except when Alex insisted that she was right*
   - *leaving the room for a few minutes to calm herself using the breathing technique was successful*

4. *Other*
   - *reducing the instruction portion of the lesson and involving Alex in the lesson helped to maintain Alex's attention*
   - *enforcement of the hands-up rule, group praise, and cuing were successful with all of the children, with Alex blurting out answers only one or two times per lesson*
   - *Choice was given in lessons and units — Alex appreciated it*
   - *monitoring Alex's levels of agitation, giving individual attention, and offering praise helped to prevent conflicts*
   - *using "I-messages" made Alex less defensive and giving choices about behavior gave her a sense of control*
     The "broken record" technique worked and helped to de-escalate the conflict
     Proximity control and individual attention helped keep Alex focused
   - *Alex enjoyed the conversations before school*

DECISIONS

- *continue the plan until June*
- *special education teacher and Grade 3 teacher will meet with Grade 4 teacher in the fall*

Classroom rules should be expressed as positively as possible. For example:
1. Respect yourself.
2. Respect others.
3. Respect the property of others.
However, some students need more specific instructions, such as "keep your hands and feet to yourself." These may be expressed either positively or negatively *using a calm voice*. A threatening voice doesn't work because a student may see this as a challenge to be taken up.

The 4-4-6 breathing technique helped give Alex a mental pause so that she could calm herself. She learned to breathe in for 4 seconds, hold it for 4 seconds, and breathe out for 6 seconds.

During other times of the day, the teacher chunked Alex's assignments (see page 94) because doing so made a job more manageable and less overwhelming to her. As Alex completed each section of the assignment, she was rewarded with praise and the opportunity to get a drink. Every time Alex went for a drink, the teacher reminded her of the rules (no talking and no touching). A few times Alex's drink privileges were suspended because she talked with or touched another child. For the most part, however, this technique worked.

Alex and her teacher each tallied the number of times per day that she was out of her seat without the teacher's permission. Alex was surprised that she was wandering so often and made the link between wandering and being able to finish her work in school as opposed to at home. Once she realized the relationship, she tried harder to stay on task and in her seat. Alex and her teacher decided that she could be out of her seat (other than with the teacher's permission) five times a day. She was fairly successful at it, and by the middle of February was receiving stickers every day in her planner. Her parents rewarded her with a double-scoop, chocolate-dipped ice-cream cone at the local mall on Friday if she received stickers every day that week.

The teacher provided a second desk for Alex at the back of the room where she could do her seatwork. After two weeks Alex begged the teacher to move her closer to some of the other children, and that lasted two days. Before the teacher moved her back, Alex had pushed her new desk to its previous position. She explained that she was talking too much, walking around, and not getting her work done. She had missed a day's sticker and knew her parents were disappointed. However, she joined in group work that had been structured to permit many opportunities for discussion. The teacher monitored Alex's group closely to ensure that the students' discussions remained on topic. When organizing group work, the teacher placed Alex with peers who were accepting and generally on task. They helped to model appropriate behavior and were able to de-escalate conflicts.

The teacher also watched for signs of agitation in Alex and tried to reduce conflict with her by using the broken record technique. She was amazed that the technique worked. She noted when Alex was becoming tired and angry, and tried to monitor the girl's behaviors *before* they got out of hand. She used proximity control (see page 109) and provided Alex with as much individual attention as she could give. Alex and the teacher decided on a signal that Alex could use when she was becoming agitated and needed a break. She was permitted to leave the classroom and walk down the hall to practise the breathing technique she learned from the teacher. It usually took only two or three minutes to calm down using this method.

The teacher offered more choice in some activities, including being able to stand up and work, which Alex and others appreciated.

However, one major incident occurred during the first week in February. Alex refused to do her math assignment, yelled and screamed, threw her pencil on the floor, and ran out of the classroom. The teacher followed her out into the hall and found her crying uncontrollably. When Alex had calmed down enough to talk, the teacher learned that her father was undergoing exploratory surgery. Alex was afraid he would die. Since the meeting with the parents, Alex's mother and father had explained the heart condition and the operation to her, and Alex had seemed less anxious about it. Nonetheless, Alex's mother had sent a note to the teacher to forewarn her about possible problems the day of the operation. Alex had forgotten to give the note to the teacher. In the hallway, Alex said that she was too embarrassed to return to the classroom and wanted to do her work at the office. The teacher made the arrangements, and Alex worked quietly in the office until lunch, then returned to the class. The teacher made certain that no comments about the incident were made to Alex by the other children.

Revisiting classroom management and instructional practices

Besides planning more movement in her lessons, the teacher sought to make the instructional part shorter and to involve the children more. She incorporated more questioning, more hands-on and kinesthetic approaches (e.g., the use of manipulatives in math, hands-on centres in science, drama in reading activities), and more variety in her lessons. The teacher also revamped her classroom management and discipline techniques.

The teacher recognized that, when calling on children to answer questions, she had not always followed the hands-up rule herself. She would invite the children to raise their hands, then ask someone who hadn't raised a hand. The teacher realized that her own behavior may have contributed to Alex's habit of blurting out answers. Therefore, she began following the rule consistently. She stated the hands-up rule and called only on those students who raised their hands. She called on Alex as soon as hers was raised to reinforce the link between hands up and answering. She also tried to cue Alex about raising her hand by tapping the palm of her own right hand with her left index finger. By the end of March, Alex was blurting out answers only one or two times per lesson. The teacher also used group praise ("I like the way you are raising your hands") which seemed to reinforce this behavior for everyone.

The teacher realized that instead of becoming angry, she should be calmer and more assertive. She found that using I-messages and offering choices about behavior ("If you choose to leave your seat one more time, you will lose your sticker for the day. It's up to you.") helped her remain calm. She also stopped yelling at Alex, as it made both of them angry. It was better to monitor Alex, watch for signs of agitation, provide a few seconds of individual attention, and praise for staying on task. The breathing technique also worked for Alex.

One other strategy the teacher began using with Alex and two other students was daily check-ins. In a health class, emotional awareness was reviewed to provide a common vocabulary for the class. Ways to manage emotions and behaviors were also discussed, which was helpful for Alex and a few others. During the check-ins, which occurred when the students arrived in the morning and after recess, the teacher asked Alex how she was feeling. Alex would indicate her emotional state and if she was angry or upset about something, time was taken to discuss it. Alex was usually fine when she arrived at school; however, she could be upset after recess. The daily schedule allowed for a 10-minute cool down period after recess in which students wrote in their journals. On days when Alex indicated being angry, she and the teacher would sit at the back of the room and quietly discuss the situation from Alex's perspective, then from the other person's perspective, discuss possible solutions and possible effects, and come up with a way to resolve the situation. During these conversations, the teacher tried to listen and lead Alex to solving the social problem instead of imposing a solution.

Finally, in an effort to develop a rapport with Alex, the teacher made a point of talking to the girl each day about non-school matters. She learned that Alex had recently done well at a swim meet and that her name was in the community newspaper. The teacher cut out the article and with Alex's permission tacked it

An important skill for a teacher to learn is how to work with one child at her desk and still watch the other students. I try to position myself in such a way that I have my back to the least number of students, watch the ones in front of me, and turn around periodically to monitor those behind me.

Decisions
- continue the plan until June
- special education teacher and Grade 3 teacher will meet with Grade 4 teacher in the fall

on the bulletin board. She was striving to develop a positive attitude towards her student.

At the end of March the teacher invited Alex, her parents, the special education teacher, and the principal to a second meeting. She described the outcomes of the plan and stated that Alex's disruptive behaviors had decreased and that academically she was doing above-average work. Alex's mother reported that Alex had seemed happier at home and was no longer showing aggressive behaviors towards her younger brother. Her mother explained that at home, they were trying to help Alex use her words to express anger instead of communicating the feeling through physical means. She also revealed that Alex did enjoy the ice-cream cones and that chocolate and ice cream were strong motivators for her daughter. Alex's father reported that all had gone well with the exploratory surgery, and he had resumed his normal activities. The anxiety everyone had felt about his health had subsided. It was decided to continue the plan until the end of the year, as Alex was proud of the stickers and wanted the weekly ice-cream cone. It was also decided that the special education teacher and the classroom teacher would discuss the plan with Alex's Grade 4 teacher the next fall.

Opportunities to Shine

Erik

A case conference is an *informal* meeting between the school staff, the parents, and the student to discuss the student's progress and ways to improve it.

A week after the September Grade 7 staff meeting at which Erik's computer, math, and music abilities were noted, a case conference was set up with Erik and his parents, the homeroom teacher, the music teacher, the vice-principal, and the special education teacher. It was decided that Erik would not be referred for testing, but that accommodations would be made.

Between October and June, Erik took advantage of many opportunities presented to him. His homeroom teacher, also the supervisor of the Engineering Club, informed the entire class of the meetings. He then privately invited Erik to attend. Erik was initially shy about going, being a Grade 7 student mixing with some high-school students, but he met another Grade 7 boy who shared his interests, and they became "regulars." He enjoyed the problem solving, learned how to upgrade his family's computer, and discovered more about careers in engineering and in the high-tech sector. He also attended a weeklong enrichment camp held at the local university in May and spent the week in the new technology faculty. Finally, the teacher began having the students do daily brain teasers and a longer problem to be solved by the end of the week for a mark out of 5. Erik enjoyed these questions and noticed how popular he was by Thursday as his peers went to him for help with the weekly questions due on Fridays. In the area of computers, Erik did three extra projects, one of which was entered into the school's science fair. He was awarded second prize for the intermediate students. (A Grade 8 student won first prize.)

Few children are *globally gifted*, that is, excelling in all academic areas. These children are usually provided with an enrichment program at school. However, some students have a gift in just one area, which also needs special nourishment.

In music Erik really shone. Although he had never had musical training other than singing in the elementary schools he attended, he became passionate about the saxophone. He happily practised at home and finished the Grade 7 book by the end of March. The music teacher gave him extra sheet music and started him on the Grade 8 book in April. Erik joined the Grade 7 Band and met more friends. In the early spring Erik began practising with the Grade 8 Jazz Band, and he was amazed to learn that they would be competing in a local festival.

At a case conference at the end of the year, Erik and his parents decided against testing. Erik clearly had gifts in math, computers, and music, but to be admitted

Planning Sheet

NAME: *Erik* IMPLEMENTATION DATE: *October*

GRADE: *7*

STRENGTHS WEAKNESSES

- *math and computers*
- *music*

GOALS

1. *Math and Computers*
   - *encourage Erik to join the Engineering Club*
   - *provide enrichment activities in class and ask open-ended questions*
   - *encourage Erik to do one extra project in computers, which would be entered in the school's Science Fair*

2. *Music*
   - *encourage Erik to join the Grade 7 Band*
   - *work at his own pace through the Grade 7 music book, offer tutoring, give sheet music of more challenging pieces*
   - *informally acknowledge him as the first saxophonist of the Grade 7 Band; find pieces for the saxophones*
   - *possibly encourage him to join the Jazz Band*
   - *speak to Erik's parents about private lessons*

3. *Other*
   - *encourage Erik to attend the enrichment camp held at the university each spring*

POST-IMPLEMENTATION RESULTS: *June*

1. *Math and Computers*
   - *did join the Engineering Club, participated in contests*
   - *did three extra projects in computers, with one entered in the Science Fair (Second Prize)*
   - *enjoyed the enrichment questions*

2. *Music*
   - *joined the Grade 7 Band*
   - *finished the Grade 7 book in March, began working on the Grade 8 book in April*
   - *joined the Jazz Band*

DECISIONS

- *individual ability testing will not be done*
- *special education department will monitor Erik's progress and will inform future teachers*
- *continue using the planning sheet to organize accommodations*

into a gifted program, a student needed to have a global IQ score in at least the 98th percentile. With Erik's only above-average marks in English his composite score was unlikely to be that high. Beyond that consideration, Erik did not want to move to another school where the gifted program was offered as he now had some good friends. He didn't want to have to break into a new social scene. He did want to continue with the Engineering Club, the Grade 8 Band, and the Jazz Band the next year.

It was decided that the special education teacher would monitor Erik's progress over the next few years and inform future teachers about some of the ways the program could be enriched. Although an individual education plan was not written, the planning sheet developed by the homeroom and music teachers became the reference point for making accommodations for Erik.

Meanwhile, Erik's parents had quietly been searching for appropriate summer camps for their son. They had found one computer camp at the local university and a jazz camp offered by a community group. These were both weeklong day camps, which Erik agreed to attend. Erik's parents had also looked into private saxophone lessons, which would begin the following September.

Key Principles Distilled from the Case Studies

Three important principles can be derived from the case studies presented. These principles can be summarized as follows: (1) work with others, (2) strive to develop a sense of academic and social belonging among all your students, and (3) caring teachers can make a difference. They should guide our attitudes and actions in relation to all students but, in particular, those who require accommodations in our classrooms.

Work with others

Given the range of student abilities and needs, it is impossible for one person to meet all those needs effectively. You will have to enlist the support of the student's parents, the child, teaching colleagues, and administrators such as the principal. Know and draw upon the skills and experiences of others as you collaborate with colleagues and parents.

As was shown in each of the case studies, the teachers discussed their observations and ideas about possible accommodations with the special education teacher. The special education teacher can provide valuable ideas about how to make minor adaptations to your teaching strategies and the curriculum.

A second source of support is a child's parents. In each of the case studies, the parents provided either active or moral support for the work of the teacher. At the same time, the teachers listened attentively to what the parents had to say. Most often, parents are grateful that a teacher made certain observations and is willing to help implement a plan to assist their child. The importance of the home and school working together to provide remediation, a supportive environment, or enrichment for a child cannot be emphasized enough.

The third partner is the child, who will either accept the assistance or reject it. In all case studies presented here, the students were willing to collaborate, and in one case, the student wanted to be an equal partner in the development of the "extra work." The old maxim states that you can lead a horse to water, but you can't make it drink. This saying is particularly appropriate when working with teens and pre-teens because they often worry about being perceived as different from their peers. The adaptations for these students must be fully acceptable to them; otherwise, the students will not cooperate.

The final partner consists of administrators, such as the principal, who may provide moral support for your work; other teachers, who will join you in implementing accommodations for a student; paraprofessionals, who may be available to assist you in putting into practice certain programs; and other professionals, such as a speech language pathologist, who can provide information and ideas. Therefore, although the classroom teacher takes the lead role in making the adaptations, the success of the plan frequently depends on the teacher's ability to work with others.

Strive to develop a sense of social and academic belonging

We all want to belong and even though a student's words or action may not suggest it, they too want to experience social and academic belonging. As we saw in Chapter 1, teachers need to develop positive relationships with each student, and you can do this by checking in with the students and talking informally about non-school topics (Alex's teacher did this). By developing a positive relationship, the student learns to trust that you genuinely want them to succeed, that you will not humiliate them in front of their peers, and that you will help them be accepted by others. Within the classroom (and school), the norm should be acceptance of others, where negative comments about others are not tolerated. The adage "If you don't have anything positive to say about a person, then don't say anything at all" can be introduced. Teachers can also encourage students to participate in extracurricular activities that align with their interests to meet others who share those interests (e.g., Erik), thereby providing an opportunity to develop friendships as Erik did.

Students also want to experience academic success and for struggling students, a few accommodations that are useful for everyone (e.g., using manipulatives, typing assignments, standing while working) can easily be implemented. Using them for all students ensures that the students who need them are not singled out. When students feel they can do the work, they are motivated to begin it and persist (we saw this with Andrew).

Caring teachers can make a difference

In each of the case studies, an observant and caring teacher initiated a plan and guided its implementation. As a caring professional who is concerned about ensuring that all students are engaged in learning, meeting the curriculum expectations, and thriving socially, you, too, can make observations, develop a plan of action, put it into practice, and make the plan work. Doing it involves time, energy, and a commitment to providing the best possible opportunities for each child.

Caring teachers such as those who taught Andrew, Alex, and Erik look beyond the delivery of the curriculum to review the academic performance and social connectedness of each student and consider ways of making them better. In other words, they look beyond their own needs and examine the needs of others. They reflect on their own practices and decide what is helping children learn and what is not. They have the courage to abandon those practices that are not working and to seek better ones. They also take the time to work with others to develop accommodations, make adjustments in their teaching methods and curriculum, find ways to strengthen peer relationships and their own with the student, and follow up on students' progress. The fact you are reading this book suggests that you are one of them.

The keys to working with at-risk and exceptional children are easily stated. First, you need a sense of commitment to children and to the teaching profession. Next, you need to take the time to make observations, develop a plan, implement it, reflect on how it is working, and do the follow-up. Finally, you have to be a sufficiently flexible thinker to see the strengths each child possesses instead of just their deficits and the problems they create for you.

These ideas are easily stated but not always easily implemented. Success depends not only on you, but on the child, the parents, and other people in the school. Is it worth the time and effort of striving to meet the individual needs of your students? Of course, it is. But it takes a caring teacher to initiate the process and adopt appropriate teaching practices and accommodations. Some of these are outlined in Chapters 6 to 14.

Summary Checklist for Working with a Student Whose Exceptionalities Have Not Yet Been Identified

Identify and systematically observe any student whose academic performance is well above or below the standard or whose behavior is inappropriate over a period of time.

1. Making Observations

☐ Collect data on the student's strengths.
☐ Collect data on the student's weaknesses.

2. Formulating Goals

☐ Prioritize areas to be remediated or that require coping skills.
☐ Decide on areas for enrichment.
☐ Decide which behaviors to modify.

3. Developing Adaptations

☐ Meet with the special education teacher.
☐ Develop accommodations.
☐ Meet with the parents, the student, the special education teacher, and the school administration.
☐ Decide on a time frame to try the accommodations.

4. Implementing the Action Plan

☐ Implement the plan.
☐ Collect data on the effectiveness of the intervention.

5. Reviewing the Action Plan

☐ Decide whether the interventions are working or not. If not, make changes and try again.
☐ Meet with the parents, the student, the special education teacher, and the school administration.
☐ Decide on the next steps.

Pembroke Publishers © 2022 *Finding a Place for Every Student* by Cheryll Duquette ISBN 978-1-55138-360-6

Planning Sheet

Name: _____ Date: _____

Grade: _____

Strengths	Weaknesses

Goals

Adaptations

Post-implementation Results

Decision

Pembroke Publishers © 2022 *Finding a Place for Every Student* by Cheryll Duquette ISBN 978-1-55138-360-6

CHAPTER 6

Learning Disabilities

In discussing learning disabilities (LDs), a definition by the elimination of other disabilities is used: learning disabilities are *not* primarily the result of impairment of vision, impairment of hearing, physical disability, intellectual disability, primary emotional disturbance, or cultural difference. However, a learning disability results in significant discrepancy between academic achievement and assessed intellectual ability, with deficits in one or more of the following: receptive language, language processing, expressive language, or mathematical computations. *Dyslexia*, perhaps the word most often associated with learning disabilities, is a particular type of disability that relates to a person's ability to read, spell, and write.

After several decades of discussion, there is no universal agreement on how to classify the problems that come under the general term *learning disability*. Psychologists focus on dysfunctions in areas such as perception, processing, memory, and attention. Medical researchers emphasize genetics and brain organization and function. And teachers zero in on academic difficulties. Despite this lack of agreement, the primary causes of learning disabilities have been identified.

Causes of Learning Disabilities

Some children develop at a slower rate, and consequently they are unable to do the expected work. Eventually, their achievement profile may resemble that of a person with learning disabilities — e.g., scores in reading and math that are two years below grade level. However, these students may not have a learning disability. With remedial assistance, they may be able to improve their scores.

Experts agree that learning is hindered due to slow processing of information. Why it does is unknown. Several causes of learning disabilities are outlined below.

Nervous System Disorders: Some children with normal vision and hearing may misinterpret everyday sights and sounds due to some unexplained disorder of the nervous system. Researchers postulate that learning disabilities are linked to a problem in the brain's wiring that interferes with the ability to function. For example, studies have shown that adults with dyslexia exhibit greater than normal activity in the visual areas of the brain when reading than in the auditory sections of the brain. People without dyslexia show widespread activity in both the sight and hearing areas of the brain.

Head Injuries and Illnesses: Some learning disabilities are accounted for by head injuries at birth or in childhood. Illnesses or disorders linked to learning problems are high fever, encephalitis, meningitis, and diabetes.

Prenatal Exposure to Alcohol: Individuals whose birth mothers consumed alcohol while pregnant may be diagnosed with a learning disability.

Premature Births: Children born prematurely and children who had medical issues soon after birth sometimes have learning disabilities.

Genetic Factors: Genetic makeup can make a child vulnerable to developing learning disabilities which are then triggered by an environmental factor such as birth trauma. However, there is strong evidence that learning disabilities that involve reading difficulties (dyslexia) can be passed from one generation to the next. Chromosome 15 has been related to dyslexia, particularly in the development of word identification, and chromosome 6 is linked to phonological segmentation, or the ability to divide a word into its sounds.

Types of Learning Disabilities

The main academic areas that serve to identify students with learning disabilities are reading, writing, and mathematics. The speaking and listening areas can also provide evidence that will help identify students with exceptionalities.

Reading: Dyslexia

Reading disabilities are often referred to as *dyslexia*. They reflect a persistent deficit rather than a developmental lag. Lyon (1995) found that, of those children who had a reading disability in Grade 3, approximately 74 percent continue to read significantly below grade level in Grade 9. Hence, dyslexia is generally a condition that a person does *not* grow out of. People with dyslexia often have difficulty decoding words and are unable to identify the main idea of a passage. Some adults learn to compensate for their inability to identify the main idea of a passage by drawing on their previous life experiences to bring meaning to it. People with dyslexia may also experience difficulty recalling basic facts and events in a sequence and making inferences or evaluating what they have read. As many females as males have dyslexia; however, schools identify three to four times more boys than girls, largely through initial observations of behavior problems.

Here's how a person with dyslexia typically fares with the four steps in the reading process.

1. *Phonological awareness* is an understanding that words are made up of different sounds (44 in English). It also involves the ability to segment words and syllables into sounds, or phonemes. The ability to decode single words accurately and fluently is dependent upon this ability to divide words into their basic sounds.

   Many individuals with dyslexia lack phonological awareness and are unable to segment words into phonemes. For example, they may not understand that the word *bat* is made up of three sounds: /b/, /a/, and /t/. Instead, a person with dyslexia may perceive the word as having only one sound. For an undetermined reason, the brain of a person with dyslexia has difficulty translating a written word into phonemes. Hence, a person with dyslexia tries to read relying heavily on visual memory rather than on auditory abilities.

2. *Phonics* involves linking sounds to letters of the alphabet (sound–symbol association). This process can be confusing for some people as the English language has many letters and letter combinations that have multiple sounds. For example, the letter *c* has a /k/ sound in *cup*, but an /s/ sound in *ice*. Longitudinal data show that individuals with dyslexia benefit from one-to-one instruction in phonics rather than being immersed in a whole language approach.

3. When sound–symbol association becomes automatic, the decoding of words becomes fast and accurate. However, some students with dyslexia take more time than the average reader to develop the links between sounds and letters; they may never become fast readers who read every word correctly.

Can dyslexics be helped? With early intervention, some people can improve their reading abilities; however, poor reading is likely to be a lifelong condition.

4. Comprehending a passage depends on the ability to decode words rapidly and accurately. A fluent reader focuses on the meaning of the words rather than what the individual words are. People with dyslexia spend so much time and effort decoding words that they can't focus on the meaning of a passage; they read words, rather than extracting meaning from the text. Furthermore, some individuals with dyslexia find it difficult to identify the main idea due to their poor abilities to think abstractly and organize their thoughts.

Speaking and listening: Language difficulties

Language impairments may also be found in the areas of oral expression (speaking) and listening comprehension. Common oral language problems include difficulty in coming up with the right word (word retrieval), slowness in answering questions, and the use of simpler structures and words in sentences than that of peers. A student with learning disabilities may process language more slowly than others or may misinterpret the meaning of the message. Not following instructions, appearing to be balky, or daydreaming, and the like may be misinterpreted as behavioral issues rather than as listening difficulties. Students with learning disabilities may also miss nonverbal cues and may not understand jokes, something that can contribute to difficulties in social situations.

Mathematics: Dyscalculia

Dyscalculia refers to a learning disability related to problems making math calculations and reasoning. Students may have difficulty understanding and working with the four operations, the concept of zero, regrouping, place value, and basic math concepts (e.g., one-to-one correspondence, sets), as well as solving math problems.

Dyscalculia is sometimes accompanied by visual-motor problems, which make it difficult for the student to pick up on how to count using manipulatives or a number line. Visual perception problems may make it hard for a student to align numbers in columns, copy numbers correctly, or see an inscribed triangle. Finally, a person with dyscalculia may reverse numbers (e.g., *23* instead of *32*).

Writing: Dysgraphia

A person with learning disabilities may have *dysgraphia*, which refers to problems in printing or cursive writing. Writing may be labored, slow, messy, and illegible, reflecting poorly developed fine-motor skills. Some students with learning disabilities may also experience persistent difficulties with spelling and written expression (including creativity, grammar, and sentence structure).

The Effects of Learning Disabilities on General Academic Performance

Although the primary characteristic of a learning disability is a significant difference between a child's achievement and overall intelligence as measured by an individually administered IQ test, learning disabilities typically affect these general areas:

- Spoken language: delays or disorders in speech and language; problems in expressing ideas in speech

- Written language: difficulties with reading (decoding, main idea), spelling, and writing (written expression or handwriting)
- Arithmetic: difficulty in performing arithmetic operations or understanding basic concepts
- Reasoning: difficulty in organizing and integrating thoughts; may demonstrate limited vocabulary, little ability to think abstractly, problems in identifying similarities and differences, or few age-appropriate social-cognitive abilities
- Memory: difficulty in remembering information and instruction in written or oral form; problems in sequencing
- Spatiality: challenges with visual discrimination, laterality (distinguishing left from right), telling time using an analogue clock, fine- and gross-motor coordination, and body image
- Attention: inability to concentrate for long periods; easily distracted
- Performance: inconsistent, that is, knows something one day but not the next

Characteristics of Elementary Students with Learning Disabilities

Every student with a learning disability will have an individual profile of strengths and weaknesses. In other words, every case is different. Nonetheless, there is a general rule when identifying LDs: that a significant difference exists between performance and potential. If you suspect a student of having a learning disability, you need to observe the child over time to determine frequency and clusters of certain behaviors. Be sure to record your observations in a private journal or on a checklist that can be filed securely.

Your observations may be important in initiating the assessment process, which may result in determining that a child has a learning disability. In many districts, a student must be identified before extra support will be provided. The identification process typically involves (1) the classroom teacher, who makes informal observations; (2) the special education teacher, who does a screening assessment; and (3) the psychologist, who administers an individual IQ test. The results of the IQ test are examined for strengths and significant weaknesses and are compared to the student's academic achievement.

The characteristics outlined on the next two pages will not be demonstrated by every student with a learning disability: each child demonstrates specific clusters of characteristics.

No student will exhibit all the above characteristics; however, clusters of behaviors that are displayed frequently and over time may indicate that a child has a learning disability.

Developing Social Connections

Every student wants to feel as though the teacher likes them and will help them do well in school (including adults). As described in Chapter 1, it is important for the teacher to reach out to those students with LDs and welcome them to the class and discuss the academic accommodations they may require. As you would with any student, approach them with acceptance and kindness. Find out their

What to Look For in Students Suspected of Having a Learning Disability

Elementary Students

Reading

☐ difficulty in segmenting the sounds of a word
☐ problems in associating sounds and letters
☐ loses place regularly (tracking problem)
☐ makes "wild" guesses (comprehension)
☐ does not attempt to decode a word and looks at the teacher
☐ ignores punctuation and other cues
☐ makes up words and inserts them into the passage
☐ reverses the letters of words (e.g., *was* and *saw*)
☐ transposes words (changes the order of the words in a passage)
☐ loses meaning of a sentence from beginning to end
☐ has difficulty sequencing events in a story
☐ makes incorrect inferences
☐ does not identify the main idea
☐ identifies only a few supporting details

Work Speed

☐ frequently does not complete the written work
☐ works more slowly than age and grade peers
☐ has difficulty beginning a task
☐ is frustrated under time pressure

Work with the Alphabet and Penmanship

☐ may confuse letters in recitation and writing
☐ mixes lower and upper case letters
☐ mixes manuscript and cursive styles, or will continue to use manuscript long after peers use cursive
☐ has poor printing or handwriting: may be illegible
☐ often mirrors or reverses letters
☐ shows awkward movement of a pencil or pen

Remembering

☐ often forgets or misplaces things
☐ needs constant reminding (and has often trained family, teachers, or friends to do this)
☐ may know something one day but not the next

Pembroke Publishers © 2022 *Finding a Place for Every Student* by Cheryll Duquette ISBN 978-1-55138-360-6

interests and strengths so that you can plan lessons that will include them. Having an interest in the subject or some prior knowledge sets a foundation for learning and improves motivation. Conduct daily check-ins with them to ensure that they are understanding the concepts and keeping up with the work. Also monitor how they are feeling emotionally. Be patient with them, especially when things need to be repeated several times, and demonstrate acceptance to the entire class.

Some students with LDs experience difficulties making friends. They may understand every word literally and therefore not get jokes and may have challenges solving social problems. While you cannot explain every joke, you can avoid confusing phrases, such as "Let's get the show on the road." "What show?" and "What road?" could be questions the student asks. Use clear language to give instructions, such as "Let's get started on …" Teaching all the students strategies to manage social conflict as part of your social and emotional learning formal or informal curriculum will help students with LDs. As well, encourage the students with LDs to talk to you about social problems and how they might be solved. You can review the strategies and help the student select one or two that might work. Social acceptance is important for all students and with your support students with LDs will be well positioned to achieve it.

To reduce feelings of being different or deficient among students with LDs, select high-quality instructional strategies that will benefit the entire class, such as those in Chapter 2 and the ones that will be described in this chapter. When these strategies are used with the whole class, the students with LDs will not feel singled out and different. Some students are reluctant to use speech-to-text software for fear of teasing by peers. Making it available to all students in the class will ensure the student who needs it does not feel humiliated. As well, ensure that you follow the class schedule and routines so that the student with LDs will not feel worried or anxious about what will happen. Eliminating these types of worries allows more energy to be focused on schoolwork.

Find a strength in each student with LDs; for example, the student may be a skilled soccer player or show talent in art. Ensure that you showcase these abilities for peers to see, so that the student with LDs has an opportunity to shine and gain acceptance. Some students with LDs have difficulty making friends, and pairing students with LDs with kind, task-oriented, and accepting peers will help them feel a social connection within the class.

You will find that a feeling of social belonging and positive relations with you and peers sets a foundation for academic success. The strategies described in the next sections provide ideas on how to promote learning for students with LDs and their peers. When a student feels they are learning, they feel that they are academically connected to the classroom, that they can contribute, and they begin to develop a sense of self-confidence.

Ways to Help Elementary Students with LDs Learn

In this section, we discuss reading skills, both basic and advanced; spelling; printing and handwriting; note copying; written expression; written assignments; mathematics, including counting, mathematical facts, operations, and problem solving; listening and following directions; ways to remember; and organization. These strategies will help your students with LDs and their peers.

Reading skills

Basic Skills: The first step in learning how to read is to understand that letters and words have sounds; therefore, it is important to work on phonological awareness. Teach rhyming words, have the students listen to rhyming words, and prompt them to say their own rhyming words. As children become familiar with the concept of rhyming, pause before each rhyming word to allow them to predict what the next word might be.

Next, teach segmenting sentences into words and words into syllables. Use wooden sticks, blocks, or counters to hit or point to as each word in a sentence or syllable in a word or sentence is said.

Move on to identifying the sounds within words. For initial, ending, and middle sounds, teach the sounds, then delete the sound, and substitute the sound. Then teach the sounds of blended letters: for example, *cl-a-p* has three sounds.

Immerse the children in the printed word by reading to them every day, labeling classroom objects, and displaying books and other printed materials, such as catalogues or newspapers, in the classroom.

Create a word bank for the children to assist them in their writing. The words may be generated through discussions with your students or may be from word lists that accompany a reading series. Write the words on paper, cut them out, and tack them on a wall or the board. They may be arranged alphabetically or by category, such as nouns or verbs. You may want to write these words on small cards so that pairs of children can use them as a drill activity where one child says the words to a partner. This peer-tutoring approach permits immediate feedback and individual attention.

Another technique is to write sentences on strips of chart paper, using key vocabulary words. The children then read the strips. The words on the strips can also be cut, and the children can assemble sentences in a logical order and read them.

In your classroom, make available books that have varying reading levels and that might appeal to the students who are struggling to read or who have learning disabilities. Use software that can help develop reading skills, as well. The strategy here is to give students many opportunities to read — repetition is the key to learning.

If the resource teacher is available during your reading block, it may be possible to use a response to intervention (RTI) approach to reading (see Chapter 2). The students can be divided into two groups with the smaller one requiring more intensive instruction on basic skills (Tier 2). You can work with the larger one (Tier 1), and the resource teacher can focus on re-teaching basic reading skills using explicit instruction. Regular informal testing should be done and students whose skills improve can be moved back to the Tier 1 group, and students whose skill levels are not showing improvement may be candidates for Tier 3 interventions (usually one-to-one instruction).

Advanced Skills: The focus of your accommodations is on helping students understand the story or novel. Do your best to select a novel or story that will interest the students. If you have novel groups, choose high-interest, low-vocabulary novels for the weak readers. Pre-reading activities could include teaching the key vocabulary so that the children will recognize the words and understand what they mean. Discuss previous experiences or knowledge that will give the students a context for the story and a basis for understanding.

Novel: Key Words

If formatted as an advance organizer, key words such as these can be used to provide scaffolding for students:

Setting
Main Characters
Plot
    Introduction
    Rising Action
    Climax
    Falling Action
    Resolution

To support the processing of written language during novel or story study, allow students to listen to an audiobook while following printed text. Listening to the audiobook speeds the reading process, improves comprehension, and increases attention span. When an audiobook version of the novel is not available, I have read the novel to students so that they can hear it, see the words on paper, and follow the words with a finger, thereby using the multisensory VAKT approach.

After reading the story or chapter, discuss the story with the students to ensure understanding of plot, characters, setting, and so on. You might even have students dramatize specific scenes. Then ask the students to write their responses to the questions on these story elements.

Introducing the use of scaffolding would help the students organize the parts of the novel or story. *Scaffolding* is a technique that helps students move from working with direct assistance to working independently. An example of a scaffold, or support, is an advance organizer formatted with key words or headings that help the students organize their ideas. The scaffold provides direct support for the student through the key words, which act as prompts. For a novel or story, a table with the following headings could be made: Setting, Main Characters, and Plot, which could have the subheadings Introduction, Rising Action, Climax, Falling Action, and Resolution. You could demonstrate how to fill in the form, then organize the students into small groups, where they would discuss the story and write points under each heading either at the end of the novel study or as you read each chapter. This strategy will help the students with LDs, as well as the others.

Spelling

Select a spelling series that focuses on word families. Through the repetition of word families, such as "-ight," the students will see patterns that may be applied to their everyday spelling. Some students may also need a *multisensory* method of teaching (VAKT). You could write the words on flipchart paper (visual) and introduce them by reading them aloud (auditory) and pointing to them. Then, have the students say the words as you point to them. Discuss the words and look for similarities and differences. Highlight these with different-colored markers. Have the children write the words in their notebooks (kinesthetic). Finally, ask them to trace the letters of the words using Scrabble tiles or laminated letters (tactile).

For spelling tests, some of your students may require a reduction in the number of words learned each week. You may find that a student can manage only 10 of 20 words. When dictating the words, break the words into syllables so that the students can focus on small chunks of the word at a time. For example, if the word is *computer*, say the whole word first. Then say *com*, then *put*, and finally *er*. Say the word again without breaking it into syllables. This is the *whole-part-whole* method. If pencil is not permitted, encourage the students to use erasable pens. When marking the spelling test, award two points per word: two points, if the word is perfect; one point, if the word is incorrect but the student can correct it. Indicate the score as a portion of a whole, for example, 16/20 instead of so many wrong.

Encourage your students to use spelling aids such as a dictionary they have made or a word wall where commonly used words are arranged alphabetically. Encourage them to learn how to type their projects — many software programs teach keyboarding. Teach them, too, to use the spell-check and editor features on

To improve word recognition, teach the child to look for familiar parts in multisyllabic words. For example, *returned* may be segmented into the prefix, root, and suffix:
re turn ed.
The child can find the familiar parts and put them together when sounding out the word.

Beyond that, provide lists of grade-appropriate words, or write words on flash cards so that the students may practise them.

Novel Study Form

Name: _____

Novel: _____

Setting:

_____

_____

Main Characters:

_____

_____

_____

_____

Plot:

1. Introduction

_____

_____

2. Rising Action

_____

_____

_____

_____

3. Climax

_____

_____

4. Falling Action

_____

_____

5. Resolution

_____

_____

the computer. Using a computer for assignments, such as stories, will increase the number of correctly spelled words. It may also improve the students' spelling as they see that their version is not correct and discover how to spell the word correctly.

Printing and handwriting

When teaching printing to your students, use the *continuous flow* method instead of the ball and stick method. With the continuous flow method, the student does not have to lift the pencil — the alternative is drawing a circle, lifting the pencil, and trying to draw the line so that it touches the ball. Students experiencing delays in fine-motor development or who have deficits in visual-spatial abilities find the continuous flow method easier to do than the other.

An example of the continuous flow method

When teaching a specific letter, such as *a*, do pre-writing activities: for example, saying the name of the letter, listening to and producing the sound of the letter, noting how the mouth feels when saying the letter, and brainstorming words that begin with *a*. Then print an *a* on flipchart paper or the board, then another *a* while you describe your motions, and then a final *a*. When breaking the instruction into parts for the letter *a*, you might say: "We begin our circle at the 2 o'clock position [point to the clock so that the students can see the 2]. Curve to the left and make sure the bottom of the circle touches the lower horizontal line. Finish your circle by going upwards to where you began and begin a straight line to the above horizontal line. Then make a straight line down to the bottom horizontal line through the line you already started." Write the numbers 1, 2, and 3 in a different-colored marker or chalk on one of the *a*'s to show the steps. Then print another *a*, quickly summarizing the method. Tell students to print a letter *a* in the air a few times or on individual chalkboards, if they have them. When they begin printing *a* in their books, have them whisper the steps to themselves in their own words. Ask them to print three or four of their best *a*'s. As they work, move from student to student, checking pencil grip and the correct method of forming the letter. Make any corrections immediately.

This suggestion on how to teach printing is also an example of how to use VAKT — a multisensory approach using visual, auditory, and kinesthetic/tactile learning modalities.

Here are a few ways to help children remember how to print letters. For all students, tack an alphabet at the front of the room with arrows that show how the letters are formed. Some students also benefit from having a copy of the alphabet taped to their desks. Others need as much practice printing the letters as possible, which can be done through classroom written work and use of commercially available worksheets. Some children learn best by touching or manipulating things: teach printing to these children by having them trace letters that are cut out of sandpaper and glued onto cardboard cards. To improve the way a child holds a pencil, attach a rubber pencil grip to the pencil so that the student learns how to hold it properly.

Copying

If a student is slow copying notes from the board, there are three things you can do. You can reduce the amount of copying by providing a typed copy of the note in which key words are left blank. The child reads the note on the board or screen and fills in the blanks on his paper. Alternatively, ask the child to copy as much as possible from the board or screen, then provide a typed version of the note from which they may finish copying that evening. The third practice is to give extra time for copying. For example, if a note is assigned to be copied in the morning, let the child know that there will be time in the afternoon to finish the copying.

Each of these techniques serves to reduce the anxiety a student feels when he knows that they can't finish the copying within the usual time limit.

Written expression

Pre-writing activities can help all students with their written expression. For example, if you want the children to write a story on a favorite activity, then have a large-group discussion on people's experiences. Some children simply don't know what to write and discussing helps them to generate ideas. Write students' ideas and key words on the board, screen, or flipchart paper for reference. Before the children write their stories, direct them to develop an outline by completing a chart with the following headings: Introduction, Action, and Resolution (see page 95 for a sample; a reproducible version appears on page 96). They then write their points under each heading. As they write their stories, have them check off each section on their charts.

For editing, introduce the COPS method: **C**apitals, **O**verall appearance, **P**unctuation, and **S**pelling. You may use the form found on page 97 or write COPS on the board or on the inside cover of a child's notebook to serve as a reminder of what to look for when self-editing. Some students need to read their stories out loud to detect spelling errors and missing words or parts of sentences.

For peer editing, match the struggling student with someone who is patient and has a solid understanding of spelling and grammar rules.

As far as producing a good copy goes, if a student has trouble writing the story, you may have to scribe it. Alternatively, encourage older students to type their stories.

Written assignments

Before the students begin working on an assignment, such as researching a topic to answer questions, it's wise to do the following: (1) Read the instructions to the class and orally summarize them; and (2) discuss your expectations for answers, if necessary, demonstrating on the board how to format answers. These two techniques help the students know what is to be done and how to do it. They also help the entire class.

Individual students may need special attention. Go to their desks and ask them to repeat the instructions back to you. Discuss the answer to the first question and ask the student you are focusing on to write it down. Place a check mark beside the answer if it is correct. This technique provides instant feedback and motivates the child to keep working. Discuss the answer to the next question and leave the student to answer it, returning a few minutes later to check the answer. Then assign the next two or three questions and return to the student's desk within a specific time to monitor the work.

This technique, called "chunking," may also be applied to longer assignments. Basically, you divide the work into manageable chunks, check each section as it is completed, and provide immediate feedback. The technique effectively reduces the anxiety of doing a long assignment, and frequent checking provides opportunities for positive feedback, thus motivating the student.

Other techniques can help students complete written assignments, too: reduce the number of questions (but not the quality of answers), give more time to do the assignment, and insist on seeing rough copies of projects on which you can provide descriptive feedback. To make projects look neater, encourage students to type them or use an erasable pen. Alternatively, structure your lessons to give

Story Planner

Name: _Amanda (Gr. 5)_

Title: _The Soccer Tournament_

Introduction (Include where and when the story takes place, who the main characters are, and briefly what is happening):

— _house league soccer practice, late summer, final tournament is next weekend_

— _Aliyah, the goalkeeper, and Jen, a forward, talk about everybody working on passing and shooting at the park after school_

Action (Describe the problem or conflict and how the main character handled it):

— _Saturday Game 1 - played a game against really good players, never started passing - chasing the ball, lost 4:0_

— _Game 2 - won 3:2, passed in second half, Jen got two goals_

— _Game 3 - tired, played a weak team, Aliyah made some good saves, Jen got all three goals by passing the ball_

— _Sunday Semis - played same team as in Game 2, Aliyah made great saves, Jen helped on both goals, 2:1_

— _Finals - same team as in Game 1, Jen scored just before the end of the first half, was tripped, sprained ankle, can't play, talks to team during half time, score at 1:0 for them_

— _Last two minutes player on other team gets a breakaway_

Resolution (Tell how the problem or conflict was resolved):

— _Aliyah jumped and made the save — they won the tournament_

Story Planner

Name: _____

Title: _____

Introduction (Identify where and when the story takes place and who the main characters are; briefly outline what is happening):

_____
_____
_____
_____

Action (Describe the problem or conflict and how the main character(s) handled it):

_____
_____
_____
_____
_____
_____
_____
_____
_____
_____

Resolution (Tell how the problem or conflict was resolved):

_____
_____
_____
_____
_____
_____
_____
_____
_____
_____
_____
_____

Pembroke Publishers © 2022 *Finding a Place for Every Student* by Cheryll Duquette ISBN 978-1-55138-360-6

COPS Strategy

Name: _____

Title of Work: _____

The COPS strategy provides a way for the reader to look at a person's written work and check that the writer has observed key rules and conventions that apply to writing. Review the work with each criterion in mind, and then make check marks on the editorial summary chart below, where appropriate.

C — *Capitalization:* Does a capital letter appear at the beginning of each sentence and as the first letter of every proper noun?

O — *Overall Appearance:* Is the work neat and formatted attractively?

P — *Punctuation:* Have all the rules for punctuation been followed?

S — *Spelling:* Are all the words spelled correctly?

Editor	C	O	P	S
Self				
Peer				
Adult				

Pembroke Publishers © 2022 *Finding a Place for Every Student* by Cheryll Duquette ISBN 978-1-55138-360-6

students the choice of demonstrating their learning in ways other than writing, for example, through an oral presentation, dramatization, a drawing, or a model.

Mathematics

This section outlines techniques to help your students learn basic mathematical concepts, counting, arithmetic facts, operations, and problem solving. I have found that students with LDs learn mathematics better with teacher-directed lessons rather than with exploratory activities done in groups. The suggestions in this section are based on this observation. Before moving to those specific areas, though, here is a summary of fundamental techniques for teaching students who are experiencing general difficulties in math.

- Let the children use manipulatives, for example, counters or an abacus for counting, or measuring tapes and containers to teach measurement.
- For slower working children with difficulties in math, assign fewer questions if the concept is understood.
- Review concepts, procedures, and facts frequently. Repetition is important to building long-term memory.
- Tape a number line to an individual student's desk and have them use it by touching the numbers as they count.
- Teach the procedures for adding, subtracting, multiplying, and dividing by demonstrating each step. Write the procedures on flipchart paper posted in the classroom to remind students of the steps (also known as an "anchor chart").
- Help students, especially older ones who may never know the arithmetic facts, by providing fact tables and permitting the use of calculators.
- Distribute graph paper or notebooks formatted in graph paper to help those students who have difficulty aligning columns of numbers.
- If a student has difficulty with copying (e.g., reversing numbers), give them a photocopy of the assignment to eliminate problems in copying the questions.
- Pair a child with a partner who can read directions and answer quick questions about the work.
- Have students work in small groups to solve problems. Encourage them to explore different ways of solving problems and to discuss with each other how they came up with the solutions. However, monitor the group to ensure that the student with LDs is participating and has not allowed the stronger students to monopolize the activities and discussion. When a student disengages from the activity and is not directly involved, they are not likely learning much.
- Teach estimation so that the student may assess whether their final answer is remotely correct.

Counting: Use a *multisensory* method (VAKT) to teach students how to count. Post a number line (a visual approach to counting) at the front of the classroom and on the student's desk so that they may see the numbers (visual). Orally count with the child so that they hear the numbers (auditory). Have the child point to the numbers as they are being said to establish a relationship between what is said and what is seen (kinesthetic). Use manipulatives to teach counting so that the student may touch the objects when counting and put them into groups, such as five of something (tactile).

Repetition is important when working with children who experience difficulty in counting. Therefore, provide as many opportunities to count in the classroom

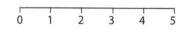

A number line: a visual approach to counting

as possible. Finally, encourage students to play board games that involve counting, such as Snakes and Ladders, and software that reinforces counting.

Mathematical Facts: Many children who have difficulty remembering their facts benefit from a multisensory approach and much repetition. To teach facts effectively, have the children touch manipulatives so that they can understand that $3 - 2 = 1$, for example. Have them say the math fact so that they hear it and write it so that they see it. Older students may want to use a number line which they touch with their index finger when answering questions involving addition and subtraction facts.

Use the principle of going from the known to the unknown when teaching multiplication and division facts. Teach multiplication as addition, for example,

$$3 + 3 + 3 + 3 = 12, \text{ or } 3 \times 4 = 12$$

Teach division as subtraction, for example, 8 take away 2 four times gives us four groups of two, or $8 \div 2 = 4$. Let the children work with counters to reinforce the concepts.

For students who have difficulty remembering the facts, provide opportunities for review. Using the peer-tutoring approach, students could work with partners using flash cards. They receive one-to-one attention and receive immediate feedback. Setting aside the first five minutes of each math period for review is another option. After you write 5 to 10 fact questions on the board, direct the students to copy them into their notebooks and answer them. Then take up the answers by writing the correct numbers on the board and asking children to check their own work. You could also distribute a sheet of various math facts and see how many questions students can answer in one minute. Once the sheets are corrected, let students graph their own progress using the inside back cover of their notebooks. A good idea is to have students make special folders in which to place the sheets they accumulate.

Operations (adding, subtracting, multiplying, and dividing): Teach each procedure in a step-by-step manner. Use flipchart paper to show an example and number each step beside the spot in the calculation where it is shown. Use a different-colored marker for labeling steps. Direct the children to copy the example into their notes with the steps labeled; it will later serve as a guide when they're working independently. Next, write three practice questions on the board and ask the students to do them at their desks. Then correct the work together by having students explain how they arrived at their answers and review the procedures. The final step is independent practice whereby the students answer questions on their own. At the end of the lesson, post the flipchart paper in the classroom as a reference for students.

Encourage any students who have difficulty remembering the steps to the operation to whisper the steps to themselves and to use counters for some of the adding or subtracting. The multisensory approach helps a student receive the message from a variety of learning channels (auditory, visual, and tactile). Furthermore, during the seatwork period, check the work of any student who frequently finds it hard to remember to ensure that the student understands the procedures and can do the work correctly. Place check marks beside correct answers to give instant positive feedback.

Problem Solving: When instructing students on problem solving, teach the words and phrases that alert them to specific operations and post them in the classroom.

- *how many, total amount* (adding or multiplying)
  Examples: How many points do the boys have? What is the total amount of the bill?
- *how many more, how many fewer, how many are left* (subtracting)
  Examples: How many more slices of pizza are in the large size than the small size? How many fewer toy cars does Rashid have than Amanda? When Dylan takes away his cards, how many are left?
- *how many does each have* (dividing)
  Example: If the pencil crayons are divided equally among the students, how many does each have?

Some ways to help students who are struggling with problem solving include underlining key words, having someone read the problem aloud, and making up problems that have some relevance to students' lives. In the latter case, you might develop math problems related to buying pet food or taking a dog for walks. Teach a viable method for solving problems, such as *read, think, draw, solve,* and *write*. (Page 107 outlines a variation.) This method serves as a good way of demonstrating problem solving to individuals or the entire class.

Listening and following directions

Before you begin teaching, ensure that you have the students' attention and that they are listening to you.

- Tell all the children to put away their materials and listen. You might reinforce this by having a traffic light made of construction paper posted on the board. A magnetic arrow pointed to the red circle will reinforce no talking.
- For the student who is finding it hard to listen, make eye contact, seat them close to you, use a special cue, or say their name quietly. Ensure that all distracting material is off the desk.

During the lesson, involve the struggling listener as much as possible through question and answer or by helping you demonstrate something. Shorten the length of your presentations to prevent loss of focus by distractible students, and vary the activities in your lessons (e.g., teacher-centred, small-group, and large-group activities).

When giving instructions for an assignment, use plenty of visual support: hold up the textbook at the correct page or hold up the worksheet, write the page number on the board, write the instructions on paper, the screen, or the board, and demonstrate what you want done. Paraphrase the instructions printed in the book or on the sheet in simple language. You might have a student repeat the instructions back to you. Some students also benefit by having a written copy of the numbered instructions, which can be checked off as they are met.

Remembering

There are four ways you can help students remember what they have been taught: by motivating them, taking a multisensory approach, using mnemonic devices, and providing *lots* of repetition.

Drawing diagrams for problems involving perimeter and area works well.

If big numbers confuse a student, suggest that they substitute smaller numbers (e.g., from 1 to 10) to figure out which operation to use, then solve the problem using the correct numbers.

For younger students, limit the time you spend presenting material to less than 10 minutes. Changing activities every 10 minutes is another viable option.

To motivate students, let them know what will be studied and why, and show them how this new information relates to their own lives. Write the name of the topic on the board. Teach from the known to the unknown and begin the lesson by asking the students questions based on previous work (known). The question-and-answer technique involves them immediately in the lesson and helps them remember information that will be helpful in learning the new concept.

When teaching the new concept (unknown), use as much visual and tactile support for your words as possible. Taking a multisensory approach helps all students receive the message through three different channels, one of which should prove to be a strength. Involve a student as much as possible in the presentation of the concept through questions or demonstration of points.

While teaching, present ways for students to remember the points through mnemonic devices, for example, the acronym HOMES for the great lakes (**H**uron, **O**ntario, **M**ichigan, **E**rie, and **S**uperior). Encourage the students to think of their own ways of remembering facts. Some children like to make up songs to help them remember lists.

After teaching the lesson, provide opportunities for review through repetition. For example, in the Think-Pair-Share technique (also known as "Turn and Talk"), pairs of students take two to three minutes to think about what they have learned and then share it with their partner. You might provide students with books taken out from the school library on the topic and have software or links to websites available for review of material. You could begin future lessons by reviewing previously learned concepts on a topic.

Organization

The most important thing you can do to help a student who is disorganized is to provide a very organized environment. Here are some ideas you can implement to help a student organize notes.

- ☐ Punch all handouts and give class time (30 to 60 seconds) to permit students to insert them into their binders. Provide five minutes for any handouts you want glued. If you *don't* give class time, then the papers will not be in the notebooks.
- ☐ Check the student's notebook often to ensure that it is complete. If not, photocopy notes from other students and have them copy or insert them.
- ☐ Pair each student with a "study buddy" who may be telephoned during an absence to get the homework.
- ☐ Put class notes, assignments, test dates, and other important information on the class website.
- ☐ Have a model notebook available so that students can organize their notes following the pattern and photocopy any notes they are missing.
- ☐ When a class assignment has been given, go to the student's desk. Discuss the first question and either watch them write the answer or return to check it. Provide positive reinforcement after you check the answer.
- ☐ For longer or out-of-class assignments, type all instructions and assessment criteria, distribute them to students, and (up to senior elementary) have parents sign the page. Give marks for each segment of the project, including the outline, the rough draft, and the final draft. This technique helps you to monitor student progress and give feedback.

Andrew's English teacher used the collateral approach with her class.

Using written agendas with *all* students who can read is a good idea. The agenda also helps keep *you* on track! As for non-readers, simply tell them what you will be doing.

Older students still enjoy being read to, and benefit from the practice. Sometimes, recordings of the story are available; however, you usually have to make them yourself. Reading individually with a recording speeds up the reading process, improves comprehension, and increases attention span.

Encourage the student with poor organizational skills to have one set of textbooks and a pencil case for school and another for home. Adopting this practice overcomes the problem of forgetting things. For older students, the collateral approach works well. As mentioned earlier, if a student forgets a pen, lend them one with collateral, such as a shoe. At the end of the class, exchange items.

Having a designated place for classroom materials promotes better organization. Younger students can place all their materials in a large plastic tub stored under their desks. This practice helps keep a child's things confined to one area. Older students can color-code their textbooks and binders to help them bring the correct ones to class. Sometimes, students find it easier to carry one binder for the morning subjects and another one for afternoon classes.

It can be helpful for older students to organize their three-hole notebooks with a table of contents and page numbers. When they do so, you can see what notes are missing just by looking at the contents. You can aid organization further by photocopying review sheets on colored paper and tests on buff, which helps to identify the beginning and ending of units in the notebook. Prompt the students to study for unit tests from the colored sheets at the end of each unit.

Help students know the class schedule, too. For non-rotary classes, post the weekly schedule so that the children can see it. Older students should have copies of personal timetables in their lockers, on their telephone, in pencil cases, in binders, and at home. Having quick access to the schedule helps students know where to be when.

At the beginning of each lesson, write an agenda on the board and review it. The agenda reduces anxiety and worry about what activities will be done in a period and helps students mentally prepare for the work. It also helps you stay on track and supports the development of a task-oriented atmosphere in the classroom.

You can take concrete measures to help students overcome difficulties in organizing their homework. At the end of the day or class period, take five minutes to list the homework and information on projects and tests on the Homework section of the board. Direct the students to copy the information into their planners or agendas or type it into any telephone, computer, or tablet they may have. You may have to sign some agendas in order to indicate to parents that all the homework is recorded. Putting the homework on the class website, along with all notes made during class, is also helpful for parents and for students who may have been absent. Give younger students a minute or two before the final bell to place homework in their backpacks. Some students may need a partner to check off the homework as it is placed in the backpack. Providing class time for students to organize their homework helps them to get it home and sends a message that you are serious about it.

Ways to Help Intermediate Students with LDs Learn

Reading skills

Novels, Plays, and Short Stories: In English class, effective pre-reading activities include discussing new vocabulary words and personal experiences that relate to the plot, and viewing a video version to gain a general understanding of the plot. Read the novel, play, or short story to the students during class time or provide an audiobook to take home. Encourage the students to visualize the action and characters and discuss the elements of the story with the class. To further enhance comprehension, arrange for students to work in small groups to dramatize scenes from the story.

Text in Content Areas: To improve comprehension of printed text, provide the students with a copy of new vocabulary with definitions. Discuss the terms with the class. When choosing a textbook, try to select one that is digitized so that the content is audible. Also consider the value of subheadings and margin notes that help summarize information.

Two strategies, RAP paraphrasing and SQR3, will help students improve their comprehension of text.

RAP Paraphrasing
Read one or two paragraphs.
Ask yourself what you just read.
Put it into your own words. (Write point-form notes, if necessary.)

SQR3
Survey — Skim material to get an idea of the topic. Look for headings, subheadings, and words in boldface.
Question — Ask yourself questions about the material you will read.
Read — Answer the questions you just asked.
Recite — Cover the book and ask yourself questions about the section you just read. Some people find it helpful to write point-form notes.
Review — When you have finished reading the material and making notes, review the passage and notes.

Both methods actively engage readers in the process of making sense of words by having them question what was just read and make notes about the key ideas.

Spelling, grammar, and handwriting skills

Some accommodations that help younger students also help intermediate students. To help a student deal with everyday spelling, permit use of their telephone to check the correct spelling of a word. For out-of-class assignments, encourage the student to type them, using the spell-check and grammar-check functions. If a student's handwriting is poor, encourage them to write on every second line and to space out the letters so that you can read their writing. You might also permit some students to use a computer in the classroom, which will improve the quality of in-class assignments. For students with very poor spelling skills, consider limiting the number of marks deducted for spelling and grammar errors.

Written assignments

As you plan the assignment for the students, consider dividing it into stages of work, such as planning, draft, and final copy. In other words, "chunk" it. Give marks for each stage. Doing this enables you to keep track of each student's progress and motivate students through the feedback you give them. When you introduce a big assignment to your students, it's best to distribute a typed sheet with instructions that specify exactly what is to be done when, the rubric or assessment criteria, and mark weightings. Read the instructions to them. Having

With older students, the focus is less on remediation and more on teaching coping skills. It is believed that once a student is beyond Grade 6, more of the same kinds of remediation activities will not make much of a difference in performance. Therefore, the student is taught how to work around specific weaknesses.

Andrew's English teacher used many of these ideas with him.

A resource such as *Information Transformation* by Tricia Armstrong, published by Pembroke, may help you.

What to Look For in Students Suspected of Having a Learning Disability

Intermediate Students

Basic Reading Skills and Reading Comprehension

☐ lacks fluency, accuracy, speed
☐ loses place, skips words or lines
☐ repeats words
☐ shows discrepancy between oral and silent reading
☐ confuses similar letters, words, sounds
☐ follows with a finger, ruler, or pencil
☐ is unwilling to read aloud
☐ has difficulty finding main idea and making inferences

Spelling

☐ spells the same words in the same passage in different ways
☐ reverses letters
☐ faces difficulty in associating sounds with letters
☐ puts letters in words in incorrect order
☐ omits last letters, capitals

Writing Skills and Written Expression

☐ handwrites illegibly
☐ shows inability to stay on the line
☐ handwrites slowly
☐ writes and prints in the same assignment
☐ omits dates and underlining
☐ has poor sentence structure and general expression of thoughts as compared to peers
☐ does not seem to show on the page what is in the mind
☐ doesn't complete or submit written assignments

Oral Skills

☐ speaks hesitantly
☐ forgets common words
☐ has poor grammar compared to peers
☐ has generally poor verbal expression as compared to peers
☐ avoids oral participation and discussions

Listening

☐ misunderstands ideas and directions presented orally
☐ remembers information poorly
☐ has difficulty sequencing instructions
☐ confuses similar sounds
☐ takes no notes or poor notes from oral presentations

Pembroke Publishers © 2022 *Finding a Place for Every Student* by Cheryll Duquette ISBN 978-1-55138-360-6

Mathematics
- ☐ reverses numbers
- ☐ experiences difficulty in aligning numbers in columns
- ☐ has not mastered basic facts or operations
- ☐ makes careless errors
- ☐ has difficulty with mental calculations
- ☐ struggles with reasoning and math concepts
- ☐ finds problem solving difficult

Behavior
- ☐ short attention span, easily distracted
- ☐ impulsive
- ☐ frequently late for class
- ☐ "class clown"
- ☐ quiet or withdrawn
- ☐ sullen or angry
- ☐ disorganized or forgetful
- ☐ inconsistent in performance
- ☐ immature
- ☐ easily frustrated, notably by time pressure
- ☐ difficulty accepting change
- ☐ very literal, may not understand jokes
- ☐ difficulty generalizing (e.g., instructions must be repeated for similar tasks)

Social Relations
- ☐ has younger friends
- ☐ has false friends
- ☐ is ridiculed, teased, or avoided by peers
- ☐ says the wrong thing at the wrong time
- ☐ wants instant gratification
- ☐ is unable to interpret nonverbal behaviors
- ☐ is socially naive; unable to distinguish between sincere and sarcastic or deceptive remarks
- ☐ cannot predict the consequences of behavior
- ☐ makes poor social decisions
- ☐ finds it hard to solve social problems

Motor Skills
- ☐ poor handwriting and drawing
- ☐ clumsy
- ☐ accident prone
- ☐ poor eye-hand coordination

No student will exhibit all of the above characteristics; however, clusters of behaviors that are displayed *frequently* and *over time* may indicate that a student has a learning disability.

Pembroke Publishers © 2022 *Finding a Place for Every Student* by Cheryll Duquette ISBN 978-1-55138-360-6

the parents of intermediate students sign the sheet ensures that they are aware of the assignment.

Before the students begin work, discuss ideas for the assignment with the entire class or with particular students. Demonstrate exactly what you want done and provide an example of a completed assignment, if possible. If your students need to know, teach them how to research a topic using the library and the internet. As well, develop a form that will help students organize their information on a topic into headings which will later become sections in a report. Teaching students how to write a five-paragraph essay expressing a point of view may also help them. (Andrew's teacher did this; see page 60.) Learning to write a five-paragraph essay may seem a rather narrow goal, but at the Grade 10 level in Ontario, for example, students are required to compose an essay of at least three paragraphs when taking the mandatory literacy test.

Andrew's English teacher used the procedure for extensions and gave him some opportunities to present orally with positive results.

Some students may require extra time to complete the assignment. As one student with a learning disability told me, an extra day can make a big difference in the quality of the work. When it comes to negotiating an extension, be clear that the student must approach you *before* the due date and that the two of you will decide on a new date. Announce your policy to the class before the assignments are under way. Some students benefit from using speech-to-text software to get their ideas on paper. You can make this option available to all the students so that the student with LDs will not feel singled out. When the students are at the editing stage, provide consultation with specific feedback to improve content, expression, and mechanics. Finally, consider giving a student who has great difficulty completing written work the choice to do part of the assignment in oral form. Some people can express what they know much better orally than on paper.

Mathematics

As mentioned previously, a student with LDs in the area of mathematics may not demonstrate much engagement in group activities, and without engagement, there will be little learning. I have found that using explicit instruction is a better approach for students with LDs, and it is explained here. Be sure to introduce a new concept or procedure systematically. First, write the title on the board or screen. Review what has already been learned to help the students feel confident about beginning something new and to contextualize the new material. Work through an example on the board, showing *all* the steps and numbering them, preferably in colored chalk or marker After completing your example, verbally summarize the procedure while pointing to the steps. Direct students to do two or three examples in their notebooks. Take up the answers on the board and repeat the procedures, while students make any necessary corrections. Then, assign them the work, stating the page number and writing it on the board, as well as all the questions to be answered. Be sure to discuss how to solve the more difficult questions. While the students are working, move from desk to desk, monitoring and providing one-to-one assistance.

Some students will require accommodations in math. A number of them will not know their facts (and may *never* know them all) so permit them to use a calculator. When teaching integers, encourage students to refer to a number line and to use an index finger to count the numbers. Recommend to students who have difficulty aligning numbers in columns to bring a notebook entirely of graph paper. Consider having students work in pairs or in mixed-ability groups of three or four so that math concepts and solutions may be discussed. Stronger students will also demonstrate to others in their group how they solved the problem and weaker students will be able to follow along. However, you will need to monitor the groups to ensure that the struggling students are actually following the lead of the stronger students. You should also provide as much one-to-one assistance as possible and have regularly scheduled extra help sessions for all students.

> ### Mathematical Problem Solving
>
> Here is a logical, five-step approach you can introduce to students who experience difficulty with problem solving.
>
> 1. Read the problem and underline key words.
> 2. Think about what information you know and what you have to find out.
> 3. Draw a sketch to show the information. If you find big numbers difficult to understand, mentally replace the big ones with small numbers to help you decide what operations are necessary.
> 4. Estimate what the answer should be.
> 5. Solve the problem and compare it to your estimation.

When correcting daily work, ensure that the answers are said aloud and written on the board. Doing this accommodates the needs of both auditory and visual learners. For longer solutions or problem solving, have the students write them on the board or on flipchart paper. As you correct them, review the steps that were followed. Insist that *all* mistakes be corrected to ensure that the notebook is a record of accurate answers. If group solutions are posted on the wall, have the groups discuss their solutions in turn, and ensure that you conclude the students' presentations by summarizing the key concepts. These summaries of three or four key points are important for consolidating their learning.

When scheduling a test, provide as much notice as possible so that students may study. Teach the students how to study for math: to do sample questions and check them against the answers in their notebooks. You may want to permit students to bring a "cheat sheet" to a test. In this case, specify the desired size of paper and which algorithms and formulas should be on it. The day before the test, prompt the students to bring their sheets to class for you to initial.

The period before the test, you could give the students a review sheet formatted similarly to the test. Doing the review sheet helps some students with difficulties in math to feel confident about the test. It may also be the only studying a student does. Correct the review sheet and repeat the steps in the procedures for solving questions.

Once students write the test, return it as promptly as possible to provide feedback. Correct the answers to the test together on the board and ensure that students make necessary corrections. Recommended practice is to have students in the intermediate grades get all tests signed by a parent.

The same basic ideas on listening and following directions, remembering, and organization apply to both lower-elementary and intermediate-level students.

Copying and note-taking

Give students who are slow in copying notes from the board or screen a copy of your notes so that they don't have to look up from their work, find the correct spot, and look down again. You may also consider providing students with a fill-in-the-blank version of the notes. They would then have to copy only key words from the board onto their sheets.

When you plan to show a video, take advantage of the start/stop features of the technology. Distribute a viewing guide form with questions and spaces for the students to write their answers. You might pause the video as each question is answered, discuss the answer with the class, and give students a few minutes to write or type the answer on their form. If you don't want to pause the video, take up the answers at the end of the video and insist that students correct their work and include all information.

If you want students to take notes while watching a video or performing an experiment, plan to provide visual support for students whose learning strength is through the visual channel. For these students, write key ideas on the screen or board; distribute an organizer with headings, subheadings, and spaces to write point-form notes; teach the students how to make notes; and encourage them to develop their own abbreviations for words. Cue students about key points by saying, "This point is important." Write such points on the board and repeat them. For students who are unable to listen and copy at the same time, provide a photocopy of your lecture notes, permit them to bring a digital recorder to class, or put your notes on the class website. Students who have poor handwriting or a poor memory should be encouraged to type their notes that evening. Adopting this practice ensures that the notes are readable and provides an opportunity for the students to review their notes.

Create an Enabling Environment

By now, you should better understand LDs, their characteristics, and ideas for accommodation. These classroom suggestions may be used with students who have been identified as having a learning disability *and* with all students.

When planning lessons, remember the four teaching methods described in this chapter: multisensory (VAKT), moving from the known to the unknown, whole-part-whole, and chunking. They will assist *all* students to better understand the concepts you are teaching. Remember, too, to demonstrate what you want done in an assignment, provide a rubric, and review procedures, concepts, and facts often. Repetition is important.

Your goal is to create an environment in which students, including any with LDs, can enjoy success and feel they belong academically in the class. To do this, you have to know the students' strengths and weaknesses. You also have to be organized and patient.

Following the suggestions provided in this chapter will go a long way to helping students with LDs develop a connection with you and trust that you will provide the academic support they require and in a way that does not make them feel different or deficient. Your relationship with the student and the ones you help them develop with classmates will also make them feel that they belong socially and that your classroom is a psychologically safe place to be. Upon feeling comfortable and accepted, they can turn their attention and energy to learning.

CHAPTER 7

Behavioral Disorders

In this chapter you will learn how to work effectively with students who act out, who have been diagnosed as having attention deficit hyperactivity disorder (ADHD), or who have experiencing trauma.

Acting-out Behaviors

Calmness is strength. Remember not to show annoyance and to remain firm, but fair.

We all know the frustration of working with students who exhibit acting-out behaviors. They not only challenge our authority and disrupt the classroom, but they also take valuable learning time away from the well-behaved students. Although most people want to be liked and accepted by others, some choose inappropriate ways to try to achieve this goal. Dreikurs and Cassel (1992) suggest that children misbehave for the following reasons:

- to gain attention
- to seek power
- to exact retribution or revenge for real or perceived injustices
- to conceal a feeling of inadequacy

Attention Seeking: If you suspect that a student is misbehaving to seek attention, try not to give attention if it's a minor inappropriate behavior, such as excessive pencil sharpening, finger tapping, or playing with a toy. Instead, use *proximity control* and move towards the child. Standing close to the student usually causes the inappropriate behavior to stop. You may also have to say the student's name in a quiet voice. Your behaviors send a message to the student to stop the inappropriate behavior without giving them attention for misbehaving. On the other hand, give attention to the student for positive behaviors, such as bringing learning materials to class, sitting properly, and not pushing in line. Doing so reinforces the desired behaviors. With older students, state praise in a quiet voice to avoid embarrassment.

Power Seeking: Sometimes, the student misbehaves as a way of seeking power. Knowing this, try not to argue with the student — this is what they want. Rather, use the *broken-record* technique. In a calm, firm voice, positively state the expected behavior, perhaps "In our class, we clean up our messes." Move close to the student and be sure to look them in the eye as you repeat the statement of expected behavior. Remember that you don't have to have the last word in a discussion.

One way to deal with the power issue is to share power. In a non-threatening voice, offer *choices* to the student, for example, "You may do this assignment individually or with a partner" or "Please take out your notebooks. This is the work that has to be done, and you may do it in any order."

You can also present *logical consequences* for behaving a certain way. Have a few clearly defined rules that you enforce at all times: one might be no talking during a test. If a student breaks one of the rules, state the rule and the consequences, then offer a choice of action. For example, if you notice that two students are whispering to one another during a test, walk over to their desks and quietly remind them of the rule and the consequences if it's broken. You might say something like this: "During the test there is no talking. If you choose to talk anymore during this test, then you will each receive a zero. The choice is yours." If they force you to invoke the consequences, their quarrel is with the rules, not you.

If you state the rules, describe the consequences, and give choices, you are unlikely to feel guilty about administering consequences. You'll be able to administer them in a calm way because it is clear to others in the classroom that a student has chosen to break a known rule. The subjective element is gone.

Below are some typical classroom misbehaviors that violate rules, along with their consequences. They would be administered after re-stating the rule at least once as a reminder.

Elementary Level
- Excessive talking that is unrelated to the work: Work alone at another desk or seat.
- Touching others during circle time: Move away from others.
- Pushing in line: Move to the back of the line.
- Not completing work: Take it home for homework with a note written in the agenda or planner.
- Playing with a toy (not a fidget) during instruction: Place toy inside the desk, or place toy on the teacher's desk to be returned at recess.
- Deliberately knocking over furniture or throwing things in the classroom: Clean up the room.

Intermediate Level
- Late or lack of submission of assignments: Marks will be lost.
- Late to class: Have a detention at the office (as a school rule) or make up the missed time after class.
- Excessive talking: Move to another seat or work alone.
- Fighting or swearing: Go to the office (a school rule).

Revenge Seeking: Yes, you may encounter a student who seeks revenge on you for whatever reason. I had a student who exacted revenge on a teacher because a request did not include "Please." Although you may feel hurt by the student's meanness, try not to reveal your vulnerability. As hard at it may be, find something positive about the student and use it constructively in class; for example, an interest in science may be applied to a variety of subject areas. Try to develop a positive relationship with the student by talking with them about personal interests, too.

Do your best to show that you like the student, but not the disturbing behavior. You might say: "Olivia, I like you, but when you talk while I'm giving instructions, it makes it difficult for the others to hear. And they may not know what to do. It's not fair to them. Please listen when instructions are given." When Olivia is silent or behaves appropriately, offer praise. You could quietly make a comment or write something positive in the margin of an assignment.

Don't give students any openings to think about revenge. Being polite to all students and never centering anyone out blunts any student's inclination to seek revenge. It's especially effective to treat older students in this way. However, once a teacher has yelled at a student in class, the student may decide they have the perfect reason to "get back" at the teacher. Reminding students of the rules, stating consequences, offering choices, and showing respect for your students will eliminate rationalizations for revenge.

Feelings of Inadequacy: A student prone to such feelings may misbehave in order to get out of doing work or to delay starting work that they doubt they can complete successfully.

What is needed here is much encouragement and praise. Observe the student so that you know their strengths and plan activities in which you know they can be successful. For example, let the child help you when you are teaching or demonstrating a skill, perhaps in the arts or physical education.

Another useful technique is chunking. Break the work into smaller components, give a short time limit to complete each segment, help the child get started, leave, return after the allotted time, correct the work that is done, and offer praise. Assign another section of work, leave, and return. Repeat this process and gradually increase the length of time between visits. You can also cover some of the work and reveal it gradually. Chunking may also be used with students who have learned helplessness and want you to do the work for them.

Provide encouragement for the student as they start the work. Say, "You can do this." Give praise or acknowledgment for completed work. You can also promote the use of positive self-talk. For example, have the student repeat in their head, "I can do this. There may be some problems, but I can get it done." It is important that the student knows that you have faith that they can do the work, which may support feelings of academic belonging.

Twenty-Five Ways to Minimize Behavior Problems in Your Classroom

Establishing a positive relationship with your students is likely the most effective strategy you can use to promote desirable behavior in your classroom. All students want to feel that they are liked by the teacher and that this adult can be trusted not to make them look bad in front of others. A positive and trusting relationship is the basis for the work of the classroom: teaching and learning.

The second-best way to foster good behavior is through lesson planning and preparation. Develop lessons that follow the curriculum, incorporating the students' interests and including activities in which they will be successful. Ensure that you have all your materials ready for use so that there are no "dead" spots in the delivery. As well, offer students choices about how to demonstrate their learning (e.g., written assignment, oral report, or dramatization) or how they may do their work (individually, groups, sitting, or standing). Below are more ideas to help reduce behavior problems in the classroom.

1. Model respectful behavior. When asking a student to do something, use the words "please" and "thank you." Always speak positively of others and treat others the way you want to be treated. Avoid raising your voice for

long periods of time or yelling. Some students find the volume unsettling and others will laugh at you because you've lost control of your emotions. Remember that you need to model appropriate behavior and once you have established a tone of respect, the students will follow your lead.

2. Know the students' strengths, weaknesses, and situations that trigger an outburst. Avoid these situations as best as possible.

3. Help the students feel good about themselves. Convey the idea that you like them, but not the problem behavior.

4. Find areas of strength in each student and provide opportunities for them to demonstrate their strengths so that peers see them too.

5. Provide students with opportunities to make choices. For example, say: "If you speak politely and respectfully, you may work with this group, or you may complete the assignment alone at your own desk."

6. Develop a few classroom rules, for example, respect yourself and your property, and respect other people and their property. Establish logical consequences for misbehavior and enforce them *consistently*.

7. Pinpoint and analyze a student's misbehavior (e.g., hitting others, wandering in the classroom). Make observations of the student through tally counts to determine frequency and duration. Use these data to hypothesize reasons for inappropriate behavior and to make a plan to change the behavior. For example, perhaps you notice that a student talks to others and wanders around the classroom to avoid tasks they do not enjoy. You may decide to provide some one-to-one attention to that child when doing those tasks: reviewing requirements, helping them get started on the work, checking questions frequently, and providing feedback.

8. Involve students in monitoring their own behavior (*self-monitoring*). Pinpoint a specific behavior, for example, calling out answers. On a sheet of paper, have the student do a tally count each time they engage in that behavior. You should also try to keep track of the behavior using the same system. At the end of class or an agreed-upon time frame, discuss your observations with the student. This method helps to make the student aware of the frequency of the behavior, which may lead to a decrease in it. You may also want to reward the student for having correctly counted the number of infractions, that is to say, your totals match. Self-monitoring might also be used as part of a reward program for the student.

9. Closely supervise the students to ensure that misbehavior does not occur. Consider being in your classroom at all times to ensure that incidents, such as fights or bullying, do not happen there. Also monitor hallways, locker bays, the lunchroom, the playground, or anywhere students may engage in teasing or bullying.

10. Observe the student who is having a tantrum or outburst to determine the triggers that may have caused it, the actual behavior, and the aftermath. As mentioned previously, follow the A B C method (A = antecedents; B = behavior — description of the behavior, duration, intensity, and frequency; and C = consequences). For example, a student may feel overwhelmed by two boards of writing to be copied, show signs of frustration, overturn their desk, and storm out of the classroom. Once you know that copying is difficult for the child, you may either give the student a sheet on which the notes are typed but the student has to insert key words in blanks, or ask the student to copy as much as possible and later provide a photocopy of the full note.

Alex's teacher (see Chapter 3) recognized Alex's skill in swimming and posted a newspaper article about it on the bulletin board.

Andrew, who was asked to tally how many times he missed or came late to class, was amazed to discover how often he thought of skipping (see Chapter 3).

Using I-messages helped Alex's teacher remain calm, and nonverbal cuing helped Alex stay on task (see Chapter 3).

11. Adhere closely to routines and the class schedule. They provide security and a predictable environment for the students. Write the agenda and the homework on the board in the same spot each day. If variations to the schedule emerge, explain them to the students ahead of time.

12. If you find yourself in an argument with a student, move to a location where you can speak to that student alone. A hallway may suffice. Remain calm and lower your voice. Try to de-escalate the conflict. Whenever possible, allow the student to "save face."

13. Some students may require opportunities for physical movement within an activity. For some students, getting out of their seats and placing completed work in the inbox is all that is required. Others need to manipulate objects in math and science. Another possibility is to organize your lesson so that the students meet in small groups, which involves getting up from their desk, or in centres to which the students rotate every 10 to 15 minutes.

14. Use I-messages to express concern about a student's behavior. You might say: "I am concerned when you throw your pencil in the class because it may injure other students. I want you to keep your pencil in your hand or in your pencil case." Avoid "you" messages, such as, "You are always disturbing the class." Be sure to speak calmly and firmly.

15. Use nonverbal cuing and proximity to correct minor misbehavior. For example, to remind a student to be quiet, place your index finger at right angles to your lips. Most students will respond and engage in appropriate behavior. I have always found that moving close to a student who is misbehaving will send a message to stop. You can also move a student close to you to monitor and manage behavior (e.g., during circle time, move the student next to you).

16. Provide as much genuine and specific feedback as possible. Try to use words that praise the student's work, such as "I like the way you have shown all your work when answering this math question." Positive feedback helps to shape appropriate behaviors because students know what you want. Negative feedback only tells them what you don't want, and they have to guess at what you want. It's simple: tell them what behavior you expect *before* the event happens or the work is assigned (e.g., during this assignment you may work in groups and talk quietly). Acknowledge appropriate behavior.

17. Make students accountable for their actions. Beyond using proximity control (moving near the student whose behavior is disruptive to the functioning of the class) and nonverbal cuing, adopt the practices outlined below.

How to Make Students Accountable for Their Actions

Behavior in Focus: Talking while you are instructing the class

1. State the student's name and the behavior expected. For example: "Nicole, I would like you to stop talking so that the others have an opportunity to learn." Say this in a firm, but non-threatening tone of voice. Usually, the student will stop talking.

2. If the student continues to talk, offer her a choice: "Nicole, you may sit where you are and not talk, or take a seat at the back of the classroom away from the others." The student will likely stop talking, or she may take a seat at the back with some bravado.

3. If the student continues to talk in either location, state firmly: "You have chosen to continue to talk. You will have to leave the room and

> go to the office." The student will likely leave in a huff. Contact the office and tell the staff that the student should be expected. Resume teaching.
> 4. After class, find out what happened at the office. During or immediately after the next class, talk to the student privately. Ask her why she misbehaved and how she will change her behavior.
>
> Note that, in this case, Nicole is aware of the expected behavior and is making choices as to how she is going to behave. At all times, remain firm but non-threatening and calm. You are just enforcing rules and consequences. You are not punishing the student, but rather she is choosing to disrupt the class, and known consequences apply. If she decides to comply at any point, privately acknowledge her behavior.

18. Watch for signs of frustration in students. By intervening when you observe that a student is becoming frustrated, you may be able to defuse a potentially explosive situation. Johns and Carr (1995) describe four stages of frustration; appropriate responses are also outlined.

    1) *Anxiety stage:* The student shows nonverbal signs, such as sighs and putting their head down. Respond by listening actively and talking in a nonjudgmental fashion.
    2) *Stress stage:* The student often shows frustration through minor behavior problems, such as tearing paper or tapping a pencil. Use proximity control to redirect behavior or boost the child's interest and motivation by providing assistance with the assignment.
    3) *Physical stage:* The student has lost control and begins to threaten others, throw objects, or hit others. Remind the student that they still have choices, escort the student from class, get help from other staff, protect the safety of the other students, and restrain the student if necessary.
    4) *Tension reduction stage:* The student releases tension through crying or verbal venting. In a private discussion, show empathy and help the student gain insight into their feelings and behavior. Discuss ways to manage similar situations in the future.

Alex's teacher found that it was far more constructive to monitor the girl for signs of agitation and intervene early than to wait till yelling became "necessary" (see Chapter 3).

Students may be confused and frightened by their lack of self-control during stressful situations. They are often receptive to those who respect their dignity while providing assistance.

19. A teacher's response to a particular behavior can escalate or de-escalate the problem. If you react by presenting an ultimatum (e.g., "Don't say another word or I'll throw you out of class"), the student may take the challenge. Colvin, Ainge, and Nelson (1997) recommend that when a student displays defiant, challenging, or inappropriate behavior the teacher do three things using a calm voice:

    1) State the rule or expectation.
    2) Present options for the student on how to address the problem.
    3) Request explicitly for the student to "Take care of the problem."

This course of action provides a way for the student to back down and save face in front of peers.

20. Train yourself to cue students to demonstrate the correct behavior. For example, during a large-group discussion when the students are talking out of turn, you could do the following:

   1) *Decide* exactly what behaviors you want to see, such as raising their hands and waiting to be called upon.
   2) *Tell* the students what behavior you want to see. For example, say, "Raise your hand if you want to speak and I'll do my best to call on you" or "I'll only call on those people who choose to raise their hands."
   3) *Phrase* your questions as follows: "Raise your hand if you can tell us . . ." This phrase cues students to raise their hands and tells them that you are serious about having them do it.
   4) *Call on only* those students who raise their hands.

21. Involve the students as much as possible during a lesson through questioning, doing work on the board or screen, or hands-on activities. Learning is enhanced and off-task behaviors minimized.

22. Use chunking, where you break down the task into smaller units and ensure that each segment is completed to the required standard. For certain assignments, marks can be given for the completion of each segment. This technique helps motivate the child to stay on task instead of trying to avoid the task because it looks daunting.

23. Give precise instructions. Using simple words, tell the students exactly what has to be done and demonstrate how to do it. Ask specific students to repeat the instructions back to you. Furthermore, state the expectations for quality of work and behavior while working on the assignment. This technique eliminates guessing at what is to be done and what you consider to be appropriate behavior.

24. Provide *meaningful* activities for "fast finishers" or those who require enrichment (see Chapter 8 for more ideas). Such activities extend the skill or concept so that the student can explore the topic further or deeply. Give students opportunities to earn marks for successful completion of enrichment assignments. Having these activities ready when students finish their work before the others ensures that they are occupied in appropriate ways.

25. Look beyond the behaviors a student is exhibiting to consider whether an underlying problem is not being addressed. For example, a student who doesn't seem to pay attention to oral instructions may have a mild hearing impairment or a learning disability involving the processing of oral language.

Chunking, coupled with a system of rewards, enabled Alex to complete longer assignments successfully (see Chapter 3).

One reason that Erik's homeroom and music teachers wanted to provide him with enrichment activities was to avoid the development of behavior problems (see Chapter 4).

In Andrew's case, the behavior problems stemmed from the student's feeling that he could not do the written English work (see Chapter 4).

Classroom Behavior Taboos for Teachers

Remember: You always want to serve as a positive model for your students. If your behavior isn't up to par, you can't expect theirs to be.

- Never nag. Students stop listening to you.
- Don't issue threats or ultimatums. You usually lack the power to carry them out.
- Avoid making hasty judgments and acting without thought. Take time to calm down before you speak to a student whose actions disturb you or the class.
- Don't overreact to minor incidents.

- Avoid arbitrary or inconsistent enforcement of the rules.
- Don't yell, scream, or even talk very loudly.
- Do not implement inappropriate or harsh punishments. If you do, you will set yourself up as a target for revenge.

Attention Deficit Hyperactivity Disorder

While it is technically a mental health condition, students who have attention deficit hyperactivity disorder (ADHD) present as having behavior difficulties and display a persistent pattern of inattention and/or hyperactivity-impulsivity. ADHD is a neurologically based disorder that impedes the learning process and interferes with social interactions. Early medical and psycho-educational assessment will help ensure more positive and constructive experiences for the student with ADHD, as well as for the other students in the class. Usually, a combination of medication, individual and family therapy, support groups, and an individual education plan (IEP) is recommended. If you have a student with ADHD in your classroom, focus on the child's strengths and teach the student strategies to complete academic tasks, such as chunking, and to learn social skills that will enhance interactions with peers and authority figures. However, most importantly, develop a positive relationship with the student and avoid a deficit frame of mind. Try to see the positive aspects and strengths of the student (e.g., a sense of humor, talent in sports or the arts) and allow the student to demonstrate them whenever appropriate. Letting them "shine" strengthens the bond between you and the student, while allowing peers to see their strengths.

Characteristics of students with ADHD

Although students with ADHD have symptoms of both inattention and hyperactivity-impulsivity, one or the other pattern is predominant. The appropriate subtype should be medically diagnosed. Furthermore, to meet the definition, the symptoms must interfere with or reduce the quality of the student's functioning and some of the symptoms must be present before the age of 12. The symptoms would have to occur in at least two different settings (e.g., home, school, extra-curricular activities, with friends) and not be accounted for by some other reason (e.g., a mental disorder). Diagnosis of one of the two subtypes is based on the *Diagnostic and Statistical Manual of Mental Disorders* (Fifth Edition), commonly known as DSM-5.

What to Look For in Students Suspected of Having ADHD

When observing a student you suspect of having ADHD, make systematic observations (see Chapter 3). Note the frequency of behaviors over a period of six months. If a student is suspected of having ADHD, clusters of behaviors will be observed *often*. According to the American Psychiatric Association, when observing a student for signs of ADHD, there are two main categories of behaviors to look for: (1) inattention and (2) hyperactivity and impulsivity.

Inattention

The student has difficulty maintaining attention to their work and is easily distracted by other things (e.g., background noises, unrelated thoughts). They may also procrastinate or avoid tasks that require him to maintain concentration for longer periods of time, for example, a long assignment or homework. Once the attention shifts from the work, it is hard to get the student back on track. They have difficulty organizing their work, lose materials (e.g., notebook, pen), and make careless errors in their work. Their work may be messy, as if they were not completely focused on it. When you give instructions, they do not seem to be listening and do not follow the instructions or complete the work, even though they may be close to finishing it. The student may also be forgetful in daily activities and may miss due dates for assignments or leave their lunch or physical education clothing at home. Students who demonstrate these symptoms but not hyperactivity or impulsivity are usually diagnosed as having attention deficit disorder (ADD).

Hyperactivity and impulsivity

A student who is hyperactive may constantly fidget with their hands or feet, may jump up and down or move head, arms, and legs, or talk, often at times when they should be quiet. They may also walk or run around the classroom, gym, or outdoors at inappropriate times. Not surprisingly, you may observe that the student has difficulty engaging in quiet activities, such as reading. An impulsive student has trouble waiting for a turn, interrupts you when you are speaking to someone else, or blurts out answers before listening to the entire question.

Your observations may be an important first step in an assessment process that could lead to the diagnosis and treatment of ADHD. However, a student must exhibit many of the characteristics over a longer time — not just a two-week period. Keep in mind, too, that some of these characteristics may be due to other factors, such as the child's developmental stage or high anxiety (as we saw with Alex in Chapter 4).

How to Help Students with ADHD

One of the most important things you can do to help any student with ADHD is to provide a *structured and predictable* environment.

After she reflected upon her own practices, Alex's teacher used these techniques (see Chapter 4).

Problem: Fidgety Behavior — Seat the fidgety student near you when you're teaching so that you may monitor their behavior. When giving instructions, make eye contact with the student; say, write, and demonstrate what is to be done; and have the student repeat the instructions back to you. If necessary, place the student at a desk away from others during seatwork to reduce the amount of sensory stimulation or to decrease the disruption to the other students. Emphasize that moving is not a punishment; it is a way to help them complete their work.

When the students are engaged in activities, observe the fidgety student often for signs of fatigue or loss of interest, and stop the activity before it breaks down. Ignore minor misbehaviors, such as pencil tapping. Always ask yourself: "Is this bothering me or the entire class?" You will frequently find that during the time you pause to mentally ask this question, the behavior has stopped. You will also discover that more often than not, the misbehavior is bothering only you. Unless you ignore minor misbehavior, you will end up nagging the student, and after a while they will likely ignore you. If you must speak to the student about fidgety behavior, do so in a quiet and calm voice.

Problem: Short Attention Span — When working with a student with a short attention span, plan your lessons carefully, monitor the student's behaviors, and give positive feedback. As you develop your lessons, plan a variety of activities, such as teacher-directed, small-group, and individual work. Use a multisensory, or VAKT, approach; for example, say and write important points, plan activities in which students can move around, and use manipulatives in math and science. Cue the student that it is time to listen and look them in the eye. Involve the student as much as possible in the presentation of the lesson by serving as your helper to distribute materials or by demonstrating a skill. Keep your presentations short and change activities about every 10 minutes.

Explain seatwork clearly. For example, in math write the assignment on the board and say it to the class. Then do the first question on the board or screen to show the students how to set up their work. You can use the *say, write, and demonstrate* approach for every subject area. To ensure that the student with a short attention span understands what to do, ask them privately what the assignment is. The student may also benefit by chunking, or breaking a longer assignment into manageable parts.

Remember to encourage with praise whenever possible. Say: "I see that most people are listening. This is good because they will hear the instructions. We'll wait for the others to listen too." Monitor the class for on-task behavior and quietly praise individual students who are on task. For example, for younger students, quietly tell them that you are pleased to see that they are doing what is required and to keep it up. Beyond that, try to schedule interesting or rewarding activities to follow more difficult tasks, for example, a one-minute trip to the water fountain after a reading lesson.

Problem: Impulsive Approach to Tasks — Have the student sit near you when you give instructions, make eye contact, and quietly say, "I need you to listen." Make sure that you say, write, and demonstrate all instructions. For example, say, "Write on every second line, place the title in the middle of the top line, and add the date at the left." Then demonstrate this on flipchart paper, the screen, or the board, while repeating it. Next, ask the student to repeat the instructions back to you.

Use chunking, where you break down the tasks into smaller parts, present one part at a time, check the work, offer praise, and assign the next section. Always insist that the student does their best work. When something below standard is submitted, ask the student for their opinion on whether this is their best work. Tell them how to improve it while stating you know they can do a better job.

Sometimes, students complete work in slapdash fashion so that they can be the first to finish or to have time to do a preferred activity. Ensure that any student inclined to do this shows you their work before they engage in the other activities. If the work is messy, incomplete, or incorrect, explain how it must be changed, and ask them to show it to you when they are finished. The student with ADHD may require individual assistance to get started on the corrections.

Problem: Selective Listening — If the student is not paying attention, calmly request that they stop what they are doing. Get down to the same level as the student, and when you make eye contact, state the direction clearly, speaking calmly in short sentences. Then ask the student to repeat the instruction back to you. Reinforce the instruction by saying, writing, and demonstrating exactly what you want done. If possible, show the student a sample of a finished product. Monitor the student's progress with the task and give positive reinforcement.

Problem: Refusal to Complete the Task — Provide a balky student with individual assistance to help them get started. Sometimes, you may have to compromise on the amount of work assigned. For example, instead of every question, tell the student to do every second one. However, use this technique sparingly as the child may refuse to work in order to do less.

If you think confidence is an issue, encourage positive self-talk, whereby the child says in their head that they can do the work. Monitor the student's progress with the assignment and encourage them by offering positive feedback.

If you feel that the refusal is strictly an issue of power, offer choices to the student. When you offer choices, you're sharing power with the student and the conflict will de-escalate. Say: "You can do the work now or for homework. It's your choice. If you choose to do it for homework, you must be quiet so that others will not be disturbed." If the student chooses to do the work later, then it must be noted in their agenda. You *must* check the work the next class. If it is not done, then consequences are administered, for example, loss of marks, a detention, or a phone call home. Following through on the consequences is important.

Problem: Wandering in the Classroom — Allow regular movement breaks so that the student can release energy. Sharpening a pencil one or two times during a designated period (perhaps the time between morning recess and lunch) may serve as a break. If necessary, give the student two pencil passes, one to be given to you every time they get up to sharpen a pencil. If you use breaks for pencil sharpening or getting a drink, make sure that the student knows the rules: remaining in the classroom, being quiet, and keeping their hands to themself.

Another technique is self-monitoring, where the child makes tally marks to record the number of times they are out of their seat. You also keep track and compare your numbers at the end of the period or other agreed-upon time. While self-monitoring may not eliminate the behavior, it usually serves to draw it to the student's attention, which may help to reduce it.

Alex's teacher came to realize that she had not consistently followed the hands-up rule and may thereby have contributed to Alex's habit of speaking out of turn (see Chapter 4).

Problem: Calling Out in Class — When you are questioning your students, insist on the hands-up rule. Cue students by prefacing your questions with the phrase, "Raise your hand if you can tell us . . ." You can also use a visual cue, such as pointing to your arm. Ignore responses that are spoken out of turn. You *must* call only on those students who raise their hands. When you see the student with ADHD raise their hand, call on them immediately to reinforce the link between hand raising and answering.

Problem: Disorganization — To help a younger student organize their books and materials, place everything in a large plastic tub beneath the desk. Ask older students to color-code their textbooks and binders or to keep morning subjects in one binder and afternoon subjects in another. Another technique is to permit the student to have a set of textbooks at home and one for school, which eliminates forgetting.

To help a younger student organize time, post the weekly schedule in the classroom and follow it. Older students should have multiple copies of their timetable, perhaps keeping it in their pencil case, on their phone, on a computer, on a tablet, in binders, in locker, and at home. When assigning work, tell the students how much time they will have to complete it. When 10 minutes remain in the period, say, "There are 10 minutes left." Announce when only five and two minutes remain, as well.

Write the homework assignment in the same spot every day and review it orally with the class. Give the students time to copy it into their agendas. You may have to sign the agenda of the student with ADHD to ensure that the homework is recorded and to show the parents that you have checked it. Posting homework and dates of tests and information about assignments on a class website is also a useful practice. It helps parents keep their children organized.

Be sure to follow up on assigned homework. Check notebooks often and give marks for neatness and completeness. Some students also find it helpful to have access to a model notebook to check the order of notes and to borrow notes for photocopying.

Provide class time for students to place handouts where you want them.

Working with Students Who Have Experienced Trauma

It is estimated that one-third to one-quarter of children experience some adversity. When a child experiences stress or trauma within the environment of a supportive relationship with an adult, the child will likely get over it. However, some students experience prolonged adversity due to physical or emotional abuse, caregiver substance abuse or mental health issues, neglect, natural disasters (e.g., wildfires, severe flooding), experiencing and witnessing violence, and poverty. Intergenerational trauma should not be dismissed. It exists and affects students in many ways. The effects of trauma are cumulative and may result in trouble with self-regulation, difficulty trusting adults, inappropriate relations, explosive behavior, withdrawal, and negative thinking. The student may communicate their distress through behavior such as aggression, avoidance, and disengagement. Their emotions may seem to explode for an unknown reason. Not surprisingly, students who have experienced prolonged trauma can't learn if they don't feel safe, emotionally and physically, and cared for. It is these children who benefit from a trusting and protective relationship with an empathic teacher.

A strong relationship with a student who has experienced trauma is fundamental to successful outcomes. To build trust, ensure that you have created a predictable environment. The daily/weekly schedule should be followed. The student needs to be assured that things will occur in a predictable way; a reliable routine provides a sense of control and security. Your reactions to outbursts and inappropriate behavior should also be predictable. The student should know the expected behaviors and consequences for breaking the rules, which should be administered consistently to all students. Equally important, the student should know that pro-social behaviors and achievement are also acknowledged. Students need to be assured that positive results will happen when they follow through. Teachers can also provide predictable attention during independent work times. After checking with the student for understanding after teaching a lesson, the teacher may say, "I will be back in five minutes." Return in five minutes to ensure the student knows that you are attentive to their learning needs.

As stated elsewhere in this book, the teacher should spend time talking informally with the student about their interests or common ones, such as animals, sports, computer games, or music. These conversations can help to build a relationship with the student who has experienced trauma.

When the student is learning new skills and concepts, emphasize that mistakes will be made, and they are part of learning. Teachers should make a point of acknowledging and praising effort put forth by students. Appropriate reactions to making a mistake may also be modeled by the teacher, who can use the opportunity to analyse their behavior out loud for the students. They can state, "Did you notice that I made a mistake with the spelling of this word? Did I become upset over it? What did I do?" Students will likely explain that you calmly checked the spelling and corrected it.

See also Chapter 10 for information about post-traumatic stress disorder (PTSD).

If the student is showing signs of agitation and distress while working, go over to them and ask how they are doing or how the assignment is coming along. If the student seems frustrated by the work, provide assistance with it. You can also establish a signal between you and the student to let you know that they need a break. Some teachers set up a calming area in the classroom where there may be pillows and headphones with calming music. In some cases, the student may want to leave the classroom to do some deep breathing and positive self-talk (e.g., "I know this work is hard, but I can do it. I just have to keep trying. The teacher is there to help me.").

Building a trusting relationship with a student who has experienced trauma will take time and the positive, caring, and predictable behaviors you demonstrate are cumulative. If a student does not seem to respond immediately, recognize that trust will develop slowly and that you need to understand that the behaviors are symptoms of trauma. You need to be that patient, consistent, caring, and respectful teacher who provides a supportive relationship and environment.

Notice Various Behaviors — and Examine Your Own

You will likely be aware of the behaviors of those students who show signs of ADHD or of defiance long before you notice their well-behaved and quiet peers. When identifying the students who may have ADHD, make careful, systematic observations over four to six months (see Chapter 3). Share your data with the special education teacher or the principal to determine if assessment procedures should be done. Read the student's file to see whether there is a history of a particular behavior. Describe the behaviors to the parents and inquire as to whether the student shows them at home. Be aware that, if a parent responds that the behaviors are not shown at home, (1) the behaviors may represent a peer or academic problem or (2) the parent is in denial. In either case, you may not have much support at home for your actions. This lack of parental support will limit your success in helping the student to demonstrate appropriate behaviors.

With students who may have experienced trauma, also note the behaviors, potential triggers, and ways you have successfully re-directed or calmed the student. As with students who may have ADHD, share your observations with the administration and/or the resource teacher. There may also be some important information in the student's school file. If appropriate, contact the parents or caregivers and describe your observations. Ask them if they have noticed similar behaviors at home or if there have been any incidents that might be causing these behaviors. In some cases, you may learn that the death of a loved one or last summer's wildfire has had an effect on the child. In such instances, you may recommend some services that may be accessed by the family.

Remember to examine your *own* behaviors, too. Ask yourself if you're ever intolerant or impatient. Consider what you can do to make the classroom more *positive*, *consistent*, *safe*, and *secure* for all students. You may have to make changes in your teaching techniques to bring about positive changes in the students' behaviors.

It takes courage to critically assess your methods and make changes that will promote an environment in which behavior problems cannot thrive. The fact that you have read this chapter shows that you are willing to make some changes, if necessary, to help students with behavior problems feel they belong academically and their strengths are acknowledged, and this will help give them a sense of social belonging with you and peers.

CHAPTER 8

Giftedness

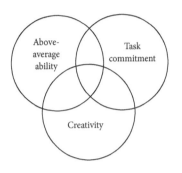

Renzulli's model of giftedness from *What Makes Giftedness* (1979)

Giftedness has traditionally referred to superior intelligence as measured by a standardized, individually administered test. Students scoring two or more standard deviations above the mean and who show superior performance in an academic area are usually identified as being gifted. *Creative* and *talented*, considered as subgroups, are not usually recognized, as these abilities cannot be easily measured using a test.

Current Approaches to Determining Giftedness

The traditional approach described above has given way to one based on the work of Renzulli (1979) and Gardner (1983, 1999). These researchers rely less on the results of standardized tests; instead, they focus on a variety of indicators of giftedness. Renzulli's model consists of three interlocking clusters of traits: above-average ability, creativity, and task commitment. The interaction of the elements is the key to creative and productive accomplishments. Gardner, who uses the term *intelligences*, has identified eight areas of abilities or gifts that a person may have. These intelligences are logical-mathematical, linguistic, musical, spatial, bodily-kinesthetic, interpersonal, intrapersonal, and naturalistic. According to Renzulli and Gardner, if students are identified as having strengths in a particular area, they should be given opportunities to develop their skills in that area.

The approach based on the Renzulli and Gardner models recognizes that a student is not gifted in every subject area. These models focus more on the provision of enrichment for students with varying gifts within the regular classroom, as opposed to the creation of special pull-out programs or congregated classes.

Regardless of the approach, some people feel that no extra programming or accommodations need to be made available to gifted children. However, these students *do* need adaptations for them to reach their full potential and to avoid becoming bored and frustrated in school. Such feelings can lead to underachievement, withdrawn or acting-out behaviors, and a general dislike of school.

Identify gifted students

You may be in a situation where you will be helping to identify students who are gifted. Some children may be very easy to spot as gifted; however, others who are underachieving, do not speak English, have a disability, are economically disadvantaged, or are of a cultural or racial minority may be more difficult to identify. You will need to make careful observations of these students as their gifts may be masked.

Students who demonstrate many of the characteristics identified on the next page *frequently over time* may be academically gifted. Many children will display

Characteristics of the Gifted Student

☐ exceptional speed of thought, rapid response to new ideas

☐ ability to learn quickly and to process information correctly; little need for detailed explanations

☐ good memory with apparent lack of need to rehearse

☐ large knowledge base on a variety of topics

☐ advanced problem solving and conceptualization, logical thinking; makes good educated guesses

☐ extensive vocabulary

☐ superior reading ability

☐ intellectual curiosity; asks many questions

☐ has varied or intense interests

☐ has a vivid imagination

☐ searches for a challenge, wants to delve more deeply into a topic, enjoys games of thought, plays with ideas and words

☐ flexibility in thinking: sees other ways of viewing problems and generates original ideas and solutions

☐ persistence and goal-directed behaviors, well-developed attention span, ability to work on a task or project for a long time, ability to delay closure

☐ ability to work independently; has a high tolerance for ambiguity

☐ fondness for elaboration; embellishes ideas, concerned with detail

☐ awareness of relationships among diverse ideas, ability to see connections between parts

☐ may be impatient with slower peers

☐ has a keen sense of humor, idealism, a strong sense of justice, high expectations for self, feelings of being different, exceptional emotional depth and intensity, and sensitivity to the feelings of others (These are considered *affective* characteristics.)

these characteristics; what separates the gifted from the bright student is the degree or intensity of the characteristics.

How to Enrich the Learning of Gifted Students

Strive to establish a classroom environment in which gifts are valued. You can achieve this by modeling acceptance of students who have knowledge and abilities in specific areas that are greater than your own. Permit these students to contribute to discussions or to demonstrate skills in physical education or the arts; avoid discouraging their comments, even though what they say may be beyond the comprehension or interest of others.

Students identified as gifted who have an IEP need opportunities for enrichment to support a sense of academic belonging. You can imagine how frustrating it must be to have to wait continually for your peers to understand a concept after you got it in the initial presentation. Gifted students learn at a faster pace and do not require a lot of repetition. To ensure that your gifted student does not become bored or worse, disengage or become disruptive, you can provide enrichment activities in your classroom. For example, if you are studying the solar system in science, you could require that the student do some research on a topic related to the subject and produce a report, graphic novel on space adventures, or a play. The actual product would be determined through a discussion with the student, who would be expected to demonstrate deeper thought, critical analysis, and creativity. The student would be given the option to present their product to the class.

While not identified as gifted, you may have students who are passionate about a particular topic and would welcome the opportunity to do extra research on it. They too may be willing to discuss the products of their research to their classmates. Other students may be mildly interested in a particular science, math, or social studies unit and could be encouraged to engage in activities such as reading more about it, developing games, or doing word searches. These activities would be done after work completion. You could also use tiered activities, as described in Chapter 2, where the second and third tiers, or levels, of activity involve higher orders of thought.

You may be tempted to employ gifted students as teacher aides. Don't. Serving as an aide is not enrichment. Similarly, remember to focus on letting gifted students go more deeply and broadly into a topic. You can do this by compacting or compressing the curriculum to provide time for a student to work on individual projects. For example, if your students are studying triangles in the junior division, have the student do every second question in the seatwork and correct their answers themself. With the time remaining in the period, they can work on an individual project whereby they examine architecture in ancient Greece in terms of geometric shapes.

If any students are withdrawn from class for enrichment, avoid having them do all the work that was missed. Instead, select those assignments or parts of those assignments that embody the most important concepts or skills. The key idea in both the above suggestions is that students who are identified as gifted do not require endless repetition. Suggestions on providing enrichment for gifted students in the regular classroom appear on the following pages. Some may also be appropriate for those who possess gifts in specific areas, but who have not been formally identified as being gifted.

Younger gifted students

Permit gifted students to work on independent or small-group research projects that are related to the unit being studied. After the students have completed the class assignment, they may work on their research projects. Be sure to discuss the topics for these projects with them and permit them to choose something that interests them.

If you are studying data management with your class, you and each gifted student could establish a learning contract whereby you and the student discuss the product/outcome (e.g., a report on a survey of students in the school), the process for reaching the goal (e.g., developing the questionnaire, collecting the data and analyzing them), and the way the project will be assessed (e.g., teacher and self-assessment).

Sometimes, gifted students may become very involved in a given project or writing assignment. Provide extra time for students to complete it. For example, the students in a Grade 1 class may require 30 minutes to write a three-sentence story and draw a picture; a student who is gifted may require 90 minutes spread over two days to write a five-page story with three detailed illustrations. The student may work on it if finished their other work early or they may take it home.

If possible, use cross-curricular instruction whereby you integrate several disciplines into one unit. For example, integrate an exploration of pulleys and levers, novel study, and medieval history into a unit. Doing this helps the students understand how subject areas may be linked to solve problems or to provide a deeper and broader understanding of a topic. Consider using overarching themes, such as adaptation, community, cooperation, exploration, conflict, heroism, and survival, to provide a framework for study and to help the students understand how many things may be viewed from a different and possibly unusual perspective. For example, with an elementary class you may adopt the themes of survival and adaptation as you study animals and habitats in science, pioneers in history, and Susanna Moodie's *Roughing It in the Bush* in language arts.

Instead of a steady diet of questions that ask students merely to recall facts, incorporate higher-order thinking skills into your questioning, as well as into the assignments. Ask questions that require students to apply, analyze, synthesize, and evaluate information. (See Bloom's taxonomy for more information.) For example, ask them to apply a set of characteristics to a particular event in history (application) or describe how two characters in a novel are similar and different (analysis). You might also require students to produce a graphic that embodies the concepts learned in a unit in health (synthesis). Perhaps have them assess and explain whether certain industrial or agricultural practices are ecologically sound (evaluation). You can also ask open-ended questions that permit students to speculate on things, such as the ending to a story, or ask "What would happen if . . ."

Encourage gifted students to take on extra responsibilities. For example, one might serve as an editor of a class newspaper or group project. You might also recommend that a student join a club or the choir, or try out for a school team, if that's where the student's strengths seem to lie.

Maintain high standards of academic work and of behavior. As with all your class, these students should follow the rules and be held accountable for their actions. Beyond the classroom, they could work with a mentor in their field of interest. For example, a student with an interest in creative writing may be given the opportunity to correspond through email with a prominent author or poet.

Bloom's Taxonomy

Briefly, Bloom (1956) identifies six cognitive levels from less complex to more complex:

1. Knowledge
2. Comprehension
3. Application
4. Analysis
5. Synthesis
6. Evaluation

The first two levels are considered to be lower levels of thinking because they involve memorization of information; the remaining levels are higher levels of thinking because the student must demonstrate an understanding of material.

Erik's teachers recognized his strengths in math, computers, and music. They encouraged him to explore these areas further than the regular curriculum by joining the Engineering Club and the Grade 7 Band.

Older gifted students

In the classroom, ask gifted students higher-order questions that require more than factual recall. In your questioning and on assignments, ask students to apply concepts to real-life problems, analyze material, synthesize ideas, and evaluate positions. Beyond that, ask open-ended questions that require the students to speculate or predict based on known data, solve problems, and create new products. You can also provide opportunities for gifted students to investigate topics related to a unit of study independently. For example, in a unit on light you can permit a student to research the use of lasers in cosmetic surgery or photonics. An extra project can be substituted for another assignment or completed for bonus marks.

Encourage such students to develop leadership skills through courses and workshops and to take an active part in extracurricular activities at school and in the community. Some gifted students will embrace the opportunity to become involved and thrive in balancing a broad range of school and community activities with schoolwork. Other gifted students may want to participate only in specific clubs or activities. Still others may choose not to participate at all. As a teacher, you can highlight specific activities or appeal to a need to socialize, but you cannot make your students join.

Special courses can also provide enrichment opportunities. If available, encourage gifted students to take high-school courses at the most advanced, or International Baccalaureate (IB), level. As with club involvement, some students will want to take these kinds of courses and others will not.

Gifted students might benefit from taking part in a mentoring program. Before you begin arranging something, talk with a student to determine interest. Perhaps the student could communicate in person or electronically with a prominent person in a field of interest. To identify someone, you could explore a university website or conduct a google search. If, for example, you had a student who found social history absorbing (e.g., the work of suffragettes), you could introduce this student to a historian who shares similar research interests and agrees to some short-term mentoring of the student.

Social considerations

It is not unusual for a student identified as gifted to feel "different" even before the assessment. It is possibly because they have different learning needs than their peers, such as rapid grasp of new concepts and a desire for a quicker pace and opportunities to go more in-depth. However, they share the same wish for friends and social belonging as their peers. Some gifted students (e.g., girls and Black males) will hide their intelligence and broad knowledge so as not to attract unwanted negative attention. They may choose not to raise their hands to answer your questions during a lesson, or they may deliberately score in the average range on a test or submit a mediocre assignment to manipulate their grades. As well, some gifted students will remain silent in a group so as not to say something that might provoke teasing (e.g., "You're just a know-it-all").

To support a sense of social connection, get to know these students and find out about their interests and how they are feeling about the results of the testing. Also conduct regular check-ins with them and allow them a say in their individual projects to give them an opportunity to voice their feelings and ideas. Let them know that you care about them. Ensure that enrichment activities are available to everyone to avoid singling out students who may be reluctant to reveal their intelligence. To avoid them feeling like an outsider, pair them up with students who have similar interests to complete assignments. It is possible that a friendship will develop from these pairings or small group encounters. As well, if the gifted student would prefer to blend in, respect this decision, but at the same time, encourage them to find individual projects that are suited to their interests and desire to go into depth on the topic.

Encourage *All* Your Students

Gifted students need opportunities for enrichment, but some teachers are reluctant to adapt their teaching style or curriculum: they think that doing so is too much work. The suggestions in this chapter about providing individual projects and opportunities to join clubs or other activities are *easy* to implement. You may find that students who have not been identified as gifted want to take part in enrichment activities, too. Encourage *all* your students to develop higher-order thinking skills, to pursue their interests, and to wonder about the possibilities. In doing so, you will find that your students are engaged in their schoolwork, which will strengthen their sense of academic belonging.

CHAPTER 9

Developmental Disabilities: Intellectual Disability, Fetal Alcohol Spectrum Disorder, and Autism

A developmental disorder is not a temporary developmental lag. It is an impairment that manifests before the age of 18 years. It is lifelong. While symptoms may improve, there is no cure. In this chapter, we will examine intellectual disability, fetal alcohol spectrum disorder, and autism.

Intellectual Disability

Intellectual disability is characterized by significant limitations both in intellectual functioning and in adaptive behavior, which covers many everyday social and practical skills. This disability originates before the age of 22 (American Association on Intellectual and Developmental Disabilities [AAIDD], 2021). *Intellectual functioning* (or intelligence) relates to general mental capacity, such as learning, reasoning, and problem solving. It is measured by an IQ test, and a score of 75 or less indicates limitations in intellectual functioning. *Adaptive behavior* refers to how a person responds to environmental demands, which are affected by age and culture. It consists of three skill types: (1) conceptual (e.g., language and literacy; money, time, and number concepts), (2) social (e.g., interpersonal skills, social responsibility, gullibility, social problem solving, abilities to follow rules and to avoid being victimized), and (3) practical (e.g., activities in daily living, occupational skills, healthcare, travel/transportation, safety, use of money, and use of a telephone) (AAIDD).

Intellectual disability is a type of developmental disability and is classified into four categories: mild, moderate, severe, and profound. Children with mild intellectual disability are usually educated in regular classrooms with little support. Those with moderate, severe, and profound intellectual disability are placed in special education classrooms for most of the day and are integrated into regular classrooms to improve social behaviors. These students will be accompanied by a paraprofessional, and you will not likely be required to provide educational programs for them. Hence, the focus of this section will be on characteristics and strategies related to *mild* intellectual disability.

Characteristics of students with mild intellectual disability

Most children diagnosed with mild intellectual disability (MID) will be educated in regular classrooms, with or without the support of a paraprofessional or other professional personnel. These students learn at about one-half to three-quarters of the rate of their normally developing peers. Over time, some of these students may be capable of doing work in academic subjects up to the higher elementary grades. General achievement ranges from the second to the fifth grade level.

Nevertheless, many of these students can be taught functional English and math, and they may learn job-related skills through direct training and supervised cooperative education placements. The checklist on page 131 lists characteristics that may be displayed by students with mild intellectual disability in the classroom.

Down Syndrome

Children with Down syndrome typically have some degree of developmental disability — mild, moderate, or severe. Down syndrome is a genetic defect causing limitations in physical and intellectual development. It is caused by an aberration in chromosome 21: in most cases, there is an extra copy of this chromosome instead of the usual pair (one each from the mother and father). The condition is usually recognized at birth, on the basis of characteristic features or through chromosome testing. Common observable features include upward sloping eyes, a protruding tongue due to a small mouth cavity, a head that is flattened at the back, a short flat nose, short fingers — particularly the fifth — a wide space between the first and second toes, low muscle tone, and a short stocky build. Children with Down syndrome also have higher rates of congenital heart defects and leukemia than the general population.

How to help students with mild intellectual disability

As with all students who have identified exceptionalities, do the essential research and work cooperatively with others. Read the individual education plan (IEP) of the student in focus and talk to the student's paraprofessional, if one has been assigned, and previous teachers. Work with other professionals, such as the occupational therapist, resource teacher, reading specialist, speech-language pathologist, and behavior specialist. Meet with the parents or caregivers to discuss the teaching approaches and behavior modification programs that have proven to be effective. Discuss, as well, the goals the parents have for their child. These become very important during adolescence because transition plans need to be developed and implemented. A transition plan identifies academic and vocational goals for the student and outlines the steps and agencies involved in meeting them. The transition plan is usually developed by the special education or guidance department with the parents and the student. (Additional information on transition plans is found in Chapter 14.)

As with all students, developing a positive relationship with the student who has mild intellectual disability (MID) is an important step in helping the student feel a sense of belonging. You can begin by smiling and greeting the student each morning and talking to them about activities they did on the weekend or the night before. Through your speech and actions, you will model acceptance of the child with MID for the other students in the class.

Providing a structured, predictable environment is one of the most important things you can do in the classroom to help the student with MID feel comfortable. That's because it helps to reduce student anxiety about not knowing what to expect. As part of this effort, post the weekly schedule in a place that is visible to all the students and *follow* it. At the beginning of the day, point to the day of the week on the schedule and read the names of the subjects that will be taught. Highlight any schedule changes, such as an assembly being held instead of social

How to Identify Students with Mild Intellectual Disability

The following are criteria to consider when wondering whether a student has mild intellectual disability:

- ☐ has a poor memory, for example, can perform a task one day, but not the next; has difficulty remembering a series of instructions or the sequence of numbers
- ☐ has immature language patterns and uses simple vocabulary
- ☐ may have delayed and slurred speech
- ☐ may have difficulty understanding body language, such as facial expression and tone of voice
- ☐ has difficulty grasping abstract concepts; is clearly oriented in the present and not in the past or future
- ☐ has difficulty generalizing and transferring information to day-to-day activities, for example, may be able to add, but can't total purchases in a store
- ☐ displays learned helplessness, is reluctant to try new things, and may try to manipulate someone else to do a given task
- ☐ requires extrinsic motivation to do things
- ☐ may be disorganized and has difficulties keeping track of personal belongings
- ☐ is slow to complete academic work, something that may be due to slow processing of information and/or short attention span
- ☐ may have low self-esteem and may make negative statements about self
- ☐ has difficulty making a transition from one activity to another, for example, moving from recess or physical education back to the classroom
- ☐ may exhibit specific anxieties, such as going to the washroom, or specific compulsive behaviors
- ☐ may be aggressive due to lack of success, fear of failure, low self-esteem, resistance to transitions from one activity to another, or excessive stimulation such as is found in a school cafeteria

Pembroke Publishers © 2022 *Finding a Place for Every Student* by Cheryll Duquette ISBN 978-1-55138-360-6

studies. A timetable with pictures and words could also be taped to the student's desk.

Be aware that transitions from one activity to another are sometimes difficult for students with developmental disability. It is not unusual for them to want to perseverate, or continue a task past the desired time. One way to ease transitions is to give a ten-minute warning that you will be finishing one subject and moving on to another. Give further warnings at the five- and two-minute marks. To reinforce this with the student with developmental disability, go to their desk and quietly say how many minutes are left and what will be done after this activity.

When teaching a lesson, gain the student's attention by directly asking them to look at you. Quietly say, "I need you to look here." Explain why the student needs to know the information or skill you will be teaching and relate it to their own life. In physical education you can say, "Think of when you are playing basketball. You can't throw the ball because the other team is around you. So, you can pass it. Today, we're going to learn how to do one type of pass."

As much as possible, involve the student in the lesson through hands-on activities and questions. Phrase questions simply and allow sufficient "wait time" for the question to be processed and the answer to be formulated. Encourage the child to use their language through use of open-ended questions that require more than a mere "yes" or "no." The student can also help demonstrate a particular skill (e.g., a chest pass).

When giving instructions, speak in short, simple sentences and privately ask the student to repeat the instructions. Demonstrate exactly what you want to be done. For this student, you may also have to give instructions one at a time and couple each one with positive feedback and a short break. Do the same for tasks. (See the information on chunking in Chapter 2.) For example, after the student has completed a certain amount of work, offer praise and permit the student to get a drink of water.

When the student is working on assignments, select a peer as a partner to assist with non-instructional tasks, such as applying glue to a craft. By similar token, give as much individual assistance to the student as possible to ensure that they are on task, understand the work, and are making progress.

Planning lessons for a student with mild intellectual disability

A student with intellectual disability learns at a slower pace than their peers, and you have to modify the curriculum to reflect the student's academic and cognitive levels. Doing so ensures that the student is able to do the work and complete it, which supports their sense of academic inclusion. For example, children in a Grade 1 class may be working with numbers from 10 to 20; however, the student with intellectual disability may spend the entire year on numbers from 0 to 10. While the student can participate in the presentation of the lesson, they will likely require follow-up activities that are at the student's academic level. Avoid having low expectations for the student by just giving them pictures to color or other busy work. Also avoid providing a steady diet of computer activities for the student with MID. Although it will take extra time, plan lessons that are challenging yet achievable, advance their skills and knowledge, and ensure they feel included.

Students with intellectual disabilities benefit from the use of a multisensory approach to teaching (VAKT). You can teach by discussing important ideas (auditory), showing pictures and writing key words (visual), and providing objects that can be touched (tactile). For example, if the topic is money and you are teaching about nickels, dimes, and quarters, tell the students about each of the coins, show pictures and corresponding values, and let them work with real coins.

You may also need to shorten assignments by reducing the number of questions to be answered or the amount to be written. If the student has difficulty with fine-motor control, precut materials for crafts or partially assemble the item to avoid frustration with scissors or glue.

As noted in earlier chapters, if copying notes is a problem, give the child a photocopy of the note or a fill-in-the blank version whereby they write the key words in the spaces. You may also need to provide extra time for the student to complete assignments.

Plan to reinforce learning through repetition. You will need to review skills and information often, as things learned one day may be forgotten the next. One way to do this is by purchasing or preparing games that review such things as the alphabet, the names of the days of the week and the months, basic sight words, and number facts. Software that uses gamification to reinforce these concepts may also be purchased. Sometimes, pairing the student with a patient partner can turn the review into a game.

Evaluate the student's assignments in light of the goals for the student and the grade level at which they are working. For example, in a Grade 5 class when students are writing a two- to three-page story, the student with developmental disability, who is working at the Grade 1–2 level, may be required to write three sentences and draw a picture. Regardless of the student's academic level, always maintain high expectations for them: they *can* learn.

Managing the behavior of a student with mild intellectual disability

Expect the same standard of behavior for the student with intellectual disability as you would for other students. All students must be accountable for their behavior and know that you will apply consequences for any misbehavior that are also used with other students. For example, if the student hits another child during recess, talk to the student about what happened and how the situation should have been handled. Request that the student apologize.

You will have to review the class rules frequently as they may be forgotten. Praise the student when they follow the rules to reinforce the correct behavior. Preparing work that is at the right level for your student with MID will reduce outbursts caused by frustration with a task. You should also watch for signs of anxiety and frustration when the student is completing a task. Monitor the student frequently by watching them and going to their desk. If the student appears anxious, suggest a two-minute break or another way to do the task. You might also provide some individual assistance to help them through a difficult section of the work.

To develop appropriate behaviors, adopt the use of a simple behavior modification plan. If your goal is to have the student complete their work, explain that you will reward finished work with time to read a favorite sports magazine or use the computer, or with a check mark redeemable for a prize (e.g., a pass to shoot basketballs with a friend in the gym at lunchtime). As the student learns the appropriate behavior, you can phase out the rewards. You can also reduce inappropriate behaviors by having the student substitute socially acceptable ones; for example, to reduce unwanted hugging, ask the student to give high fives instead and reinforce this behavior with praise.

Role playing may also be used to teach appropriate behaviors. If a child is taking the lunch boxes of other students and hiding them, ask them and another student to role-play a situation in which the child with developmental disability is first, the perpetrator, and second, the victim. After each scenario, discuss how the child felt. Then talk about the acceptable behavior, have the child demonstrate it, and praise it. Discuss how it felt to do the right thing and monitor the student during the next lunch break. Encourage the correct behavior and praise them for it.

Developing self-confidence and social acceptance

Feeling good about ourselves helps motivate us to keep trying. A student with intellectual disability needs to develop self-confidence for the same reason. You can help the student by ensuring that there are sufficiently challenging tasks at which they can succeed, by providing individual assistance, and by insisting that they perform personal tasks, such as putting on their coat by themself.

Remind students of their strengths, which may range from being conscientious about watering plants to knowing their number facts. Many students who have intellectual disability claim to be "no good at anything," so you need to help sustain positive feelings and discourage negative self-talk. Teach the student to engage in positive self-talk (e.g., "It's okay if I'm slower, I will get it done." Or simply, "I can do it.").

You can help the student gain social acceptance in a variety of quiet ways. Model accepting behaviors to peers and monitor anxiety levels to avoid a blow-up or tantrum, which can be very embarrassing. A tantrum could also make the other students afraid of the child with intellectual disability. Try to monitor classroom activities as closely as possible to ensure that the student is behaving appropriately and that others are not teasing or bullying them. Also supervise activities in the hallways, lunchroom, and playground to ensure physical and verbal bullying does not occur. If necessary, speak to the class about intellectual disability and how their classmate should be treated — with dignity and kindness — the way we *all* want to be treated.

Another method of facilitating social belonging is through group work. Assign the student a task at which they can succeed — managing materials might be an example. Select group members who are accepting and patient. Successful group experiences help the student to be seen in a positive light, which may lead to friendships. In phys ed you can have them be a team leader and select the team, thereby ensuring that they will not be the last person to be picked. Students with MID can take their turn with class duties such as taking the attendance to the office or distributing art supplies for a lesson. Students with MID want friends as much as their peers and sometimes need you to help their peers to get to know them and see their strengths.

Model patience, kindness, and respect

You may feel awkward about working with a student with intellectual disability, but there is no need to feel this way. Read the IEP and talk to others about what approaches are effective. Make note of the student's academic performance and social skills. Sometimes, a student's test scores are lower than actual day-to-day performance. Use the teaching techniques and suggestions for curriculum modification to ensure that the student experiences success in your classroom and feels as though they belong academically. Have high expectations for the student but remember that they will learn more slowly than others and will require much more repetition. Knowing this, be patient and kind with the student who has MID, and you will find that peers will do the same, thereby strengthening a sense of social belonging for everyone.

Fetal Alcohol Spectrum Disorder

Fetal alcohol spectrum disorder (FASD) is an umbrella term that refers to a number of physical, behavioral, and neurodevelopmental disorders caused by prenatal alcohol exposure (PAE). PAE affects different areas of the brain with varying severity, and individuals with FASD will have different strengths and challenges ranging from mild to severe. The three major areas of impairment are cognition (e.g., memory and processing speed), executive function and self-regulation (e.g., attention and managing emotions and behavior), and adaptive functioning (e.g., social interaction, motor skills). FASD occurs when a birth mother consumes alcohol during pregnancy. Because there are usually no physical signs of FASD, it is considered to be a lifelong, invisible disability. The first diagnosis of FASD occurred about 40 years ago and while public awareness of FASD is increasing, it is not at the level of learning disabilities, attention deficit hyperactivity disorder (ADHD), or autism.

Although people working in the fields of child welfare or child protection services, foster care, medicine, and education are becoming more familiar with recognizing the symptoms and how to work with individuals with FASD, birth mothers who drank during pregnancy are often reluctant to disclose this information to them. It results in lower levels of diagnosis of FASD. Students with milder forms of FASD are often identified as having ADHD and learning disabilities, and parents and teachers do not seem to look more deeply to find out the cause of the symptoms associated with the other diagnoses. However, as prenatal exposure to alcohol results in permanent brain damage, the result is intellectual disability in more severe cases of FASD. In fact, alcohol consumption by a birth mother is the leading cause of intellectual disability not due to genetics.

Symptoms of students with FASD

Students with FASD who are in general education classrooms usually have an IQ score within the normal range, but below what would be expected for their environment and background. These individuals are often identified in school as having a learning disability (typically due to problems with decoding words, reading comprehension, and written expression) even though no one else in their family may have learning disabilities. While students with FASD may have good oral expressive skills, auditory processing is a difficulty as they may catch only every third word, something that poses challenges when oral instructions are given. These students typically have difficulties with math concepts, computation, and problem solving; time; and money — all of which have implications for adult life. Impairments in memory also cause difficulties because the students can't remember things from one day to the next and more than one thing at a time.

Students with FASD are frequently diagnosed with ADHD as they have problems with attention, impulsivity, and inappropriate activity levels. As stated above, individuals with FASD have memory difficulties, and they often do not learn from their mistakes. This characteristic is an important distinction between

ADHD and ADHD symptoms caused by FASD. In both cases, similar problems with attention, impulsivity, and movement are shown and behavioral modification is usually used to change behavior. However, individuals with FASD do not respond to the consequences that are usually applied when a student behaves inappropriately because they do not *remember* the consequences associated with their previous actions. Instead, they keep doing the inappropriate behavior over and over again. As you can imagine, if a teacher does not suspect FASD, this pattern of repeated inappropriate behaviors can cause much frustration. The teacher should not blame themself; rather, they should try to understand that the student with FASD is not necessarily doing the wrong thing willfully — think *cannot* rather than *will not*. Repeat behavioral expectations often, monitor the student's behavior, and provide as much praise as possible.

By adolescence, some students with FASD develop secondary disabilities, such as depression, anxiety disorder, and a substance abuse. Furthermore, many of them have low self-esteem, and some can be physically aggressive. Social skills are delayed, and an 18-year-old with FASD may have the social behaviors of a 10-year-old. It is often the case, as well, that students with FASD desperately want friends and end up with peers who really are not friends.

General teaching strategies for students with FASD

Students with FASD struggle in school; however, adoptive parents and individuals have told me repeatedly that a teacher who is understanding and knowledgeable about the disability can make a difference in the academic outcomes for them.

The first place to search for information on the student's specific strengths and needs is their file. There may be an individual education plan (IEP) that can point to accommodations to use with the student. You can also speak to teachers who have taught the student before to find out what works and what does not work. Talk to the student's parents or caregivers, who will likely be able to provide information on how to instruct and manage the behaviors of their child, as well. It is possible that some parents and caregivers will know a lot about FASD and what works best for their child. Be open to collaborating with them.

There are some general strategies to use when working with students with FASD or whom you suspect may have FASD. As with other exceptionalities, know the student's strengths and needs so that you can select strategies that will use the student's strengths and interests to build positive classroom experiences and address personal needs. For example, the student with FASD may have an excellent singing voice and could be encouraged to join the school choir. Or the student may show talent in visual arts and when placed in a small group learning activity could illustrate some aspect of the work. Note that you should arrange the small groups to ensure that this student is working with on-task, knowledgeable, and tolerant peers. As well, if students are permitted to choose their group members, the student with FASD may not be selected by others and may feel inadequate and frustrated due to peer rejection. Therefore, be sure to pre-arrange the groups so that no one is left out.

Establishing structure with a predictable schedule in your classroom is important so that the student is not concerned with what is coming next. Post the class schedule and tape it to the student's desk. When assemblies, class photos, and other events disrupt the schedule, inform the students the day before and explain how things will follow for the day, block, or period. Have routines for lining up, passing out materials, submitting work, and so on. Be sure to follow these routines consistently.

Consider limiting the visual stimulation in the classroom. Some students with FASD become overstimulated by the sounds and lighting in a room and in an environment with a lot of colorful items posted on the wall or with items to touch. If necessary, provide a study carrel where the student can work and noise-canceling headphones so that they can focus on the assignment and not be distracted by noise or commotion in the classroom. Reassure the student that placement here is not a punishment; it is a way for them to get their work done.

Some students with FASD will need to be taught how to notice when they are overstimulated and how to regulate their response. One approach is to label arousal levels according to engine speeds (i.e., "low gear", "just right", and "high gear"). The students are taught strategies to shift their arousal state to meet the needs of the environment. Other students with FASD may have situations in which they cannot concentrate or work. I once had a student who could not tolerate the sound of a pencil on paper, so they did their math using a pen. It's important to know the specific needs of your students and to make adjustments accordingly.

As you plan lessons, consider using a multisensory method in which you incorporate visual, auditory, and kinesthetic/tactile learning modalities (VAKT). Use visual and tactile materials as much as possible to make abstract concepts more concrete. For example, in math you can use anchor charts to guide a student through the steps in doing computations (e.g., subtracting with borrowing) and manipulatives to assist in the understanding of concepts such as parts and wholes in fractions. Plan activities in which the student will be successful, and if necessary, reduce academic expectations.

During instruction, seat the student close to you so that you may keep them involved and focused. Some students with FASD may also need to have a fidget toy to stay focused. Explain why they need to know the information or skill that is being taught and relate it to their life as much as possible. As well, include the student's interests into the lesson to motivate them to pay attention. Give explicit instructions for the seatwork, using short, simple sentences, and always demonstrate exactly what is to be done. You may also have to repeat key ideas and provide extra practice so that the student can master specific skills. Be sure to use concrete materials (e.g., math manipulatives) when teaching abstract concepts.

During the activity, go to the student's desk, ask them to repeat the directions, and watch them begin their work. Gently correct if necessary and offer feedback and positive reinforcement. You might chunk the work by breaking it down into smaller components and offer praise as each section is completed. When possible, provide choices of tasks and assignments to demonstrate knowledge or skill acquisition.

Watch for signs of frustration because it may escalate into disruptive behavior. If the student is becoming frustrated, provide individual assistance, offer a break to get a drink, or redirect the activity. Generally, supervise the student closely and anticipate potential difficulties to ensure that situations where they may harm others or themself do not occur.

When the student with FASD cannot seem to do the work, refrain from asking them to try harder. They may be trying as hard as they can to complete the assignment or understand the concept. Instead, try a different way to teach the idea or have the student complete the work. For example, incorporate more visual and tactile or kinesthetic components into your instructional strategies, summarize ideas into three or four key words, and repeat them often. As you have likely noticed, these strategies are all associated with differentiated instruction (see Chapter 2).

Social belonging

Students with FASD and their adoptive parents have repeatedly told me that having a positive relationship with a knowledgeable and caring teacher is critical for successful outcomes. That relationship will be important in motivating the student to do the work and persist when challenges arise. Students with FASD also want a teacher who is kind and patient and realizes that they may not be able to meet some expectations. They want a teacher with whom they can talk when misunderstandings and conflicts arise. That sense of attachment to you, the teacher, is important, as is conducting daily check-ins with your students who have FASD. You need to monitor their moods (see Chapter 1) and arousal levels to make sure they are appropriate to facilitate learning.

Students with FASD may not have many friends and may be ignored, teased, or bullied by others. Generally, their social and emotional skills are below age level and a 10-year-old may be functioning socially at the level of a 6-year-old. To build social skills, teach personal boundaries, such as where to stand when speaking with someone and not to touch other students. You may also have to teach conversation skills through social stories and rehearsal. Some students have difficulty with emotional regulation and need to be able to identify their mood and level of arousal, as well as ways to address them. You can find ideas on how to help the student with FASD in this area in Chapter 1. As well, as much as possible, monitor these students outside of the classroom to ensure that verbal and physical bullying do not occur.

Besides working with the student with FASD on social skills and social communication, you may also have to work with their peers on acceptance, respect, patience, and kindness. Begin by modeling these traits and insist that everyone treat others the way they would like to be treated. Also have the student with FASD work with conscientious and accepting peers on daily class work and longer assignments. I have seen these situations turn into a supportive peer group for a student with FASD that lasted into high school.

How to help older students with FASD

At the intermediate level, students with FASD will need extra time to complete individual assignments and tests. You can usually make arrangements with the special education personnel so that a student can complete assignments or take tests in the resource room. Having a laptop in the classroom or in the resource centre will permit students with FASD to type their work and use the spell-check and grammar-check functions. Some students with FASD also benefit from having a resource period every day so that they can complete their homework with the assistance of a teacher. As the content becomes more difficult, students with FASD may need a paraprofessional in the classroom to provide one-to-one assistance.

Again, watch for signs that the student is frustrated or overwhelmed and offer permission to leave the class for a short time to calm down (e.g., do some deep breathing). In order to gain credits, these students may take basic-level, vocational, and life skills courses that include money management and social skills training.

As stated before, consequences for inappropriate behaviors usually do not work with students with FASD because of memory impairments. On the other hand, positive reinforcement such as acknowledging appropriate behavior during an activity or work completion to the required standard does seem to work. Offering praise and recognition can also help to develop a positive relationship between you and the student. Repeating the rules and expectations often and being consistent with consequences while linking them to choices is also helpful. Beyond that, help students with FASD take responsibility for their actions — do not accept the excuse of "I couldn't help it" or "It was somebody else's fault."

Given their permanent brain damage and the many implications for problems with cognitive, behavioral, and social functioning, many adolescents with FASD do not complete high school. Some, however, do graduate from secondary school with a certificate or qualifications that meet the requirements for community college entrance.

Parents and caregivers of students with FASD consistently say that when teachers know about the symptoms of FASD and are willing to implement academic and behavioral interventions, their children can make progress. As well, students with FASD reinforce the importance of having a teacher who is kind and patient and who doesn't make them feel unwanted in the classroom. These are clearly teachers who value academic and social belonging and work to make it happen for all their students.

Autism

Diagnostic and Statistical Manual of Mental Disorders, Fifth Edition (DSM-5), is the authority by which autism spectrum disorder is diagnosed. Healthcare professionals use the symptoms and criteria set forth in DSM-5 to identify the disorder. Autism spectrum disorder encompasses autism disorder, Asperger's syndrome, childhood disintegrative disorder, and pervasive developmental disorder (not otherwise specified): these all fall under the one category ASD.

Autism spectrum disorder (ASD) refers to a group of developmental disabilities that affect people in different ways and range in degree from mild to severe. These disabilities affect an individual's brain and cause problems with social communication and social interaction. Symptoms also include restricted, repetitive patterns of behavior, interests, or activities. Although individuals may have similar types of symptoms, there will be a wide variation among them. ASD is a lifelong, neurological disorder of which the cause is unknown; however, it appears that contributing factors are genes and the environment. Research has shown that vaccines and "refrigerator" parenting (a "cold" mother) do *not* cause them. ASD is usually diagnosed in early childhood and may be accompanied by other disabilities, such as intellectual disabilities. The prevalence of ASD diagnoses, which is 1 in 66 children and youth ages 5-17 years (Public Health Agency of Canada, 2018), has risen dramatically in the last two decades. Males are diagnosed with ASD four times more often than females (Public Health Agency of Canada, 2018). While a reliable diagnosis of ASD may be made as early as two years of age, most children are diagnosed at about four years old.

Symptoms of students with ASD

The symptoms of ASD combine in different ways for each individual; however, people with ASD do share common symptoms: They all have (1) persistent challenges in social communication and social interaction in a variety of contexts and (2) restricted, repetitive patterns of behavior, interests, or activities. Furthermore, the symptoms limit and impair the everyday functioning of the individual.

There is no medical test for ASD, and diagnosis is typically made by a pediatrician, child psychiatrist or clinical psychologist with expertise in the area of ASD, and a speech-language pathologist. Information provided by the parents is combined with assessments from the above healthcare professionals to provide an overall picture and to eliminate other disorders (e.g., hearing impairment).

Social communication and social interaction

While many individuals with ASD develop functional speech, some do not and use pictures or synthesized speech to communicate. Other students with ASD may have delayed speech and language skills. Furthermore, their voices may be high pitched, monotone, or robot like. Some students with ASD may also repeat words or phrases over and over again. They might not understand the use of nonverbal communication, and their facial expressions and body language may be inappropriate for the situation (e.g., smiling in a very serious situation). Words are taken literally, and many individuals with ASD do not understand slang and puns. These symptoms point to impairments in the development of social communication skills.

Children with ASD also have challenges with social interaction. They might avoid eye contact and interact with others only to achieve a specific goal (e.g., to obtain food). They all show impairments in social-emotional reciprocity and may have difficulty conducting a back-and-forth conversation or taking turns.

Some of your students with ASD may not be interested in interacting with other people and may be unable to make and keep friends. It is often the case that they prefer to play alone, do not engage in pretend play, and use toys the same way every time (e.g., only lining up the cars instead of moving them). They may also have difficulty understanding other people's perspectives and feelings; talking about their own feelings; sharing interests with others; and understanding jokes, sarcasm, teasing, and personal space. Lacking empathy and the ability to "get" jokes have negative implications for making friends, especially among older students. Beyond that, individuals with ASD may avoid or resist physical contact with others and engage in self-stimulatory behaviors (e.g., hand flapping, body rocking, or turning the light switches on and off). Some individuals with ASD have *echolalia*: when asked a question, they will repeat the question instead of providing an answer. Although some students with ASD may want to make friends, they may not know how to do so, and their poorly developed social communication and social interaction skills present additional barriers.

Behavior

Individuals with ASD will likely have challenges adjusting their behavior to suit the context. They may adhere to routines excessively, practise ritualized speech and behaviors, and resist change. All these symptoms will limit their flexibility in social situations. They might also have narrow interests (e.g., trains) and not want to talk about anything else. Another symptom is hyper- or hypo-reactivity to sensory input, for example, apparent indifference to pain, heat, or cold, or adverse response to specific sounds (e.g., a pencil on paper) or the way things feel (e.g., tags on clothing). Some individuals may smell or touch objects in an odd way and be fascinated by lights or spinning objects.

Some people with ASD may exhibit hyperactivity, impulsiveness, and a short attention span. They may be aggressive towards others, have temper tantrums (e.g., if a routine is changed or if they are in an unfamiliar place), or engage in activities that cause self-injury. These types of behaviors can frighten other children and may cause them to shun peers with ASD. These individuals may also exhibit unusual eating habits (e.g., refraining from eating foods that are brown).

The text sections on symptoms were adapted from DSM-5.

The above-outlined symptoms would be present in early childhood but perhaps not detected until later. Beyond that, students with ASD may develop a mental health condition (e.g., depression or anxiety) in adolescence and young adulthood. This type of secondary disability can be managed through therapy and medication, but the symptoms of ASD cannot.

Working with students who have ASD

Given that all the above symptoms of ASD may vary widely among individuals, it is important that teachers are familiar with the specific strengths and needs of each student with ASD. Read the student's file and pay particular attention to the individual education plan to determine specific academic and social strengths and needs. Your role is to provide academic accommodations (if required), but more importantly to promote acceptance by others to enhance social belonging. The suggestions described in this chapter are for teachers working with students with milder forms of ASD who may or may not be assigned a paraprofessional to assist.

Some students with ASD do not require any academic accommodation, and some may be very knowledgeable about a specific topic. Such a student is known as a "savant." Or the student may be talented in a particular area (having "splinter skills"). If so, you can provide opportunities for this student to share knowledge or display talent when appropriate.

More often it is the case that the student is not working at grade level and may require modifications to the curriculum. When considering teaching strategies for a child with autism, four elements are critical: routine, structure, organization, and consistency. Individuals with autism may become agitated when things are out of order and routine is not followed. Hence, structure and consistency are very important to make the environment predictable and to develop a sense of control within the child. These become the stable foundation from which the student can learn.

Establish routines

Here are some measures to take.

1. Post the class schedule in a spot in the classroom so that all the students can see it. If required, use pictures to show the schedule or pictures and words. A daily schedule with pictures and words can also be taped to the student's desk.
2. At the beginning of each day, review what subjects will be covered so that the student with ASD will know what to expect. Avoid deviating from the schedule as much as possible; however, when changes are necessary, inform the class about the time of any special event (e.g., an assembly, guest speaker) and mention what parts of the schedule will be missed. Be prepared to answer questions about the event throughout the day.
3. If possible, find out when fire drills will be held and warn your students about them on the appropriate days. Tell them you can't predict at what time the drill will occur, but you know there will be one. Remind them about how to behave during the drill.
4. Be prepared to deal with any students who perseverate, or continue an action beyond a reasonable time. These actions may include rocking back and forth, stroking a lock of hair, sucking a thumb, and manipulating an object. There may be times when, due to the nature of the child or task or their mood, your

student with autism will not want to stop an academic activity and move on to the next. To address this, give a warning about when the activity will change. For example, when 10 minutes remain in the language period, tell the students that you will be moving to math in 10 minutes. Repeat the warnings at the five- and two-minute marks.

Organize the classroom

In the elementary grades, you can designate certain areas of the classroom for specific activities (e.g., group instruction and independent work). Store materials in an organized way and clearly label them with pictures, words, or both. In the student's specific area to store their coat, boots, and backpack, place their photo or some other easily recognizable cue. If necessary, include a pictorial representation of the steps to take to put on winter clothing.

Be sure to record the agenda and homework in the same spot on the board for each day or class. In senior elementary classrooms, some students with ASD also benefit from organizing their binders in different colors according to subject or to color-coordinate with their textbooks.

Modify curriculum

When you plan lessons, consider the student's strengths and needs. The child may be functioning at grade level in some areas and not in others, or they may have specific interests. Plan activities that are challenging, yet at a level you know the student can succeed. You may have to modify some in order to ensure success. For example, if planning a craft activity, you may want to precut materials and have a paraprofessional or volunteer provide help in the assembly of the craft. Consider structuring the activities so that a non-preferred activity is followed by a preferred one.

Use differentiated instruction

Provide Visual Supports

Pictures or drawings that may be used to show the timetable or choices, teach social skills, or present steps in completing an activity. The advantage is that students can refer to them whenever needed and for long periods of time, if necessary. Visual supports are more permanent than the spoken word, which is no longer available once the speaker stops talking.

Plan to teach your lessons using a multisensory approach (VAKT). Say the important points, write the three or four key ideas on the board or on flipchart paper, and use concrete objects to teach concepts. When presenting the material, use short, simple sentences and involve the child as much as possible by asking questions and inviting them to touch the objects or act as a helper. Plan on repeating key ideas and develop drill activities or purchase software that will reinforce concepts and facts. When giving instructions, state specifically what you want done and demonstrate how it is to be done. If necessary, use chunking by breaking the task into smaller sections and provide positive feedback as each component is completed. For more ideas on differentiated instruction, please see Chapter 2 of this book.

Provide one-to-one attention

During the seatwork part of the lesson, ensure that the child receives individual attention. Depending on the severity of the autism, you or a paraprofessional may provide this one-to-one attention. If necessary, use verbal or physical prompts when guiding the child's performance of a task. For example, place your hands on the child's to trace or say aloud the instructions, such as, "cut, back, cut, back" when using scissors. Fade out or withdraw the prompts to encourage independent performance. Consider, too, the value of chunking whereby you break the work into smaller tasks and give positive feedback after each is completed. Provide a short break if you notice that the student is becoming agitated or frustrated with the work. Sometimes, if the student is overwhelmed by visual distractions in the classroom, placing them in a study carrel may help improve focus.

Working with a Paraprofessional

Paraprofessionals (also known as educational assistants, teacher aides, and classroom assistants) are often cited as the most important facilitator of integration of children with severe disabilities. In many cases, the paraprofessional implements the academic and behavioral programs for students with severe disabilities.

You and the paraprofessional serve complementary roles. Your role as the classroom teacher is to understand the strengths and needs of the student, know how to adapt instruction and curriculum for the child, develop behavioral management programs, track the student's progress, evaluate the student's progress, and report to parents. You are also responsible for disciplining the child, if necessary. The role of the paraprofessional is to *implement* the instructional and curricular adaptations, as well as the behavioral management plan. However, it is recognized as good practice to involve the paraprofessional in planning the accommodations.

The need to work closely with the paraprofessional makes it imperative for you to develop a good working relationship with that person. Begin by communicating regularly and at mutually agreeable times with the paraprofessional, sharing observations, information, concerns, and ideas about working with the student. In some cases, the paraprofessional has worked with a particular student for several years and can contribute valuable information and expertise. Respect the skills and knowledge that the paraprofessional brings to the job.

Promote positive communication

Use a variety of communication methods with the student: oral, gestural, pictorial, and written. These methods may be used in combination. For example, when gaining the student's attention, move close to the child, say their name, then give simple instructions orally and combine them with gestures. When you ask a question, allow for "wait time" because the child may be slow in responding. Comment frequently on the environment and what is happening around you to provide information and encourage social interaction.

Elaborate on the child's utterances. For example, if the student says, "Hat," say, "Yes, you have a new baseball cap." Encourage the child to communicate their feelings as it may alleviate any anger and frustration. Discuss the vocabulary for feelings to give the words for happy, sad, disappointed, frustrated, and angry. Provide pictures to represent each emotion and label each one with the name of the emotion. Some children may find that using pictures and words helps them to communicate their feelings.

While some students with ASD may have difficulty communicating, others may be knowledgeable about a particular area and talk for long periods of time about it. During large-group discussions, discourage overly long comments by suggesting that you and the student discuss the topic at another time. Structure academic tasks so that discussion about the assigned topic will occur and also permit some off-task conversation. Use cooperative learning techniques whereby in group work, students have specific tasks. Ensure that the student with ASD is assigned a variety of tasks beginning with the ones you know can be done well. Also pre-select the groups so that the student with ASD is working with patient and accepting peers.

Monitor seating arrangements

Consider seating the student next to peers who are easygoing and who have well-developed social skills. Conversely, avoid grouping the student with ASD with peers who may make fun of them or bully them. Monitor activities in the classroom and hallways closely to ensure that no teasing or bullying occurs.

Enforce behavior rules

Establish reasonable expectations that the child can meet. State the expected behaviors in positive terms, for example: "Complete your language assignment and if there is time left in the period, you may use the computer." Be prepared to enforce the rules several times before the child realizes that you are committed to them. Provide positive feedback for appropriate behaviors, perhaps by spoken comments, the use of pictures, such as a happy face, or gestures, such as a raised thumb, or by both verbal and visual means.

If the student misbehaves, be sure to implement logical consequences. For example, if they spill paint deliberately, then provide a sponge for them to clean it up. Show them how to do it and ensure that they clean up the mess. If necessary, use applied behavior analysis (also known as "behavior modification"). Identify the behavior that must be changed (e.g., grabbing toys from other children). Decide on a desired replacement behavior (e.g., asking to have the toy). Describe the expected behavior to the child and explain when to use it. You will likely have to practise the new behavior with the student. Offer praise when they behave in the desired way — praise the action, not the child. If necessary, to reinforce the behavior, provide a reward (e.g., a few minutes to do a preferred activity). Find out what motivates the child and use those "carrots" to reinforce appropriate behavior. You can also plan a menu of reinforcers from which the child may choose.

Take a preventive approach

When it comes to students with ASD becoming agitated and having a tantrum or outburst, take a preventive approach. Regularly observe the child for signs of anxiety and divert their attention or provide a break to relieve the stress. You may also consider providing individual assistance, restructuring a task if it proves too difficult at that time, or suggesting that a break be taken. As well, monitor the child's interactions with other students to ensure that they say nothing that will create extreme agitation. It may be the case that other students are teasing the child with ASD due to their "weird" behaviors. The student may know they are being teased but do not have a witty reply and react aggressively. Discuss acceptance, respect, and kindness with the class and monitor their activities to ensure students are not teasing their classmate with ASD. As well, talk to the student with ASD about how to manage situations in a pro-social way when they feel they are being disrespected (e.g., speak to the teacher) rather than with physical aggression.

Some students with ASD become overwhelmed by the sensory stimuli in the classroom (e.g., the noise, group work, the lights). Consider building calming activities into the student's day to reduce anxiety: these may include listening to music with headphones, playing with favorite objects, breathing deeply, using weighted vests or blankets, or engaging in a preferred activity. Students with ASD who are in the upper elementary grades may also seek refuge in the resource room when they feel overwhelmed or at lunch when they may need a safe haven. In some schools, the resource teacher invites students with ASD to their classroom for lunch where these students can eat together and socialize without the fear of being bullied or teased by others.

Teach them how to behave appropriately

Many students with ASD do not learn social skills informally by observing others, so you can assist a student by teaching social skills directly (e.g., standing an arm's length from the person to whom you are speaking, giving greetings, and making appropriate responses). You may also want to do some role playing with the student to teach social skills. You can have the student play the perpetrator and then the victim in a scenario and discuss the feelings of the people in both roles. During the next few days, quietly remind the child of the appropriate behavior, monitor the behavior, and provide positive feedback for appropriate behaviors and logical consequences for inappropriate behavior. You may also consider breaking some activities, such as the snack, lunch, and cafeteria routines, into steps and rehearsing them with the student. How to have a short conversation with an adult or a classmate in a predictable situation (e.g., before the lesson begins) can also be rehearsed. You can teach how to interact with others through reading social stories and discussing them or working with a child while filling in the bubbles of comic-strip conversations.

Your behaviors

While students with ASD may prefer to engage in parallel play over interactive play, may want to talk about things that are of limited interest to peers, and may seem socially awkward, they want to be accepted by others and feel that they can trust the teacher. It falls upon the teacher to develop a positive relationship with the student so that they feel emotionally and physically safe in the classroom. Chapter 1 of this book provides many ways to go about building that empathic relationship with students. Try seeing the strengths of the student and avoid adopting a deficit perspective. Remember that they are not being difficult on purpose. Help them find peers with similar interests by pairing them with appropriate classmates during group work and encouraging them to join clubs aligned with their interests. To model acceptance among peers, have informal conversations with them and publicly praise their efforts, accomplishments, and appropriate social behaviors whenever possible.

If a student with ASD has an outburst, ensure that they and the other children are safe. They may have to be evacuated from the classroom. When the student with ASD calms down sufficiently to talk, ask them what happened and what was bothering them. Listen without making judgments. When the student is finished, use an active listening technique and say back to them what you think was the gist of their concern. Then ask the student how they think the other student(s) may have felt about the situation. Then begin to engage in social problem solving whereby the two of you come up with ways of managing the situation in the future. Possible outcomes of each one could be explored, and one or two solu-

Behavior is a form of communication. Students with ASD may not have the skills to tell you what they need. They may also not know what they need. Calling out and hitting others may be their way of communicating an unmet need.

tions would be selected. You may need to rehearse the situations and ways to manage them with this student. Also remind the student to come to you with their concerns so that the two of you may discuss them before an emotional outburst occurs. The rest of the students should be invited to return to the class and have a discussion with them about belittling, disrespecting, and bullying, as well as the importance of demonstrating acceptance and kindness. Students with ASD want to be accepted, and your behaviors and the actions of peers can go a long way to support this feeling of belonging.

ASD is a lifelong disorder, and with early diagnosis and treatment some individuals make solid progress in school and can interact with others reasonably well. However, other students with ASD will need more support in school, particularly in developing social communication and social interaction skills. Do work with the resource room and special education teachers at your school as well as with your district consultant on ASD. Keep the lines of communication open with parents — they likely know what strategies work best with their child and work with them to plan transitions, which are described in Chapter 14.

CHAPTER 10

Mental Health Disorders

Have you ever worked with a student who was diagnosed with a mental illness or who was frequently absent, failing, on the verge of dropping out, or seemingly troubled? Many mental health disorders affecting adults today began in childhood and adolescence. Up to 15 percent of children and teens are living with a mental health condition, which may take the form of anxiety, attention deficit, depression, substance abuse, or other disorders.

Mental health disorders are thought to be under-diagnosed and under-treated due to the stigma associated with mental health issues. It is an invisible disability, and no definitive medical test identifies it. Diagnosis is done by medical and mental health professionals through a process that includes a physical and psychological assessment. A few individuals diagnosed with learning disabilities (LDs), attention deficit hyperactivity disorder (ADHD), or fetal alcohol spectrum disorder (FASD) develop a mental health condition as a secondary disability in late childhood, adolescence, or early adulthood. Other individuals with undiagnosed disabilities discover they have LDs, ADHD, or FASD while seeking treatment for anxiety and/or depression.

Teachers need to know about disorders that may be caused by a mental health issue. As with all concerns about a student's progress or behavior, the teacher should begin by reading the student's file for psychological reports and other documents. As well, note changes in behavior, appearance, and school performance. If you notice changes, talk to the student individually and say: "I noticed … Is everything all right?" The student will likely report that everything is fine. You should then respond with: "Okay, but I'm here if you want to talk." Also check in with them regularly to see how they are feeling. Sometimes a quick chat is all that is necessary to reassure the student. It may also be helpful to consult the parents, if possible, to find out if the child is taking any medication, what the side effects are, and what strategies have proven to work for their son or daughter.

In this chapter, we will talk about anxiety disorders and depression. Along with attention deficit disorder, they are the most commonly diagnosed mental conditions among children and teens. It is very likely that you will encounter at least one student who has an anxiety disorder or depression.

Anxiety Disorders and How to Help Students Who Have Them

We all experience occasional worry, fear, or anxiety over events in our lives; however, individuals with anxiety disorders have symptoms of anxiety that are ongoing, severe, and disrupting to their daily lives. Individuals who are diagnosed with generalized anxiety disorder often have a low tolerance to uncertainty and they worry, which takes a toll on their physical and mental state. If a student seems to be so overwhelmed by their anxieties that their social and academic life is affected, they may need professional help. Below are signs of anxiety among children and youth.

- Irritability, tantrums, crying a lot
- Excessive worrying about grades
- Trouble concentrating
- Fear of making a mistake, striving for perfection
- Constant fatigue, sleep difficulties
- Avoidance of friends and social situations
- Restlessness, fidgeting
- Procrastination
- Fear of asking questions at school
- Need to be reassured
- Headaches, stomach aches
- Avoidance or refusal to go to school or recreational activities

If you notice a student exhibiting some of these symptoms, ask if everything is all right. They may be willing to talk, and if not tell them that they may come to you when they are ready. Check in with the student on a daily basis and do what you can to develop a positive relationship with them to develop trust and to provide emotional support. Suggest that the student practise mindfulness and focus on developing a plan to manage uncertainties. For example, if a student is worried about marks, you can suggest that they develop a study schedule and work plan to complete assignments. It is also helpful to have the student try to show compassion towards themselves at the same time as trying to take control over their worrying. The plan developed by the student can be a point of discussion in your daily meetings.

You can also discuss your observations with the special education teacher, administration, or guidance counselor to find community resources that may be of help (e.g., a community crisis line, clinics, school psychologist, social worker, or child youth worker). You can also contact the child's parents or caregivers to describe your observations and ask if they have noticed similar behaviors. If they have and seem interested in seeking help for their child, provide the list of community resources. If the parents are not interested in following up or deny that anything could be wrong, keep the lines of communication open between you and the child, as well as with the parents.

Three types of anxiety disorders some of your students may have are (1) social phobia, (2) obsessive-compulsive disorder (OCD), and (3) post-traumatic stress disorder (PTSD) (American Psychiatric Association).

Suggestions for working with students with anxiety disorders are organized into three main types: environment, social, and academic.

Social phobia

Students with social phobia constantly dread interacting with groups of people, giving presentations or speeches, and, in some cases, going to school. These situations evoke anxiety among students with social phobia, and they may experience physical symptoms, such as blushing, trembling, headaches, and speaking in a shaky voice. The students may arrive late for class; prefer to work, eat, and play alone; avoid volunteering answers in class; rarely ask for help with their work; walk in the hallway head down; and generally, avoid social contact with peers.

They may also complain of headaches or feeling sick to get out of going to school or may simply not attend school.

Other students may be quiet and shy, sharing many of the above characteristics, but these behaviors do *not* interfere with their day-to-day functioning. These students may simply be introverted and comfortable doing many activities on their own instead of with friends.

Environment: Students with social phobia (or those who are extremely withdrawn) may not demand much of your time, so it is easy to overlook them. However, they do need your attention and a predictable environment. Strive to organize your classroom so that it is structured, calm, and consistent. Post the timetable so that students know what will happen during the day and write the agenda for each period on the board. Post the class rules and follow them consistently. Knowing the schedule of activities and how others are expected to behave goes a long way to promote a safe and predictable environment.

Social: Create a supportive social network for students with social phobia. First, try to develop a personal rapport with such a student. Smile at them and warmly say, "Hello." Then engage the student in light conversation about sports, concerts, news events, school activities, or anything they may enjoy. Striking up a conversation may be difficult at first but persist. Second, try to acknowledge the student's academic success in the classroom in a way that does not single them out. Go to the student's desk and in a quiet voice comment positively on their work, speak supportively to them about their assignment after class, or write encouraging comments on their work. Third, conduct regular check-ins with the student to monitor feelings and address concerns (see Chapter 1 for ideas).

To help the student feel comfortable doing group work, begin with pairs. Larger groups are likely intimidating to a student who has social phobia or is very shy. Match the student with another student who is confident, easygoing, and accepting. Have them work on a task that you know the student with social phobia can do well and will enjoy. You can also try cooperative learning with only two students in a group, such as Think-Pair-Share. If you choose to have pairs complete an assignment, give each of the students a different task so that the pair does parallel work and partners interact only when putting the project together at the end or when reporting on it. Gradually increase the size of the groupings. Privately praise the student for their participation and for completing the work.

While you cannot create friendships for the student with social phobia, you can arrange that the student be paired with an accepting student in various activities, such as discussions, assignments, and physical activities. It is possible that the student will feel more socially connected knowing there are a peer and a teacher who are supportive.

Academic: Use differentiated instruction and provide choices in how work is done (perhaps individually, in pairs, or in groups of three or four) and in how work is assessed (e.g., written assignment or taped oral presentation). Having this type of choice will give the student control over the situation and the opportunity to select the process or product that will work best for them. The student with social phobia may also require extra time to complete assignments due to physical symptoms associated with anxiety: these may include an inability to concentrate, nausea, and vomiting. You might chunk the work into sections and check each section as it is submitted so that you can monitor the work production and the quality, as well as provide positive reinforcement after each section is finished.

Other: If the parents are willing to become involved, consider asking them to sign up their child for extracurricular activities the child enjoys, perhaps sports, dance, visual arts, or music. The child could then gain confidence in a particular area and become more willing to participate in similar activities at school. Parents and child might also practise how to greet peers and adults and rehearse potentially anxiety-producing situations so that the child has an idea of what to expect.

Obsessive-compulsive disorder (OCD)

Individuals with OCD are obsessed with upsetting thoughts that they know are irrational, but they cannot get them out of their heads. For example, they fear that if they are not perfect, if things are not in or done in a certain way, then they or their loved ones will suffer illness or injury. These thoughts cause anxiety, which the student tries to relieve by performing repeated behaviors (compulsions). The behaviors may be ritualized and must be performed in a certain way and order. Examples of compulsions are excessive hand washing, counting, or checking to ensure that certain things are done. These behaviors may be performed 20 to 30 times a day, and although they provide short-term relief, the irrational thoughts return to the individual's mind. As you can imagine, the compulsive behaviors can disrupt daily lives, academic performance, and social relationships.

Environment: Although you want to organize your classroom so that it is predictable and consistent as described above, some flexibility is required when working with students who have OCD. For example, you may have to permit a student with OCD to go to the washroom or use the sink at the back of the room to wash their hands more often than other students. You may also have to let them do their ritualized behaviors. Nonetheless, talk to the student about when the actions may be done (e.g., after the instruction part of the lesson) and where (e.g., at the back of the classroom).

Social: Since their unusual behaviors related to OCD may be disturbing to other students, closely monitor their interactions so that bullying does not occur. You should also develop a positive class climate in which mutual acceptance and tolerance are the norm so that the student feels safe and comfortable in your classroom. You can begin by modelling acceptance for the students (e.g., having informal conversations with them before school begins or at lunch). You can also do check-ins with the student to monitor how things are going. In addition, talk to the student about how to do their rituals in a discreet way (e.g., tap their own chair instead of all the chairs in the classroom) so as to reduce any negative attention from peers and improve the sense of social connection to you and peers.

Academic: Persistent, negative thoughts may interfere with the student's ability to concentrate, something that has implications for following directions. To help the student with OCD deal with directions, write them on the board or the assignment sheet. This strategy will also assist the visual learners in the class. If the student is obsessed with creating perfect assignments and is constantly erasing and redoing work, talk to them about perfection. Emphasize that people cannot be perfect all the time and that perfection is an unrealistic goal. You might also permit the student to type some assignments to avoid constant erasing. Some students with OCD may require extensions on assignment deadlines to accommodate the time required to perform their ritualized behaviors. They may also need extra time when taking tests or exams and a quiet, private place to write them (e.g., the resource room). Sometimes, a student with OCD procrastinates when given a lengthy assignment to do. Consider chunking long assignments into smaller sections and checking each section as it is completed. Provide positive reinforcement as each portion is finished. Chunking makes the task seem less intimidating to the student, and they may be able to complete the segments more readily than the entire project at once. These simple academic accommodations will enhance the student's feeling of belonging in the class.

Post-traumatic stress disorder (PTSD)

Some people develop PTSD after experiencing a terrifying physical or emotional event. The event may have been experienced directly (e.g., being physically or sexually assaulted, being in an accident or fire, being held hostage), experienced vicariously (e.g., violent assault, rape, or injury to people important to the person), or witnessed (e.g., observing accidents, war, or natural disasters). Individuals with PTSD may feel extreme distress when something reminds them of the event or its anniversary occurs; they may experience nightmares and flashbacks in which they relive the trauma. They may also be depressed, angry, and irritable.

Environment: Ensure that you create a predictable and calm classroom as described above to give the student with PTSD a sense of security and control. Work with the parents or caregivers to find out what activities or topics trigger a memory that produces anxiety and avoid them or talking about them.

Social: Keep the lines of communication open between you and the student with PTSD in case they want to talk and express their feelings. Avoid pressuring them to talk about the traumatic event. Be aware that students with PTSD generally react differently to the event: they may be clingy, withdrawn, or aggressive. Try to be empathic and avoid making judgments. Reassure them that you are available should they want to talk about anything. As well, check in with them regularly, either by using the color system (see Chapter 1) or by simply asking how they are.

Academic: Strive to ensure that the student with PTSD has some say about the academic activities you assign so that they can experience a sense of control. Use differentiated instruction (DI) strategies in which the student has a choice about the type of work and/or method of assessment.

Depression and How to Help Students Who Have It

Depression is a medical illness that negatively affects a person's mood. People with depression may feel sad, lonely, or guilty, and they may also have a sense of hopelessness and worthlessness. A common mental condition, it affects about one in ten adults a year and occurs more often in females than males. Depression usually begins in late adolescence or early adulthood, but a growing number of children can also have it. According to the American Psychiatric Association, this mental disorder is highly treatable with medication and counseling.

Depression is caused by the interplay of several factors, such as a particularly distressing life event (e.g., divorce, remarriage or cohabitation, death or prolonged ill-health of a parent). Depression can also be caused by abnormalities in the chemistry of the brain and genetics (it runs in families). Individuals with a pessimistic outlook on life and who have negative cycles of thought in which they ruminate on the negative aspects of life are susceptible to depression. Beyond that, environmental factors, such as continuous exposure to violence, neglect, abuse, and poverty, can lead to depression. Various events in our lives, such as the death of a loved one or the ending of a relationship, can cause sadness. The person's feelings of sadness lessen over time, but depression can continue for months and years.

Students with depression may not want to be with other people, attend school, or participate in activities. They may find it difficult to concentrate on their work, withdraw into a state of apathy, or be irritable and angry. Symptoms may also include intense feelings of guilt, sadness, and grief. While older students may abuse drugs or alcohol, even younger children may have thoughts of committing suicide.

Signs That a Student May Be Thinking about Suicide

A student may be very depressed and thinking about or planning to commit suicide. Take all threats of suicide seriously, and take notice when a student

- says they want to kill themselves;
- displays suicidal ideation — talking, writing, reading or drawing about death, writing suicide notes;
- has set a time or place to commit suicide;
- talks about not being around in the future or "going away";
- gives away belongings (because they will no longer need them);
- changes behavior — withdraws from friends and family, neglects personal appearance, suddenly engages in risky, aggressive, or hostile behavior;
- thinks there is no other way to end the pain or says there is no hope, feels trapped or sees no point in going on.

If a student displays these behaviors, ask them how things are going or directly ask, "Are you thinking of committing suicide?" Talking about suicide does not lead to someone planning to do so. If the student is not thinking about ending their life, remind them that you are available to talk with them. You should also contact the administration, special education teacher, and guidance counselor to find resources for the family. Parents or caregivers should also be telephoned so that you can describe the behaviors you have noticed, the talk you had with their child, and a list of community resources for them to follow up on.

If the student appears to be intent on committing suicide, call 911 immediately and stay with the student (or have someone else stay with the student) until help arrives. Avoid arguing with the student ("It's not that bad") or challenging them ("You're not the type to give up"). Instead tell the student you want them to live and talk about the situation as openly as possible.

Environment: Maintain a structured and predictable classroom in which the students are generally kind and respectful towards one another. You may also have to monitor the students closely to ensure that there is no bullying. Pair students with depression with peers who have similar interests, are inclusive of others, and generally have a positive outlook on life.

Social: Bear in mind that when individuals are depressed, irrational negative thoughts run through their minds, such as "Nobody likes me" or "I'm useless at everything." Regularly and gently remind the student of their strengths and ensure that they are included in class activities. Encourage them, too, to engage in positive self-talk along these lines: "It's okay if someone doesn't seem to like me. Maybe they're having a bad day." "It's okay if I make a mistake." When you make a mistake, model appropriate behavior for the whole class. Also do regular check-ins with the student to ensure that things are all right and that they are not contemplating suicide. As well, try to be cheerful, be open to listening, and avoid making judgments.

For more information on developing a sense of belonging and how to use differentiated instruction, see chapters 1 and 2.

Academic: Ensure that you know the student's interests, strengths, and needs. Incorporate their interests into the lessons, and as much as possible use differentiated instruction to offer choices in activities that play to their strengths. Do whatever you can to support the student's academic success, as it helps them develop a sense of belonging in the classroom.

In summary, the symptoms of anxiety disorders and depression persist over a long time and interfere with the student's daily functioning in the classroom. One of the first things you can do is to develop a positive and trusting relationship with the student so that they feel comfortable turning to you if they think they may need assistance. While you will not be providing therapy, you can direct the student and their parents to appropriate services. At school, you can help the student develop feelings of control over events in the classroom by ensuring that the environment is structured, consistent, and predictable. Partner the student with supportive peers and strive to be as approachable and non-judgmental as possible. Ensure that peers treat the student with respect and supervise students so that bullying does not occur. Conduct regular check-ins and be willing to talk to the student and demonstrate that you care about them. When planning lessons, use differentiated instructional strategies and provide a choice of ways students can demonstrate their learning so that they are aligned with their interests and strengths. Beyond that, offer quiet encouragement and monitor success. Finally, be available to parents, caregivers, and other professionals to share information and monitor the effects of treatment interventions such as medication and therapy. A knowledgeable, understanding, caring, accepting teacher who uses the above strategies will be able to develop a trusting relationship with a student who has mental health issues and create an environment where the student feels secure.

CHAPTER 11

Sensory Impairments

Although it is not unusual for older people to have sensory impairments, such impairments also occur among children and adolescents. Profound visual and hearing impairments are usually detected at birth, but some students with mild impairments are diagnosed later. For example, sometimes mild hearing impairment is detected due to incorrect word pronunciation and spelling, or "misbehavior," such as not following oral instructions. In this chapter, you will learn about sensory impairments and how to work effectively with students who have them.

What Visual Impairment Is

Many of us have impaired vision caused by refractive errors, such as *myopia* (nearsightedness) or *hyperopia* (farsightedness), and these are corrected by prescription lenses. *Visual impairment*, on the other hand, refers to serious visual problems that range from an inability to read newsprint with the use of ordinary glasses to total blindness. Difficulties are also said to occur with *acuity* (sharpness of images) and *field of vision* (range of vision). A person is considered legally blind if they have visual acuity of 20/200 or less in the better eye with best correction (such as prescribed glasses or contact lenses). In simple terms, the person sees at 20 feet what people with normal vision see at 200 feet. Problems in field of vision can range from seeing just a pinhole in the middle of the field to seeing only the periphery and not the middle of the object.

Students who cannot benefit from the use of print material are considered to be functionally *blind*. These students must rely on their auditory and tactile senses to learn. They typically read Braille, a system of raised characters, and use a cane for mobility. Some students may have an adaptation to a computer that allows them to type Braille and to print their work in English for the teacher.

Students who have visual impairment but who can read print are considered to have *low vision*. Their visual acuity is 20/70 or less in the better eye with best possible correction. These students require accommodations or special equipment to enlarge the print or to adjust the contrast (e.g., magnifying glasses, closed circuit TV, or software). Although most students with low vision will use print, some will also use Braille.

In the school-age population, approximately 0.06 percent of students are classified as visually impaired. Of these, about one-quarter are blind. Therefore, over the span of your teaching career, it is likely that you will have a student with visual impairment in your class.

Such a child should already have an individual education plan (IEP) because a student who is blind or has low vision will likely have been identified before entering your classroom. The IEP for a blind student will state that the student is learning Braille and will require a Brailler or special computer, as well as assistance in the classroom. The IEP for a student with low vision will contain a report from an ophthalmologist and an assessment of the student's functional vision. The medical report provides a diagnosis of the general condition, whereas the assessment on functional vision explains how the student with low vision uses their vision in the classroom. This assessment is important because two people with the same eye condition may use their vision in different ways. A student's vision in the classroom may be determined by motivation, fatigue, and intelligence, as well as environmental circumstances, such as lighting, glare, and contrast. By reading the IEP, you will gain an idea of the student's particular needs.

Teaching Students with Visual Impairment

Working with students who are blind or who have low vision poses somewhat different issues and possibilities, which are outlined briefly below.

Students who are blind

Students who are blind rely on their auditory and tactile senses to learn; hence, teachers should use a multisensory approach (VAKT) to teaching. These students need to develop a sense of independence and to learn to advocate for themselves, and you can play a role in promoting this (see pages 156–157). Blind students will likely need more time to complete tasks and may need the occasional assistance of a peer.

The major adjustment for you, as the teacher, will be to work with other adults in the classroom and to prepare lessons well ahead of time. A blind student will require the assistance of a person to Braille material. Therefore, you must be sufficiently organized to give the lesson materials to the consultant to Braille for the student before the lesson.

Here are some practical suggestions, some from the Ottawa-Carleton District School Board, on how to teach students who are blind:

- Use as many specific auditory cues as possible. For example, say, "The books are on the top shelf to your right" as opposed to "The books are over there."
- Give specific instructions, such as "Roll the large round ball slowly forward to your partner."
- Repeat instructions and check for understanding by having the child say them back to you. Remember that the child relies more heavily on auditory clues than others.
- As often as possible, teach concepts, such as roughness, using concrete objects. Have the child feel things, such as a rock or Velcro, with their hands. If the child is hesitant, provide hand-over-hand assistance.
- Maintain high behavioral expectations for the student. Do not coddle or allow the use of blindness as an excuse for not doing appropriate tasks.
- At the beginning of the day or the class, outline the agenda to students especially so that the child who is blind will have an idea of what to expect.
- When calling on other students to give an answer, be sure to say students' names so that the student who is blind can associate the sound of people's voices with their names.
- Maintain high academic expectations for the child based on the IEP and what you know the student can do.

- Provide extra time to complete assignments, if required. Always agree to a specific date or time for the submission of an assignment.
- Pair the student with a peer who will dictate notes that are written on the board and notices about homework.
- Apply the same rules and consequences to the student who is blind as to the other students.
- If necessary, ask the student to lift their head and face to you when speaking. Some children have mannerisms, such as spinning, clapping, or humming. Encourage the child to stop these as they can hinder social acceptance by other students. The student should stand in line, take turns, and keep their desk tidy like every other student.
- Encourage the student to be independent and to advocate for themself.

Beyond adopting the suggestions listed above, communicate regularly with the student's parents. Parents can be an excellent source of information about their child's condition and about effective instructional strategies. A good idea is to meet the student and his parents *before* school begins to share information and to establish a viable means of communicating, for example, electronically, by the student's agenda, or by telephone. (For more information about transitions, please see Chapter 14.)

Plan to meet often with the assistants or consultants who will be working with the child in the classroom. These people teach the child Braille and will Braille materials for the child. Your job is to be organized and to inform them of lessons ahead of time so that material is put into Braille for the student. Older students don't usually require intensive classroom assistance if they have the technology that allows them to scan print material into Braille, hear material presented on the computer (a speech synthesizer), or convert Braille into English for the teacher.

A final consideration is to ensure a safe and convenient environment. The student needs to be familiar with the physical organization of the classroom. If you change the position of the desks, give them a tour before class. Furthermore, ensure that all aisles are free of clutter and doors and drawers are closed to avoid tripping or bumping. Assign the student a locker in a convenient location, such as just outside the classroom door. Allot a specific space for their Brailler or computer and large Brailled textbooks.

Promoting Independence and Self-Advocacy

The student who is blind or who has low vision needs to be able to function as independently as possible in your classroom, in the school, and in the community. You can promote independent mobility by providing a safe and predictable physical environment in which the student can use a cane or other device. The student who is blind will likely have received mobility training from a consultant and should be allowed to move independently, even up and down staircases. You can also promote understanding in the student by providing much oral discussion on important ideas and specific directions.

Encourage the student to understand and accept their disability and to identify what teaching techniques work for them. Ask the student whether your teaching methods benefit them, and if not, invite them to tell you what changes to make. Be aware that sometimes, with fatigue or a change of rooms and lighting conditions, what was effective earlier in the day may not work later. Be prepared to alter your techniques, if necessary. Encourage the student to ask for specific accommodations, such as extra time, on their own. Developing the ability to request accommodations comfortably is a skill that the student will use for the rest of their life.

Students with low vision

Some ideas on how to teach students who are blind are also applicable to students with low vision. For example, communicating regularly with parents and consultants about your successes and concerns is valuable. Specifically, consultants may be able to provide you with strategies for promoting students' residual vision. As with students who are blind, encourage those with low vision to advocate for themselves: they are best able to know what they need.

Most ideas for teaching students with low vision centre on making words larger and clearer. If you use a screen when teaching, provide a separate monitor for the student with low vision so they can use it for close-up viewing. Use large writing on the chalk board, keep in mind that, for maximum contrast, white and yellow chalk are the best colors to use. Keep your boards clean! For white boards, ask the student which colored markers provide the best contrast and visibility. Provide copies of PowerPoint presentations so that the student has the notes. Enlarge handouts, which should feature well-spaced, dark printing on opaque, matte paper (shiny paper produces glare). Choose big books, large-print books, and audiobooks to make books more accessible. Encourage the student to use any helpful reading aids, such as magnifying glasses. As well, whenever possible, use digitized textbooks so that they may be accessed audibly.

When it comes to tests and assignments, consider ways to accommodate the student with low vision. Tests may pose particular problems for the student. When giving tests, read the instructions aloud to the class. Provide extra time for the student with low vision and permit them to write tests and exams in the resource room, if required. Consider handling some tests orally. Permitting more time to complete assignments and giving the option to present orally are also appropriate accommodations.

You will probably need to make some adaptations when it comes to copying material. Have the student copy as much as possible within the given time period but hand out a copy of the notes to relieve the stress of not completing the task. Another possibility is to give the student a copy of the note in which key words are left out. The student then reads the note and fills in the blanks. Rather than having the student copy extensive notes or diagrams, provide the diagram or map and simply let the child label it. Find alternative tasks to those that require prolonged attention to visual details; otherwise, the student will become very tired.

Discuss needs with the student privately. Each child with low vision has unique requirements that can vary at any time of the day; hence, flexibility on your part and regular communication are necessary. One thing that you can be sure of, though, is that the student will require space to hold special equipment, such as large books, a computer, and reading stands. Let the student experiment with lighting, size and color of pens and pencils, chalk, and print. If you think some tasks may be unsuitable for the student, then discuss your concerns, and together develop accommodations or alternative activities. Permitting the student to work with a peer who can answer questions or provide information about homework or assignments should prove helpful.

Social inclusion

Be sure to provide opportunities for students with visual impairment to develop social skills and connections with peers. We learn most of our social skills through observation of others, and students with visual impairment will need you to teach some social skills, such as sharing toys, giving and receiving compliments, and being a good sport. These skills can be taught or reviewed with all the students. The student with visual impairment may also need to know how to join in a conversation (e.g., listen for a natural pause) or how to start a conversation (e.g., ask, "What did you think of the …?"). Another skill that may be needed is how to leave an undesirable situation, such as being chased around the playground (say, "I'm tired. I don't want to play this anymore."). The student may also need to be taught how to hold their head when having a conversation with another person and while in a group to listen for names in the conversation to match voices to the names.

On the playground, the child with visual impairment needs to be taught how to use the equipment and some supervision on structures will be necessary. Balls with noise makers in them can be introduced to the entire class so that the student may be included in various games. They should also be taught how to speak up for themselves on the playground, especially if it seems that they have been missing their turn (e.g., say, "I think it's my turn now."). As well, learn about the interests of your student with visual impairment and if possible, encourage them to join a club to participate in activities related to it (e.g., a chess club).

Teach everyone in the class how to self-advocate — to know what they need and politely ask for it. You can also teach about differences and reinforce that everyone needs to feel accepted and respected. Peers need to know that it is not all right to make disrespectful gestures or faces at the student with visual impairment. Everyone needs to be treated with kindness. Peers will likely be curious about the student's visual impairment and a parent, consultant for the district, or a representative from a community agency could discuss the topic with the class. You should ask the student whether or not they would like to be present, and if so, then they could describe their own situation and vision.

As with all the students in your class, you will want to establish a warm and trusting relationship with the student with visual impairment. You need to check in with them to ensure that the strategies you are using to promote academic and social inclusion are working and if they are not, then new ones need to be tried. The student needs to know that you will be striving to ensure academic and social success in the classroom. Besides teaching skills, you will need to ensure that other students are knowledgeable about visual impairment and treat their peers with acceptance, kindness, and respect.

What Hearing Impairment Is

Hearing loss is a broad term used to describe a range of hearing impairment. The term *hard-of-hearing* refers to a loss of hearing in the mild to moderate range. A person who is hard-of-hearing generally has sufficient residual hearing that, when wearing a hearing aid, they are able to process oral language. *Deaf* is a term used to refer to hearing losses in the severe and profound range. Many people who are deaf communicate through sign language, a form of manual communication. Others, however, undergo auditory verbal therapy, and when fitted with hearing aids or a cochlear implant, they are able to understand oral language through speech reading and amplification or electromechanical interventions.

A child with moderate, severe, or profound hearing loss will likely be identified before arriving in your classroom. That student will also have an individual education plan (IEP). The situation is less clear cut for students with mild hearing loss — they sometimes go undetected for several years. Such students are sometimes mistakenly referred for assessment as having behavior problems, learning disabilities, or speech problems. Another issue is that some pre-teens and teens with a hearing impairment choose not to wear their hearing aids. Symptoms of hearing loss that you should be aware of are outlined in the reproducible on the next page.

The Role of Technology in Improving Hearing

Hearing Aids: These devices simply amplify sound; they do not restore hearing. Since they amplify *all* sound, including background noise, they do not necessarily make it clearer, just louder. People with mild or moderate hearing loss benefit from the use of hearing aids that are made to individual specifications and generally worn behind the ear.

Cochlear Implants: These externally worn microphones are designed for people with severe to profound hearing loss. They pick up sound in the environment, amplify it, and digitize it into coded signals. The signals are transmitted to the implanted receiver, which stimulates the implanted electrodes in the cochlea. The electrical sound information that is produced is transmitted to the brain for interpretation. When a person has a cochlear implant, that person undergoes *auditory verbal therapy* which involves learning how to speech-read and to use their hearing to understand spoken language. The person is also taught how to speak.

FM System: While in the classroom, students with hearing aids and cochlear implants will likely use an FM system, which consists of a microphone worn by the teacher and a receiver used by the students. Again, this system merely amplifies all sounds in the classroom; it does not make them clearer.

How to Work with Students Who Are Hearing Impaired

When hearing loss is detected in a child, parents select the method of communication. Some parents, particularly those who have had their child fitted with hearing aids or cochlear implants, select speech as the method of communication. In order to teach the child to make use of their hearing and to speak, the parents begin auditory verbal therapy. They become speech models and learn how to teach listening and speaking skills. Other parents choose sign language, and children who communicate using sign language will have an interpreter to sign the teacher's speech in the classroom. Finally, some children use a combination of speech and sign language.

The classroom teacher is obliged to respond to the method of communication parents have adopted. Suggestions for working with students who use speech or signing are presented on the following pages.

Symptoms of Hearing Loss

If you observe some of the following behaviors, it may point to identifying students whose hearing loss has either not yet been detected or who are trying to avoid the use of needed aids:

☐ seems inattentive during large-group discussions or when oral instructions are given

☐ is slow to answer or responds inappropriately to simple questions

☐ appears to be a behavior problem in class

☐ turns the head to one side when trying to listen

☐ asks other people to repeat oral instructions or conversations

☐ avoids group discussions and is reluctant to speak (The person can't hear the words and follow the conversation.)

☐ speaks more loudly or softly than the other students

☐ has immature speech and language that is limited in vocabulary and syntax; speech characterized by slurring, sound omissions, or substitutions and a lack of intonation

☐ spells poorly due to problems hearing the language; may be functioning below potential in school

Pembroke Publishers © 2022 *Finding a Place for Every Student* by Cheryll Duquette ISBN 978-1-55138-360-6

Students who are speech readers

Be sure to take advantage of the student's FM (frequency modulation) system. Ask for it at the beginning of class and wear it throughout. Speak into the microphone using a normal volume and ensure that the student with hearing loss is within a two to three metre radius of you to avoid picking up background noise.

When the student participates in group work, encourage the other members to pass around the microphone so that they can follow the discussion. Ensure that the student's group works in a quiet environment, such as the hallway or library, where there is little background noise. It is a good idea to assign the student with hearing impairment the role of recorder to ensure that they understand the points made by the group. When groups make presentations on their work to the class, or when at assemblies, have the speakers use the FM system so that the student with hearing loss can follow what is being said.

When talking to the whole class, remember to *face* the students, especially the speech reading student, who should be close enough to hear you as well as possible. Saying the name of the student you want to speak will help the student with hearing impairment know where to look. It's best to avoid lengthy lectures because the speech reading student may have difficulty following them. Excessive use of videos is also undesirable: with lights dimmed, the student will be unable to speech-read. If possible, pre-teach the lesson so that the student with hearing impairment has a general idea of the content when it is taught, which will make it easier to understand and remember. After presenting a lesson, check with the student privately to see whether the concepts and instructions have been understood.

A student who is a speech reader must be able to see your lips. A moustache hides the lips.

Help the student with the hearing impairment by using many visual aids. Write all important points on the board or screen, and list all homework, assignments, and test dates in the same place every day. Place all notes on the class website so that the student has a copy of them and can read them to pick up on points missed in class. When selecting videos, choose the ones with closed captioning or a written script. When assigning work, use the "say, write, and demonstrate" method: instead of merely explaining instructions orally, ensure that they are written as well and demonstrate exactly what has to be done.

You can also help the student by providing a buddy: the student's peer can take notes and quietly repeat questions and instructions as necessary. Nonetheless, it is important to encourage the student to take responsibility for their own work. Maintain high academic and behavior expectations for the child: do not permit hearing loss to become an excuse for incomplete work or inappropriate behavior.

Encourage the student to deal with their impairment actively. According to the Canadian Hearing Society, self-advocacy involves the abilities to identify one's strengths and weaknesses, set personal goals, be assertive, and make decisions. Prompt the student to self-advocate for repetition when they do not comprehend a point or to move to another location in the classroom when extraneous noise interferes with understanding. They can also accept responsibility for recharging their FM system and for having extra button batteries available for their hearing aid.

Strive to ensure that the student with hearing impairment is accepted by the other children in the class. There are several ways to promote this. You can discuss hearing loss with the class so that they gain a better understanding of it. You can also model acceptance by showing patience when repeating instructions and when listening to the child speak. Finally, encourage the student to participate in extracurricular activities, such as sports and clubs, to develop social relations and skills, as well as to have fun.

As you would with all students who have exceptionalities, communicate regularly with the student's parents and work cooperatively with itinerant teachers, teacher assistants, and consultants.

Students who have an interpreter

Remember to speak to the class, not the interpreter. Besides that, don't rely totally on the interpreter. Learn some signs to communicate directly with the child. To aid the student's acceptance in the class, discuss hearing loss with the students and explain the interpreter's role. Foster social integration by calling for small-group work and encouraging the child to take part in extracurricular activities.

Final Thoughts on Working with Students Who Have Sensory Impairments

First of all, watch out for signs of vision or hearing loss in your students. While most students with hearing impairment will have been identified as infants or toddlers, as noted earlier, *mild* hearing loss may go undetected for years. Likewise, when you notice a student squinting or asking a peer what is written on the screen or board, they may need corrective lenses or may have decided not to wear their glasses. In these cases, talk to the student about your observations and, if necessary, inform the parents. As with hearing impairments, more serious visual impairments will likely have been diagnosed before the student enters school.

Knowing that a student has a sensory impairment is not enough. You need to be aware of the student's *specific* needs. Remember that teaching accommodations may vary throughout the day so be sure to check with the student. As is true of dealing with all students with exceptionalities, work with the child, parents, and consultants to learn more about the student's needs and how to work effectively with them. Keep in mind that the student needs to function as independently in your classroom as possible and to learn self-advocacy skills.

Both visually and hearing impaired students, of course, benefit from a multisensory method of teaching: for a student with visual impairment, emphasize auditory and tactile channels; for a student with hearing impairment, emphasize visual and tactile channels. Depending somewhat on the communication method that parents have chosen for their child with hearing impairment in the classroom, ensure that the student can see your lips, that you're wearing the FM system, and again, that you use as many visual and tactile aids as possible.

Be aware of the social needs of students with sensory impairments and be prepared to teach basic social skills to the entire class, so as not to single out the student with impairments. Provide opportunities for the student to engage in play, conversations, and group work, as well as to join clubs and activities that align with their interests. As well, model kindness, respect, and acceptance to establish the norm among the class. No one wants to feel like an outsider, and your actions can ensure academic and social belonging among students with visual or hearing impairments.

CHAPTER 12

Other Disabilities

In this chapter, the other disabilities you will learn about are among those that do not occur frequently in the population but can have a major impact on a student's functioning. Since students with low-incidence disabilities are frequently educated in the regular classroom, it is likely that you will teach at least one student within this broad category of exceptionality in your career.

Most students with a low-incidence disability will have been identified before entering your classroom and will have an individual education plan (IEP). When working with a student who has a low-incidence disability, be sure to read the child's file to learn about specific strengths and needs. Talk to the student's previous teachers to find out about their experiences with the child. Beyond that, work closely with the student's parents or caregivers. They can provide support for you and information on their child's condition and what teaching strategies are effective. You will also likely need to work with a paraprofessional and other professionals in meeting the requirements of the IEP. One of the most important things you can do for many students is to talk to them privately and ask which accommodations are effective. You can also try to get to know the student, find a way to connect to them, and ensure they feel a sense of belonging in the classroom.

Tourette syndrome, epilepsy, brain injury, and physical disabilities are discussed below.

Tourette Syndrome

Tourette syndrome is a neurological disorder in which there are deficiencies in the person's inhibitory circuits, which would normally suppress certain inappropriate behaviors (e.g., obsessive-compulsive). These deficiencies are due to underdevelopment of the circuits and not to poor parenting. Some people are genetically vulnerable to Tourette syndrome, while others might develop it due to some cause such as a lack of oxygen. The syndrome is characterized by tics — involuntary muscular movements, uncontrollable vocal sounds, and/or inappropriate words. It should be emphasized that the tics are involuntary; the student is not choosing to exhibit them.

There are different types of tics. Simple tics involve a single muscle group and may take the form of eye blinking, lip licking, or shoulder shrugging. Simple vocal tics may include grunting, throat clearing, or humming. Complex tics involve more than one muscle group and could include touching objects and jumping. Complex vocal tics may appear as muttering phrases or words, including obscenities, or changing the pitch and volume of their voice (Tourette Canada).

The symptoms usually appear between the ages of two and 21; however, diagnosis usually occurs after age seven. Symptoms wax and wane according to stages in development and the particular situation; they are greatest during mid-adolescence and the twenties. They may also be more prominent in situations in which the child is nervous or is annoyed by the behavior of others (e.g., domineering behaviors). By the time the person is in their mid-twenties, however, the circuits usually catch up in development and the tics become inhibited. The person may also have learned coping strategies. It should be noted that, as yet, there is no cure, although medication will often control the symptoms.

The severity of the disorder and the concomitant disabilities will determine to a large extent how the child does in school. Besides having verbal or physical tics, a student with Tourette syndrome may have attention deficit hyperactivity disorder (ADHD), learning disabilities (LDs), obsessive-compulsive behaviors, and autism spectrum disorder (ASD). (See Chapters 6, 7, 8, and 9 for suggestions about specific learning needs and instructional strategies associated with these conditions.) The student with Tourette syndrome requires an environment where they feel they belong, with support from the teacher and peers. The student also needs to have self-acceptance, learn coping strategies, and develop self-confidence.

How to Help Students with Tourette Syndrome

Acknowledge that the student has to tic and be accepting of the student and be tolerant of the tics and possible rituals. If uttering obscenities is a tic exhibited by the student, do not take it personally. With the consent of the student, you may want to discuss Tourette syndrome with the others in the class and tell them to ignore the tics. Develop a positive and trusting relationship with the student and look for their strengths. Always model respectful behavior towards the student and monitor others' behaviors towards the child to ensure that no teasing or bullying occurs. Be sure, too, to talk with the student regularly to see how your practices are working.

In the classroom, provide breaks for the student to get away and tic after a certain amount of time. For example, permit the student to leave to go to the washroom or to get a drink so that they can tic in relative privacy. You may also want to seat the student at the back of the room where they can tic without disturbing others. Ask older students where they would like to sit to provide them with some control over the situation. Consider establishing a private signal with the student so that you will know when they need to leave the classroom to tic. Encourage the student to disguise a tic so that it looks like an everyday movement, such as brushing the side of the nose.

Plan small-group activities using cooperative learning techniques. Assign group members specific tasks that are required to complete the assignment. Ensure that the student with Tourette syndrome is assigned something they can do well (e.g., the note taker, the organizer, the spokesperson, or the resource manager). The goal is for the student's peers to view them as competent.

Do your best to be aware of any medication that the student may be taking. Find out about possible side effects, for example, sleepiness, fatigue, restlessness, depression, and any unusual difficulty in learning. When considering the child's behavior, try to take these into account and to show tolerance.

Some older students with Tourette syndrome may become discouraged about their disability. They may lack self-confidence. To address this, you might suggest that the guidance or special education department of your school help the student find a mentor who also has Tourette syndrome and who has achieved a measure of success. The student and the mentor could communicate electronically, by telephone, or in person.

Epilepsy

Epilepsy is a chronic disorder that affects the brain and is characterized by repeated seizure events. Changes in regular brain electrical activity cause seizures, sometimes called "electrical storms." Less than 1 percent of the population has epilepsy and between 75 percent and 85 percent of new cases are diagnosed before the age of 18 years. In more than half of the cases, the causes of epilepsy are unknown. However, known causes include a brain tumor or stroke that causes interruption of blood-flow to the brain, head injury that causes scarring to the brain tissue, infection that damages the nerve cells in the brain (e.g., meningitis, viral encephalitis), genetic factors, and poisoning from substance abuse of alcohol. Likewise, certain events such as stress, poor nutrition, missed medication, fever, drop in blood sugar, flickering lights, lack of sleep, and some emotions (e.g., anger, worry, and fear) may trigger epilepsy.

There are three main types of seizures: focal, absence, and generalized. A focal seizure occurs in only one part of the brain and affects specific senses (e.g., smell, sight, hearing). An absence seizure is shown when an individual appears dazed and confused, with a blank or vacant expression. It lasts about nine seconds, and the student may appear to others to be daydreaming. After the seizure, the student will return to the activity at hand; however, if instructions were given during the time of the seizure, they may need to be repeated. Generalized seizures, called "tonic-clonic seizures," occur in two stages. In the tonic phase, the muscles stiffen, and the individual may lose consciousness and fall. In the clonic phase, body extremities jerk and twitch. Consciousness returns slowly, and the individual may appear confused when they wake up (Epilepsy Canada).

What to Do in the Event of a Generalized Seizure

Generalized seizures can be very frightening to witness, but usually last only a few minutes and do not require medical attention. Here are guidelines to follow when you witness a seizure.

1. Keep calm.
2. Protect the student from further injury. Move hard, sharp, or hot objects from around them and ease them to the floor. Protect their head from injury and loosen anything that might be wrapped tightly around their neck (e.g., a scarf).
3. Do not restrain them. Do not put your arms around the individual or insert anything in their mouth (teeth may be broken). The tongue will not be swallowed.
4. After the seizure subsides, roll them on their side so that saliva may flow from their mouth.
5. Talk gently to help them reorient themself. They may also need to rest. Stay with them if they start wandering.
6. Contact the student's parents to inform them of the seizure.
7. Call 911 if the seizure lasts more than five minutes or repeats without a full recovery. Although rare, this situation is life-threatening.

Epilepsy is most commonly treated through prescription drugs that work when they reach a certain level in the blood stream. Sometimes, it is difficult balancing a level of medication high enough to prevent seizures with one that induces side effects, such as sleepiness. Other side effects may include irritability, nausea, skin rashes, lack of physical coordination, mood swings, and depression.

How to Help Students with Epilepsy

Some students with epilepsy may develop learning problems due to the seizures or medications. They may experience academic problems, for example, in reading, writing, and math; language problems pertaining to oral comprehension and speech; attention and concentration problems (e.g., a shorter attention span); slowness in completing tasks and in processing information relative to their peers; and poor long-term memory, that is, not being able to remember what was taught yesterday (Epilepsy Ontario).

To address difficulties in reading and math, specific accommodations such as audiobooks and manipulatives may be needed. Reduced curriculum expectations would be noted on the student's individual education plan (IEP). To accommodate a student with a shorter attention span, break tasks into chunks and provide a short break after each component is completed (e.g., a one-minute trip to the water fountain). To avoid putting everyone to sleep, or worse, making them fidgety, do not lecture for long periods. The student may need extensions on assignments if they are slow completing tasks or, if possible, consider reducing the length of the assignments. When asking questions, provide "wait time," or silence for 8 to 10 seconds, for the student to process the question and formulate an answer. Ask them to repeat instructions back to you to ensure that they were understood. If long-term memory is a problem, you will have to repeat information and review key concepts, procedures, and skills often. Sometimes, posting on the wall the steps for a procedure (e.g., how to carry in addition) is helpful for the student with epilepsy and other students. You can also place class notes and information about assignments on the class website to help the student stay organized and keep track of the work. For more ideas on how to differentiate instruction, see Chapter 2.

If a student with epilepsy engages in hockey, baseball, or bike riding, that person must be sure to wear a helmet.

You should also contact the student's parents and ask for a plan of action that will include who to contact in case of a seizure, when to call them, and when and if to call 911. Ask them, too, about specific learning problems their child may have and how they may be effectively addressed. If medication must be taken during the school day, ask the parents about it and possible side effects. Talk to the student about their extracurricular activities and encourage them to participate in clubs and sports (e.g., running and most other track and field sports, cross-country skiing, or badminton). These kinds of activities can relieve stress, which can trigger a seizure. You might also ask the student or the special education teacher to talk to the class about epilepsy so that the other students understand the condition, know what to do in case of a seizure, and have positive feelings about the individual. Educating peers about epilepsy is important to reducing stigma and the harmful stereotypical beliefs about this disorder. As well, it will help to relieve fears the student may have about being teased and rejected or feeling embarrassed or anxious due to the disorder.

Brain Injury

A traumatic brain injury (TBI) is an injury to the brain caused by an external force after birth (e.g., gunshot wounds, motor vehicle crashes, assaults, or falling and striking your head). An acquired brain injury (ABI) includes all types of traumatic brain injuries and also brain injuries caused by strokes and loss of oxygen to the brain (Brain Injury Association of Canada).

A concussion, the most common type of TBI, is caused by a bump, blow, or jolt to the head that can alter brain functioning. It can also occur from a fall or a blow to the body that causes the brain to be shaken within the skull. When a person suffers a concussion, the brain tissue is knocked against the inside of the skull and is bruised. Usually, there is no change in the structure of the brain, but how the brain functions is altered. Concussions are considered to be mild brain injuries, and with proper rest and management their symptoms are usually resolved in a week or two. The brain takes time to heal, however, and their effects can be serious, lingering for months depending on the person's history of head injuries, length of recovery time, timing between concussions, age, and severity (ThinkFirst).

The effects of a brain injury vary with each individual who suffers one. Some of the common effects of brain injury may be classified as cognitive, perceptual, physical, and behavioral/emotional. Cognitive changes may occur in memory, concentration, processing time, and executive functioning (attention, self-regulation, planning, completing a sequence of tasks). There may also be changes in how the senses are perceived. For example, the person may be unable to tolerate bright lights or loud noises. Physically, the individual may often feel fatigued, experience dizziness and difficulties in movement, have recurring headaches and nausea, be prone to seizures, and have problems with speech. The person may also exhibit more impulsive behavior and feel irritable, angry, and depressed about what has happened to them.

How to Help Students Who Have a Brain Injury

Given that every brain injury is different, the student who has one will require specific accommodations that meet individual needs. Depending on the severity of the effects of the brain injury, the student may or may not require an individual education plan (IEP). If the injury is severe, the student may have been hospitalized; during their time away from school, be sure to contact the parents to inquire about their child's recovery. The parents may request that an IEP be written for their child before or upon return.

If the student has been away from school for a few weeks or a month, it is a good idea to develop a gradual re-entry plan with the child and their parents. For example, due to fatigue, the student may be able to attend school only for two hours a day and will need to gradually work up to a full day.

Be aware that even students who have missed only a day or two of school due to a concussion may be able to focus and concentrate for only a few minutes at a time. You may need to chunk assignments into smaller components and offer a short break as each section is completed. More time to complete written work and shortened assignments may also be required. To help the student remember their homework, schedule class time for everyone to record it in their planners or type it in their phones. You can also post dates for tests and assignments on the class website. If memory is an issue, you may have to repeat information often. Furthermore, know the student's preferred learning modality — visual, auditory, or kinesthetic/tactile — and use it as often as possible in your lessons.

If a student's information-processing speed is slowed, you can help in a variety of ways. Provide "wait time" (e.g., 8–10 seconds) for responses to your questions. Give short, clear directions for tasks and speak slowly. Demonstrate what has to be done, something that will help all students understand the expectations. Ask the student with a brain injury to work on only one task at a time to focus concentration and avoid becoming overwhelmed. To help them organize tasks or information, provide a graphic organizer (a visual display of the information). If possible, provide a written copy of the steps to completing a task or a checklist. Monitor how the student is progressing on the list and provide acknowledgment or praise for completed steps.

Be aware that some students who have had a brain injury are sensitive to light and noise. If light is an issue, the student may need to wear sunglasses indoors for a while. Headphones can be used to block distracting noise. Sometimes, allowing the student to work in a study carrel can help manage these issues. Note, too, that someone who has had a brain injury may lose the senses of smell and taste.

Students who have had a severe brain injury may struggle with mobility, and while in hospital, have had physical and occupational therapy, which may continue for several months after coming home. For your part, contact the student's parents to find out how you can support the rehabilitation programs designed by the therapists at school. Senior elementary students on rotary may need to leave class a few minutes early to navigate the hallways to the next class.

Beyond gross motor skills being affected, the student may also experience difficulty with speech. Listen carefully and patiently to them as they talk and if necessary, respectfully ask for a repetition, explanation, or the key words in writing. Speech therapy may have been arranged for the student at school or privately by the parents, and you should be aware of how to help the child at school. The speech-language pathologist can also design programs to address any deficits in pragmatic communication, such as making requests, initiating conversations with peers, and taking turns.

As a teacher, do your best to maintain a calm, organized classroom with predictable routines. Anticipate potential problems, such as having tests at the end of the school day. When possible, schedule subjects requiring sustained concentration in the morning when the student is fresh. Provide specific praise for work or behavior and deliver it right after the event. The student may occasionally struggle with their sense of personal worth and lose hope, so strive to offer encouragement during the healing process. It is during these times that the student will need a trusting and supportive relationship with you and peers. Talk to the student and their parents regularly to find out how they are feeling and to assess how effective accommodations are and how long they need to be implemented.

Physical Disabilities

Physical disabilities range from mild to severe and may be caused by genetic abnormalities or prenatal, perinatal, or postnatal factors. Cerebral palsy, spina bifida, and muscular dystrophy will be discussed in this section. None of these conditions is contagious, and only muscular dystrophy is degenerative. At this time there is no long-term cure for any of these conditions.

The Emotional Toll of Brain Injury

Accepting and adapting to the changes in functioning after a brain injury is not easy. The student may feel frustrated about limitations, fatigue, and headaches. They may also be anxious, angry, irritable, or depressed about the effects of the injury. In some cases, impulsivity increases, and the individual may say or do inappropriate things. Friends they had before the brain injury may not be interested in socializing with them any longer and making new friends may be difficult.

Cerebral palsy

Cerebral palsy is caused by damage to the brain before, during, or just after birth and results in motor disorders (fine and large muscle control), sensory disorders (sight and hearing), and sometimes cognitive impairment. The continuum of difficulties ranges from no obvious physical difficulties or a minor speech impairment to severe motor problems resulting in no mobility and total lack of speech. Despite the damage to the motor area of the brain, most children with cerebral palsy have normal intellectual functioning and are able to learn in a regular classroom. Most care for themselves and walk unaided.

Spina bifida

Spina bifida, a congenital defect occurring during the first few weeks of pregnancy, results in damage to the vertebrae and spinal cord. By the fourth week of gestation, one or more vertebrae fail to fuse to protect the spinal cord; instead, the spinal cord and its covering membranes bulge out through the spinal column. This bulge may occur anywhere between the skull and the lowest parts of the vertebrae. The protruding sac is surgically placed within the spinal column, sometimes in utero. However, this procedure is risky and sometimes results in neurological damage. The effects, obvious at birth, may range from mild to severe. A child with mild spina bifida may have no physical signs or a clump of hair covering the area of the cleft. The effects of severe spina bifida may be paralysis, loss of sensation in the lower limbs, incontinence, and kidney problems. Environmental and hereditary factors are thought to cause spina bifida. Most children with spina bifida have no cognitive issues and are educated with their peers in regular classrooms.

Muscular dystrophy

Muscular dystrophy is an inherited condition characterized by a progressive degeneration of the muscles. At birth, the child appears to be developing normally, but for an unknown reason, the muscle fibers begin to break down and are replaced by fatty tissues. Children with Duchenne muscular dystrophy have limbs that appear normal; however, there is significant weakening, leading to an inability to walk in middle or late childhood. This progressive muscle weakness is associated with death due to pneumonia, exhaustion, or heart failure in adolescence or early adulthood. A second, less common type of muscular dystrophy is Landouzy-Dejerine, which results in weakened facial and shoulder muscles but is not life threatening. No known cure for muscular dystrophy exists.

How to Help Students with Physical Disabilities

To make students feel welcome, ensure that the classroom furniture is arranged to accommodate mobility aids such as crutches, walker, or wheelchair. Make yourself familiar with specialized equipment, such as pencil holders, book holders, page turners, or special desks, and ensure that there is a place to store the equipment in the classroom. Assign any student with a physical disability a locker in a convenient location and ensure that they know where the elevator and ramp are located. Of course, the local school may not have an elevator. In this case, the student with physical disabilities would likely attend the nearest school with an elevator or if in elementary school, be assigned to a class located on the first floor.

Since the student may miss school for medical reasons, provide work to be done at home and evaluate it. You could either arrange to have the work picked up and returned by a parent or sibling or post the class notes and assignments on the class website. If necessary, reduce the amount of work during the absences. Try to keep in touch with the student and their parents when they are away from school for extended periods. When the child returns, inquire about any side effects of medication, for example, fatigue, and if necessary, schedule short breaks between activities.

The student probably will not require many special instructional accommodations. Assuming that there are no learning difficulties or intellectual disability, the student may need only extra time for tests, exams, and assignments. If there is no behavioral disorder, the student will not require any special plans or approaches.

An area in which you can probably help the student is that of social acceptance and a sense of belonging. Model accepting behavior (e.g., informal conversations) and with the student's permission, discuss the disability with the class. Plan group work using cooperative learning techniques, arrange the group members so that the student is working with appropriate peers, and assign them a task that plays to their strengths, perhaps computer graphics, drawing, or oral presentations. For pair work, select someone who is tolerant and well liked to work with the student who has the disability. To further socializing, encourage the student with the disability to become involved in extracurricular activities, such as the school newspaper, yearbook, or a club. When it comes to the student's toileting needs and routines, ensure privacy, and if required, arrange for the help of the paraprofessional.

Understand Your Students' Disabilities

As this chapter suggests, working with students who have low-incidence disabilities is not difficult. The key ideas are to be knowledgeable about your students' disabilities, their specific strengths and needs, and any specialized equipment that may be required. Be willing to make accommodations and incorporate the student's strengths in the lessons so that they experience academic success in your classroom. As with all the students in your class, strive to develop a positive relationship with the ones with these disabilities and conduct regular check-ins to ensure that things are going well. With the permission of the student, discuss the disability with peers to increase understanding and empathy. With teacher and peer acceptance, students with the disabilities discussed in this chapter can feel socially included and a sense of belonging.

CHAPTER 13

Working with Parents

Most parents want to be involved in their child's education, and research has consistently shown that their involvement is linked to positive school outcomes for students — improved achievement in language and math, better behavior while in class, and the likelihood that an adolescent will graduate from high school. Typically, parents supervise and assist with homework; attend school activities, such as plays, concerts, and games; volunteer time and expertise; and communicate with the teacher (via email, texts, apps, planners, telephone calls, and parent–teacher meetings). Furthermore, parents' expectations for their children's achievement in school and post-school goals influence how students, including those who are struggling or who have disabilities, perform.

Teachers need to know how to communicate with and involve parents in the education of their children. Some proven and practical ideas are presented below.

Communicating with Parents of Elementary Students

Most parents know their children well and from years of experience can tell you which strategies will be effective and which will not. Moreover, many parents are eager to work with their child's teacher, particularly in the lower grades. They generally welcome the opportunity to have a two-way conversation with the teacher.

Beyond that, most parents are interested in receiving information about their child's school activities. In this section you will learn how to use class newsletters, websites, and planners to keep parents informed about curriculum, behavior expectations, and assignments. Suggestions on how to promote regular communication are also provided.

Establish lines of communication with parents of children with IEPs

It is possible that some parents of children with IEPs have received nothing but bad news about their children from the school. Consequently, they may be reluctant to engage in much communication with you. One way to open the lines of communication is to make a "good news" call to the parents. I have found that the first two weeks of the year are a "honeymoon" period and that is the time to call parents of students with IEPs so that there are only positive comments to make. After speaking to you, the parents may be more willing to talk to you, which will be important if problems develop later on. If problems do occur and a plan to address them has been put in place, be sure to contact the parents to provide updates and share their child's successes with them. See pages 174–175 for more tips on making phone calls.

Newsletters

At the elementary level a one-page newsletter at the beginning of each term, month, or week is usually an effective way to communicate class activities, such as special events, assignments, and tests. Parents appreciate knowing about these, including the dates, particularly if their child is disorganized, so that they can keep track of schoolwork and schedule appointments and activities accordingly. You might also include the topics of upcoming units of study in science or social studies in case parents can plan a trip to a museum or an exhibit that may reinforce the learning at school.

The first newsletter can serve a variety of purposes.

1. It may outline your expectations for student behavior so that parents are aware of them. Some expectations might be that students are to complete their work and show respect for everyone at all times.
2. It may include your homework policy, such as that any work not completed at school must be finished at home. You might also want to add related suggestions for parents, such as demonstrating a positive attitude towards education and school, ensuring that there is a quiet place for their child to do homework, encouraging daily reading, providing writing materials (e.g., paper, pens, and pencils), asking about events and activities happening at school, and for younger children, incorporating counting into everyday activities (e.g., counting the number of stairs to be climbed).
3. If you ask that parents sign students' planners or tests, be sure to inform them of this in the first newsletter.
4. You may also want to extend an invitation for parents to volunteer in the classroom and to become involved in special events, commemorative days (e.g., September 30 — National Day of Truth and Reconciliation in Canada), and festivals that celebrate their culture.
5. Encourage parents to inform you of any changes at home that may affect their child's progress or behavior, even for a short time (e.g., a death in the family or the absence of a parent). Assure them that this information will remain confidential.

The newsletter can be available electronically through the class website or an app, or it can be printed and sent home with the students. If you use a paper copy, consider including a section at the bottom of the newsletter where parents can sign to show they have read the newsletter. This section can be cut off and returned by the student to you. Entering the returned signature sections in a draw for a "No homework tonight" coupon might provide the incentive for students to bring them in. Likewise, parents who receive an electronic copy can send you an email to indicate that they have read the report and thereby make their child eligible for a draw for a coupon.

You will write the first newsletter, but if you are teaching the upper elementary grades, you may involve students in the preparation of subsequent ones. In this case, you will provide direction on the content of specific sections and supervision of the students' work. Essentially, you will be the editor and approve all the content for the class newsletter.

In all your newsletters, do remember to encourage parents to contact you if they have information to share or concerns about their child's progress.

Information about homework, test dates, and due dates for projects

You may find it convenient to post the homework and dates of upcoming tests and projects on the class website or on an app. Beyond that, some teachers upload all the notes from PowerPoints or the Smart Board on electronic sites so that parents have access to the content of the lessons you have taught. Having the notes available to be downloaded or printed can be helpful if a student is absent from class and may save the parent a trip to the school to pick up missed work. It is particularly useful if the student has a chronic illness or disease and will miss many weeks of school.

Your school may also provide planners for students to help them, and their parents, keep track of things. If your students use planners, write the list of homework in the same spot on the board every day, and near the end of the school day, give students time to copy it into their planners. Initial their planners and consider checking the backpacks of some students to ensure that the required books and notebooks are in them. Many teachers ask that parents sign the planner in the evening after the homework has been completed.

Some parents and teachers use the planner as a way to maintain regular and brief communication with each other about the student's progress or what's happening at home. For example, if something positive, such as improved behavior, happened at school, you could write a short comment about it in the planner. Parents may then provide more positive reinforcement at home.

Communicating with Parents of Intermediate Students

Although many parents of older children attending a high school begin to transfer much of the responsibility for schoolwork to their child, they still need to be informed about the courses you are giving. Consider preparing a course outline for each of your classes in which you state the topics to be covered, the overall objectives or expectations, how students will be assessed (with the proportion of the final grade for each assessment), behavior expectations (e.g., bring equipment to class, show respect at all times), and school or departmental policies on such things as the use of phones, absences, missed tests, and late assignments. State, too, your availability to provide extra help to students and when and where that help may be accessed.

On the first day of the semester or term, discuss the course outline with the students. If it is in paper form, parents and students can sign it at the bottom to show that they have read it, and a tear-off section may be returned to you. There might also be a section in which parents are provided with ways to support their children's academics by monitoring their homework, providing a quiet place to study and complete assignments, and helping (if asked by their child). Encourage parents to show a positive regard for education and to talk to their children about school and their future plans for postsecondary education and employment.

Discussing a Problem with Parents

If you notice that a problem is developing with one of your students, be sure to contact the parents about it. Most parents want to know if a negative pattern of poor academic results or problem behavior is occurring and are eager to work with you to resolve the issue.

The keys to a successful relationship with parents of students who are struggling or who have exceptionalities is to understand their perspective and to communicate regularly with them. With few exceptions, parents are motivated by love for their children and want what is best for them. They are also the experts on their children. Although you have the degrees, training, and teaching experience, your contact with students is episodic: you see them for only 10 months or less. Parents, on the other hand, have the benefit of a continuous relationship with their children so can be a valuable source of information about past performance and successful teaching or behavioral management strategies. Hence, they can give you insights about their children and how to work effectively with them. They will often provide support for your work in the classroom, as well.

Making contact by phone

Strive to be empathic, positive, and tactful, especially if this is your first contact with a parent. Although some teachers begin with a face-to-face meeting, as noted earlier I have found that using the telephone for the initial contact with a parent works well. Before you call, gather your records and observational data so that you will have them close by you when you speak to the parent. Mentally prepare for the telephone call by thinking of the steps you will take to help the student. Try to find a place free of loud noises and distractions and use the telephone at school instead of your personal phone so that the school's telephone number is displayed.

Begin by asking the parent if they are free to talk about the issue; if not, arrange a mutually convenient time to call back. Thank the parent for agreeing to take time to speak to you and then make a positive comment about the student, for example, "Marla has a really good sense of humor"; "Liam works well with others." It helps to set the tone for the discussion. Next, describe the behavior you have noticed over the last few weeks. Perhaps the student failed the last two tests (provide the dates and marks), has not completed homework on three occasions (state the dates and the assignments), is having trouble in reading (provide the specific details), or has demonstrated a particular behavior on three occasions (give the dates and details and the response).

Choose your words carefully. Describe the problem or issue to the parent objectively in a calm voice using plain language. Avoid acronyms and professional jargon. Be aware of the tone of your voice, too. You want to convey that you are a caring teacher who is in no way judging them as a parent. If the difficulty might have arisen before or been noticed at home, ask the parent if they are aware of the same issue. Ask, too, if anything unusual is happening at home — something that may be distracting the student, such as the death of a pet.

Listen carefully to the parent's reply. You may find out that a similar problem has occurred before and what steps were taken to address it. The parent may reveal that there is an illness in the family (such as we saw with Alex), which may explain the student's unusual behavior. Or the parent may tell you that their child has a diagnosis of ADHD and that due to a recent growth spurt, they are either not taking medication or the dosage of the medication is in the process of being adjusted. You might also learn that the student has an IEP and requires accommodations (this information tends to take a while to transfer from school to school even in the same district). In this case, you need to read the student's file and speak to the school's resource or special education teacher for further information. A parent who offers these types of responses may have some suggestions for you on how to handle the problem and is usually willing to work with you to develop a plan to address the difficulty.

You can offer your thoughts on how to resolve the problem and be open to suggestions from the parent, doing your best to incorporate them into an informal plan. If the parent offers to work with their child at home, advise them about what can done to provide support (e.g., practising reading, signing the planner to ensure that homework is done, or simply providing encouragement). Conclude the phone call by stating that you will call again in two weeks to provide a progress report. Write a note in your planner to remind yourself to call again.

Some parents may respond to your telephone call with the suggestion to meet to talk about the situation in person and with their child. Involving the student in this meeting may ensure compliance with a plan they helped to develop and ensures that everyone is sharing the same information. We saw this situation earlier with Andrew, Alex, and Erik. Parents and child can also be invited to a meeting after the informal plan has been implemented to discuss the outcomes and next steps.

If the parent disagrees with your observations, do not press the point. Politely ask if you may work with the child and implement your plan. If the parent agrees, then you can put into place the minor accommodations (e.g., providing extra time to write tests or complete assignments, allowing the students to complete assignments in the resource room, giving individual assistance). If the parent does not give permission, then put away your plan until the parent and the student are willing to work with you. Fortunately, this scenario does not happen often: many parents are grateful that a teacher is willing to assist their child in overcoming a difficulty in school.

You may be in the situation where you have made observations and discussed them with the resource teacher at your school and the two of you suspect that a child has a specific type of disability (e.g., LDs or possibly on the autism spectrum). You may want to meet face-to-face with the parents or via an electronic platform to discuss your observations and recommendation that the child be assessed. Have all your observational data available to show the parents and be prepared for a potentially hostile reaction. Some people believe that having a child with a learning difficulty is a sign of parental weakness, and they may be feeling vulnerable and angry, which may cause them to lash out at you. They may also fear that their child will not be accepted and that others will think less of them and treat them differently. At some point, they will realize that you did not cause the problem. If the parents reject the idea that their child may have a disability, other than hope that they change their views, there is nothing you can do about it for now.

Remember to keep a written record of all conversations with parents. Keep your notes in a private file to which students have no access.

Role of email, texts, and apps in communicating with parents

Email and texts are useful when you can respond to parents' questions through short answers, such as a date for a track meet or test, a referral to websites about a specific topic (e.g., learning disabilities), or parent support group. Electronic communication may also be used when conveying "good news" such as improved marks or the giving of a really strong multimedia presentation. However, if you want to talk to a parent about a problem, a telephone call or a face-to-face meeting is usually a better approach. Email is not confidential, and you cannot observe facial expressions or hear tone of voice.

If you are using email, text, or an app with a parent, ensure that your message carries a professional tone. No matter how much you like a parent, you are not their friend. Be sure to check the spelling and the grammar. You do not want the parent forwarding your message with misspelled words and poor grammar highlighted to other parents or the administration. As you reread the message before sending, ask yourself: "How would I react to this information if I were the parent?" Make any required revisions to the message based on your answer to this question. As well, try not to overload parents with emails. They may have two or three children in school and may be receiving emails from their other teachers, as well as from coaches and instructors of the out-of-school activities in which they are involved. It may be hard to keep track of them all.

How Parents Interact with Their Children's School

Most teachers prefer to work with parents who clearly seem responsible and caring; appreciative of the observations that they, the teachers, have taken the time to make; responsive to teacher recommendations for their child; and supportive of the teacher's efforts to help their child succeed. However, you will encounter other parents who don't appear to be involved for various reasons (e.g., distrust of schools, working multiple jobs, coming from a culture where parents are not encouraged to be involved, not fluent in English), and you need to acknowledge that some of these parents care deeply and actively about their children's welfare and prospects, too. Unseen by you, they may be actively promoting the importance of education at home with their child.

Some reasons why parents may appear to be uninvolved

Some teachers complain that parents never attend school activities or parent–teacher interviews and conclude, perhaps incorrectly, that the parents don't care about their child. Unfortunately, teachers just observe what goes on at school; they have no idea of the nature of the dynamics of the student's home. Some parents are reluctant to go to the school due to their own negative memories of formal educational experiences. Other parents face language barriers or cultural differences in help-seeking behaviors, beliefs about disabilities, and perceptions about professionals whose opinions cannot be opposed. It is also possible that parents cannot attend meetings due to heavy work schedules, concerns about missing time from work and about lost wages, or difficulties arranging child care.

Although parents in the above situations may not set foot in the school, they may support the school in ways hidden to teachers. Perhaps they instill in their children the value of education, the expectation of good academic performance, and consideration of future career goals. Recent research has shown that some of these "invisible" home-based actions to ensure that basic needs are met and that support the development of a positive attitude towards school can have a stronger influence on a student's academic performance than parents volunteering at school activities or sitting on the school council. So, try to look beyond the obvious behaviors before deciding that a parent is not interested in their child's education. There may be a legitimate reason they did not attend the school's open house or volunteer in the classroom.

How to increase the involvement of parents

As stated above, some parents are not comfortable or not available to meet with you in person. You might consider providing the option of a telephone call or a meeting using a digital platform that can be held on their phone. Either of these communication methods may provide more flexibility for the parents. You could also consider abandoning the traditional parent-teacher conference at report card time, and institute student-led conferences. Essentially, the parents arrive at the classroom with their child, who takes them to a designated place in the room and shows them their work. The teacher is available to have a short discussion with the parents about the child's progress. The students are involved in preparing invitations to their parents and selecting representative work samples from their individual folders to discuss with their parents or caregivers. Some schools also provide on-site babysitting and a light meal for parents and children who attend. In my experience, parents are usually available to listen to their child talk about their work. As well, the teacher should speak positively about the child to open the lines of communication with the parents. This approach to parent-teacher meetings may be the beginning of a fruitful partnership with a child's parents.

Educational advocacy by parents

While some parents are reluctant or unable to meet with teachers, other parents are heavily involved in their children's education. Parents of students with disabilities or who are gifted are most likely to be involved when they feel that the school is not meeting their children's needs. These parents may turn to advocacy to obtain what they believe their children need to succeed in school. *Educational advocacy* refers to the broad range of actions of parents of students (usually with exceptionalities) as they try to obtain the educational services and programs they feel their son or daughter requires to succeed in school. Although legislation in Canada, the United States, and other parts of the world entitles children with identified exceptionalities to appropriate programs to meet their needs, some parents may find schools "uncaring" and districts "unfair" in their allocation of them. Many have learned through experience that parents who are the fastest at figuring out the system seem to have quicker and greater access to services and programs.

As mentioned previously, parents are motivated by love and a sense of responsibility to meet their children's needs. They usually want to develop a partnership with the school; however, when they perceive that the school is unresponsive to the needs of their children, they may advocate. Sometimes, as a result of advocacy, relations between home and school can become strained. Teachers can facilitate the development of a positive relationship with parents by (a) having a knowledge of the child's disability and general accommodations, (b) reading the student's file and understanding the student's specific strengths, needs, and required accommodations, (c) showing care, empathy, and positive regard for the student, (d) maintaining high expectations for the student, and (e) communicating regularly with the parents. I have talked to many parents of children with exceptionalities, and they all remember one or two teachers who "got it" and followed the guidelines above. In turn, these teachers were able to deliver a successful school experience for their students with disabilities.

In conclusion, parents want to know that you genuinely care about their children and their children's progress in school. Although some mothers and fathers may not be involved in school activities as much as other parents, they are likely equally eager for their children to succeed. Parents of children who have IEPs are usually available to work with teachers and expect that you know about the exceptionality and are providing accommodations or modifications to the curriculum. If not, they may advocate on behalf of their son or daughter. You can develop a trusting and respectful relationship with parents through the quality and quantity of your communications with them.

CHAPTER 14

Smooth Transition Planning

Students with autism spectrum disorder (ASD) typically have difficulty with changes in routine and environment. Planning in advance for changes in schools or classrooms can reduce the inappropriate behaviors (e.g., temper tantrums and aggressiveness) caused by anxiety associated with the transition. Furthermore, parents and schools need to work together to identify post-high school goals and plan for the transition into the adult phase of the individual's life. In this chapter, we will explore how transition planning at various points in the educational journey of a student with ASD may be organized.

Note that many of the suggestions below may be used with students who have other disabilities, too. In particular, students with fetal alcohol spectrum disorder, learning disabilities, attention deficit hyperactivity disorder, sensory impairments, and physical disabilities will also benefit from strategic transition planning.

Transition to Kindergarten

If the child is diagnosed with ASD early, perhaps while attending a preschool, they may have a type of applied behavior analysis (ABA) called "intensive behavior intervention (IBI)," which is a teaching method based on behaviorism. A few months before the child enters Kindergarten, a team consisting of the Kindergarten teacher, special education teacher, parents, and therapist and/or the preschool should meet to plan the transition. This meeting is usually arranged by the parent, preschool, or Kindergarten teacher.

One of the team's first tasks is to share information about the child, any previous programs, and the Kindergarten setting. Services and accommodations can also be planned, and visits by the child and their parents to the school may be arranged. The child may need to visit the class several times before school begins, or a gradual entry may be used to ease the child's anxiety about moving to a new environment. Gradual entry refers to the practice of having a child begin school by spending an hour or two per day there and then gradually increasing the time so that the student is in class for the same amount of time as their peers.

Applied Behavior Analysis

Applied behavior analysis (ABA), also referred to as "behavior modification," is the application of behavioral learning principles to change behavior. The earlier-used term, *behavior modification*, has fallen into disuse due to its emphasis on consequences.

Applied behavior analysis focuses on the use of techniques (e.g., shaping and chaining) and reinforcers to encourage behaviors and on methods of managing inappropriate behaviors. To *shape* a behavior or task, break it down into basic skills and subskills. As the child performs correctly, immediately reinforce each small step that makes up the behavior. *Chaining* occurs when the small steps are strung together and performed. Negative reinforcement is also used to increase appropriate behaviors. It eliminates inappropriate behaviors by removing an undesirable consequence, thereby strengthening the desired behavior. For example, if a student refuses to do their work (inappropriate behavior), state that they must stay in their seat until the work is completed (consequence). Once the assignment is finished, the perceived negative aspect — in this case, completing the work — is reinforced by offering a satisfying activity, such as playing a game on the computer. Punishment, such as yelling at the student or calling for a "time out" (social isolation for a short time) can decrease a behavior. Used on its own, however, punishment teaches the child only what *not* to do. The child must also know appropriate behavior, and the teacher must reinforce it.

Intensive Behavior Intervention

Intensive behavior intervention (IBI), based on the principles of applied behavior analysis, is an intensive intervention designed for children with ASD. A trained therapist develops an individual program for the child with ASD in areas of need, such as life skills, communication, social skills, self-care, and readiness for school. Intensive behavior intervention seems to have the best results when it is begun early in the child's life (before age four years), is conducted intensively (25 to 40 hours per week), and involves the support of the parents at home. Although it is effective for some children with autism spectrum disorder, it is a very expensive intervention, representing a huge financial undertaking for parents.

Transition to a New Classroom

Once the child begins school, they may be moving to a new classroom each year, and it is important to prepare them, the parents, and the new teacher for the transition. Planning should begin at least six months in advance so that the parents, present teacher, and new teacher can meet to discuss the student and the plan. The new teacher will want to know the student's strengths, needs, interests, triggers, and successful instructional and behavioral management strategies. This teacher should also have access to the student's file, and since they will be implementing it the following year, they should participate in the annual review of the IEP. In the spring the student should visit the new classroom and teacher. Photographs can be taken of that classroom and given to the student so that they can look at them over the summer. A few days before school begins, the student and their parents can go to the new classroom, and the teacher can show them their desk, where they will place their coat and backpack, and give them a copy of the timetable. Knowing what to expect on the first day of school will help to alleviate the worry and anxiety the student likely feels.

Transition to a Middle School or High School

At some point, the student will move to a middle school or high school and have more than one teacher, set of classmates, and classrooms. They will have the responsibility of organizing their locker, binders, and textbooks, as well as getting from one classroom to the next in a short time. Once again, planning for this transition needs to begin early so that the teachers in the sending school and receiving school have the opportunity to meet with one another, the parents, and the student. It is usually the resource teacher from the receiving school who coordinates the transition from elementary school to middle school or high school. This teacher meets with the elementary teachers and learns as much as possible about the student and the accommodations that are required. The student should visit the school in the spring and just before school begins in the fall to find out where their classes are located and where to find the resource room, as well as other important places (e.g., washrooms, gymnasium, music room, cafeteria, library).

From one classroom to another

It is advisable for the student with a disability to rehearse traveling the route from one classroom to the next. If moving in crowds is a problem, it may be possible to permit the student to leave class three to five minutes before the period ends so that they can get to the next class in uncrowded hallways. They should also be assigned a teacher to whom they can go when there is a problem (e.g., feeling lost, confused, or overwhelmed); typically, it is the resource teacher who can offer immediate help. All the student's teachers should be briefed on the IEP and accommodations the student will require, too. Although not always done, it is helpful to inform other teachers, as well as the custodial and secretarial staff, about the student with ASD, as they may become agitated in school hallways. A staff member can take the student to the resource room to sort things out.

Transition to Postsecondary Education, Employment, or Community Living

Transitions from high school to postsecondary education, employment, or community living will be smoother and possibly more successful if you plan for them. Many districts require that a transition plan be prepared for students with disabilities. A team consisting of special education teachers, other teachers, guidance and administrative personnel, the student, the parents, and, in some cases, community agency representatives and employers meet to develop the plan. A *transition plan* is a written document that defines the goals for the student, actions taken to meet the goals, and the responsibilities of each team member. Goals for a student may be postsecondary studies, employment, or community living. Often, the transition plan is linked to the IEP and is discussed at least once a year to ensure that goals and the steps put in place are still relevant.

Postsecondary education

Planning for post-high school placements often begins in middle school because high school programs must be in line with the goals for the student. When planning the goals, the team considers the student's strengths, abilities, needs, and interests. Parents' expectations for their child and the student's wishes are also considered. When determining potential careers for the student, the team considers the skills, abilities, and personality traits that will be required for the job. For example, a student may love cooking at home and be interested in becoming a chef; however, if the student has trouble memorizing (e.g., recipes), can process only one verbal instruction at a time, or shuts down under pressure, perhaps working in a commercial kitchen is not suitable for them.

Once the goal has been identified, then the academic requirements for entrance into the program must be considered, and high school courses must align with those requirements. For example, if a community college program is planned, then the student may be able to include appropriate vocational courses (e.g., machine shop) in high school. University programs will require that more advanced courses be followed in high school, and if community living is the goal, then literacy, numeracy, and life skills courses in secondary school may be appropriate. If at all possible, career education and career counseling should be considered. It may also be appropriate for the student to take cooperative education courses to explore specific career possibilities. In these cases, the school should ensure that the student is placed with a supportive boss and co-workers and the student may also require a job coach. Essentially, the team defines the goal and works backwards.

See the note on self-advocacy on pages 156–157 in Chapter 11.

There are other considerations. If the student plans to attend a postsecondary education program, they will have to register with the student disabilities office to arrange for accommodations (e.g., extra time for examinations), services (e.g., tutoring), or equipment (e.g., a laptop computer). The student will also need to self-advocate to obtain the needed items and speak with their professors. It will be necessary to learn these self-advocacy skills in middle school and high school. The student will also need to learn how to master the content of lectures and classes on their own (e.g., by carefully and actively reading the text and reviewing lecture notes) and how to study for tests and exams. Furthermore, when registering with the disabilities office, the student should have a current psycho-educational assessment and attend the orientation program held in the summer for students with special needs. The student may not want to disclose their disability, but relations with professors may be smoother if the disabilities office is involved to help make them aware of their disabilities and required accommodations.

Studying for Tests and Exams: General Suggestions

It takes time to study, and students can draw upon their preferred learning modality to prepare for tests and examinations. With teacher advice on how to study, students can follow the appropriate procedures repeatedly until they have mastered the material.

Visual learners can read the class notes and the textbook and ask themselves questions about what they have just read.

Auditory learners can read the class notes and textbook out loud, listen to the tape of the textbook, and ask themselves questions about what they read.

Visual-tactile learners follow the same process as for visual learners above. They can also write or type answers to self-questions in point form, draw diagrams to summarize processes and relationships between ideas, and condense their point-form study notes.

Auditory-tactile learners follow the same process as for auditory learners above. They can say and write or keyboard the answers to questions in point form. They can also condense their point-form study notes.

Employment

If the plan is for the student to engage in employment in the community, they will need to develop good work habits (e.g., arriving on time) and social skills (e.g., how to solve problems and interact with customers, coworkers, and the boss). Skills related to the actual job can be developed through cooperative education or work–study programs that are arranged by the high school, as well as by paid and voluntary employment. If a student is in a work experience program, the school may have to provide ongoing support from a job coach and communicate regularly with the people at the job site.

The goal for some students with more severe disabilities may be supported or sheltered employment. This type of employment (e.g., custodial work in hotels, restaurants, and hospitals) may involve an individual working with a job coach. It may also take the form of a work enclave, where a small group performs specific tasks in a business (e.g., washing cars or re-webbing lawn chairs); a mobile work crew, which works for various nonprofit organizations and does simple maintenance tasks (e.g., grounds keeping); or a small business enterprise, where the person with a disability receives training to perform specific jobs (e.g., chip wagon). In all cases, the workers are supported by a supervisor who visits the job site regularly or who accompanies the workers at all times.

Community living

The post-high school goal for some students with more severe disabilities may be living in a group home. Typically, six or fewer residents live in a house in a community with support workers who provide 24-hour supervision. The residents follow the normal routines of adults living in that community, for example, taking the bus, going to work (supported or sheltered employment), shopping, and engaging in leisure activities (e.g., bowling). Unfortunately, there are insufficient placements for young adults in group homes, and many youth who earn a high school completion certificate graduate to a waiting list and remain living at home.

An Eye on the Possibilities

As a classroom teacher, you should be aware of the content of students' transition plans. It may be possible to discuss how some of the skills and concepts you present in class are related to the future careers and programs of some of your students. This type of discussion may result in increased motivation on the part of students with disabilities.

Furthermore, do consult a student's file and transition plan before counseling them to drop math just after Grade 9. They may want to have the option of applying to a program that requires Grade 12 math, so dropping the subject early could have very negative consequences which may be unknown to the student and their parents. If math is a weakness for the student, first recommend peer

The Role of a Job Coach

A job coach is a teacher who meets with the employer before the student arrives to prepare the employer and co-workers for the student and to analyze the tasks involved in the job. The job coach then teaches the student how to perform the skills so that they may be done independently. Once the student is at the site, the job coach makes visits and meets with the employer and student to ensure that things are running smoothly. Sometimes, the student needs additional support from the job coach. Working as a job coach is time-consuming and labor-intensive.

tutoring or hiring a tutor. If this option does not work out, then discuss the situation with the student and parents so that the plan may be revised.

In this chapter, we looked at transition planning at various stages in the life of a student with ASD. Planning helps to reduce anxiety when a student moves from one educational setting to another, open up the lines of communication between sending and receiving teachers and schools, and ensure that long-term goals are identified and a plan to achieve them is in place. As noted at the beginning of the chapter, this type of planning also applies to and benefits students who have other disabilities.

References

American Association on Intellectual and Developmental Disabilities [AAIDD]. Definition of intellectual disability. https://www.aaidd.org/home

American Psychiatric Association. (2013). *Diagnostic and statistical manual of mental disorders* (5th ed.) [DSM-5]. Washington, DC: Author.

American Psychiatric Association. Types of anxiety. https://www.psychiatry.org/patients-families/anxiety-disorders/what-are-anxiety-disorders

American Psychiatric Association. Symptoms of depression. https://www.psychiatry.org/patients-families/depression/what-is-depression

Bloom, B. S. (Ed.). (1956). *Taxonomy of educational objectives: Handbook 1: Cognitive domain.* New York, NY: David McKay.

Brain Injury Association of Canada. Acquired brain injury. https://braininjury-canada.ca/en/node/3

Canadian Hearing Society. (2013). Self Advocacy. https://rarediseases.org/organizations/canadian-hearing-society/

Colvin, G., Ainge, D., & Nelson, R. (1997). How to defuse confrontations. *Teaching Exceptional Children, 29*(6), 47–51.

Dreikurs, R., & Cassel, P. (1992). *Discipline without tears* (2nd ed.). New York, NY: Plume.

Epilepsy Canada. Types of seizures. https://www.epilepsy.ca/

Epilepsy Ontario. Academic difficulties. https://epilepsyontario.org/

Gardner, H. (1983). *Frames of mind.* New York, NY: Basic Books.

Gardner, H. (1999). *Intelligence re-framed: Multiple intelligences for the 21st century.* New York, NY: Basic Books.

Johns, B., & Carr, V. (1995). *Techniques for managing verbally and physically aggressive students.* Denver, CO: Love.

Lyon, G. (1995). Research initiatives in learning disabilities: Contributions from scientists supported by the National Institutes of Child Health and Human Development. *Journal of Child Neurology, 10*(1), 5120–5126.

Maslow, A. (1970). *Motivation and personality.* New York, NY: Harper & Row.

Public Health Agency of Canada (2018). Prevalence. https://www.canada.ca/en/public-health/services/publications/diseases-conditions/autism-spectrum-disorder-children-youth-canada-2018.html

Renzulli, J. (1979). *What makes giftedness: A reexamination of the definition of the gifted and talented.* Ventura, CA: Ventura County Superintendent of Schools Office.

Sternberg, R. (2008). Applying psychological theories to education practice. *American Educational Research Journal, 45*(1), 150–165.

ThinkFirst. (2013). Concussions. https://www.thinkfirst.org/concussion

Tourette Canada. Types of tics. https://tourette.ca/

Index